William B. Smith, Joseph Gatch Bonnell

On Wheels and how I came there

A real Story for real Boys and Girls

William B. Smith, Joseph Gatch Bonnell

On Wheels and how I came there
A real Story for real Boys and Girls

ISBN/EAN: 9783337115999

Printed in Europe, USA, Canada, Australia, Japan

Cover: Foto ©ninafisch / pixelio.de

More available books at **www.hansebooks.com**

ON WHEELS

AND HOW I CAME THERE

A REAL STORY FOR REAL BOYS AND GIRLS

Giving the Personal Experiences and Observations of a Fifteen-year-old Yankee Boy as Soldier and Prisoner in the American Civil War

BY

PRIVATE W. B. SMITH

Of Company K, 14th Illinois Volunteer Infantry

EDITED BY

REV. JOSEPH GATCH BONNELL

Of the St. John's River Conference, Florida

" Neither shall they learn war any more."—BIBLE.

NEW YORK: HUNT & EATON
CINCINNATI: CRANSTON & CURTS

TO

MY AGED PARENTS,

WHO TEARFULLY GAVE THEIR ONLY BOY AT FIFTEEN

IN RESPONSE

TO OUR NATION'S CALL DURING THE CIVIL WAR,

AND WHO

JOYFULLY WELCOMED HIS RETURN AT THE RETURN OF PEACE,

THIS VOLUME IS AFFECTIONATELY

DEDICATED.

AUTHOR'S PREFACE.

IN writing *On Wheels: and How I Came There*, I have studiously avoided inserting anything concerning which there was the least doubt. If even my comrades can detect any errors I am positive they will be but slight matters of dates, which cannot affect the truth of my story.

Of every injury to myself or assistance received from my comrades which I have mentioned there is a record on file in the Pension Department at Washington. No fictitious names appear anywhere in the book. The persons and places mentioned are real, and the experiences and events related actually occurred.

I had no thought of writing a book until after the following occasion. One afternoon, while sitting in my chair in my Florida home, I thought of some beef heads which were issued to us at Andersonville Prison during the winter of 1864. Being unoccupied at the time, I concluded to write a short description of the circumstances for my children. I gave the story this title: "The Fate of a Beef Head at Andersonville, as Witnessed by a Boy Prisoner." It appears in this volume, substantially as I then wrote it, as Chapter XXX. The evening after I wrote it I received a call from a journalist, a personal friend, who, after listening to the story, urged me to have it published. This indorsement, together with the facts, in themselves interesting, that while a mere boy I was in the army, was captured and confined in different Confederate prisons, led me to believe that possibly I might write an account of my experience and observations as a boy soldier and prisoner that both young and old would read. I did so, and herewith submit this humble volume to the public. If its perusal shall in any way contribute to a genuine patriotic sentiment the author will be amply rewarded.

WILL B. SMITH.

LAWTEY, FLA., *May*, 1892.

INTRODUCTION.

HERE is a book that every boy and girl in all this nation ought to read. Its universal circulation would be a national blessing. Abraham Lincoln was fond of telling of his indebtedness to *Weems's Life of Francis Marion,* in forming his character and kindling in his soul the fire of patriotism.

If this republic has future struggles before it, and is to come out victorious in them all, we must see to it that the children of each generation know by heart the glorious history of their country.

The boys of '63 were in the army by the ten thousands. How they got there was a mystery. The legal age for enlistment was eighteen, and yet thousands of them were only seventeen, sixteen, fifteen years old.

The beautiful poem, "Driving Home the Cows," is founded upon a true story of a mother who sent her boy to perform this duty years before. He obeyed at last, but in the meantime he had been to war and back again. That boy was in his teens.

Lieutenant Cushing was but twenty-one when he blew up the *Albemarle* and sent her to the bottom of the river. The *Albemarle* was a powerful rebel cruiser which was about to put to sea to prey upon our commerce, when this boy, at deadly peril to his life, ended her career before it was fairly begun.

This book, *On Wheels: and How I Came There*, is a story of one of the boys of that period. He was only fifteen when he entered the service of his country, and the war was over before he was seventeen.

The story of his marches, battles, and prison life will hold the interest of the reader from the first page to the last.

If you want to buy for any American boy or girl a gift that will rival in interest the romance of *Robinson Crusoe*, select the *true* story told by the author of *On Wheels: and How I Came There*.

C. C. McCabe.

CONTENTS.

CHAPTER I.
ENLISTED.................................... 15

CHAPTER II.
UNIFORMED................................... 24

CHAPTER III.
OFF FOR THE WAR............................. 32

CHAPTER IV.
JOINING MY REGIMENT......................... 39

CHAPTER V.
CAMP LIFE................................... 48

CHAPTER VI.
ON TO CAMP COCRAN........................... 56

CHAPTER VII.
OFF FOR THE MERIDIAN RAID................... 64

CHAPTER VIII.
ON THE MARCH THROUGH JACKSON................ 73

CHAPTER IX.
THE SKIRMISH................................ 82

CHAPTER X.
THE BATTLE.................................. 89

CHAPTER XI.
AFTER THE BATTLE............................ 100

CHAPTER XII.
AT MERIDIAN.................................... 110

CHAPTER XIII.
A FORAGING EXPEDITION 118

CHAPTER XIV.
OUR RETURN MARCH............................... 127

CHAPTER XV.
AGAIN AT VICKSBURG.............................. 136

CHAPTER XVI.
OFF FOR A NEW FIELD 147

CHAPTER XVII.
OUR MARCH TO ROME, GEORGIA...................... 155

CHAPTER XVIII.
GUARDING RAILROAD IN SHERMAN'S REAR............. 165

CHAPTER XIX.
BUSY BEHIND SHERMAN............................. 176

CHAPTER XX.
BATTLE OF MOON STATION AND CAPTURE 186

CHAPTER XXI.
MARCHING TO PRISON.............................. 198

CHAPTER XXII.
ARRIVAL AT ANDERSONVILLE........................ 208

CHAPTER XXIII.
ENTERING ANDERSONVILLE PRISON................... 220

CHAPTER XXIV.
ANDERSONVILLE EXPERIENCES....................... 233

CHAPTER XXV.
Removed to Millen Prison.................... 244

CHAPTER XXVI.
Removed to Blackshear Prison................ 252

CHAPTER XXVII.
Flying from Sherman.......................... 261

CHAPTER XXVIII.
Again in Andersonville....................... 270

CHAPTER XXIX.
Diversions of Prison Life.................... 279

CHAPTER XXX.
The Fate of a Beefhead at Andersonville, as Witnessed by a Boy Prisoner.................. 288

CHAPTER XXXI.
Last Days in Prison.......................... 296

CHAPTER XXXII.
Released from Prison......................... 304

CHAPTER XXXIII.
The Bliss of Freedom......................... 314

CHAPTER XXXIV.
Homeward Bound............................... 323

CHAPTER XXXV.
Home at Last................................. 331

ILLUSTRATIONS.

THE AUTHOR; "ON WHEELS"......................FACING TITLE

ARMED AND ACCOUTERED........................FACING PAGE 54

ANDERSONVILLE PRISON.........................FACING PAGE 222

ON WHEELS:

AND HOW I CAME THERE.

CHAPTER I.

ENLISTED.

THE first gun of the great American Civil War, fired upon Fort Sumter in the spring of 1861, which thrilled our entire country with wild excitement, found me, a wiry lad of thirteen, attending school in the little town of Naples, Ill., which is situated on the eastern bank of the Illinois River, some one hundred miles north of St. Louis, Mo.

I had listened to one of the famous debates between Abraham Lincoln and Stephen A. Douglas, which occurred in our town in the year 1858. Upon that occasion Mr. Lincoln took dinner with my uncle, Mr. John White, then one of the leading Republicans of the community, and being present I heard the conversation between these two great men on the exciting political topics of the time, which I now recall with pleasure.

In 1860, during the lively political campaign which resulted in the election of Mr. Lincoln to the presidency of the United States, I was the youngest member the uniformed Lincoln Wide Awake Club of ...les.

...any circumstances conspired to incite me to the ... of a soldier. In my early life I had listened to the thrilling Indian stories of one of my grandmothers, who, with her family, had lived ten years among the Pottawattamie Indians, and to the war stories of one of my grandfathers, who was a soldier in the War of 1812, and of other relatives who served in the Mexican War.

During the summer of 1861 I became familiar with the work of enlisting soldiers and raising companies and regiments for the Union army. During this year the then Colonel U. S. Grant, afterward the great Union general of the Civil War, and still later President of the United States for two terms, having been placed in command of the Twenty-first Illinois Infantry Regiment for purposes of discipline—the regiment being a difficult one to manage—marched it across the country from Springfield to Quincy, Ill., and while *en route* held it in camp at Naples for some days. During their stay I witnessed the attractive drilling and maneuvering of the regiment by its gallant commander, who rode with grace and managed with ease his large, light-colored claybank horse, a color to which I was by no means partial, being an admirer of dark bays, jet blacks, and dapple grays.

I was often about the colonel's tent, where I could see him at close quarters, and noticed his slouch hat, plain blue blouse, and quiet bearing, and, like many other boys of the town, I thought if I were the governor I could have selected a much better looking horse, and, notwithstanding his good horsemanship, a much better looking rider as commander of the regiment.

While at Naples Colonel Grant had his son Fred, since United States Minister to Austria, with him. Being about the same age, Fred and I soon became acquainted, and were together much of the time during their stay, and greatly enjoyed such sports as bathing, boating, fishing, etc.

In addition to these experiences, many of my comrades and schoolmates were enlisting and going to the army, which had a decided tendency to keep me in a feverish state of excitement, and to beget an eagerness to trade my Lincoln Club torch for a musket and march to Dixie.

But with all my stretching and measuring and marking I could not, during the earlier years of the war, reach the required standard of height for soldiers, and, although I was actually growing rapidly, it seemed to me as if by some means I had become stunted and that my growth was checked.

In the meantime the soldier boys who came home sick, wounded, or on furlough had many thrilling experiences to relate, which were eagerly listened to, especially by the boys, and had a tendency to make me the more eager to quit school and join the fellows at the front.

The exciting months sped by, and I made real progress in growth, though to me it seemed very slow. The year 1863 found me fifteen years of age, and barely measuring up to the required soldier standard, five feet and six inches, with not a fraction to spare.

About this time Captain W. W. Strong, of Company K, Fourteenth Illinois Infantry, whose regiment was lying in winter quarters at Camp Cowen, in the rear of Vicksburg, Miss., was at home in our county raising recruits for the army, and visited Naples. Frequent meetings were held in the little old church, where I had attended Sabbath school and church services from my early childhood, for enlisting recruits. Now, instead of the sweet, peaceful songs of Zion, lined by the venerable minister in clerical black with white cravat, and sung fervently by the devout worshipers, the rostrum was occupied by the stalwart Union officer in blue with shoulder straps of gold, patriotic war songs were heartily sung, and stirring speeches were made. Martial music of fife and drum filled the air and all was enthusiasm and excitement.

A number of my schoolmates and other associates were enlisting, among them my chum and seatmate, Hardin Abrams, and the influence upon me was overwhelming. I decided to enlist if the recruiting officer would accept me and my parents would give their consent; for, with all my eagerness to go, being the only son of a crippled father, I did not want to leave him without his consent.

On the evening of December 21, 1863, in the old church, its pulpit gracefully festooned with the stars and stripes, just after the singing of the patriotic song,

"Yes, we'll rally round the flag, boys,
We'll rally once again,"

I stepped forward, and with pen in hand signed the enlistment roll as it lay on the communion table. The next morning our measure was taken, and now the only thing to impede my onward march to the enchanting fields of military glory was my age. But Captain Strong told me if I should not pass the required surgical examination he would take me as his private clerk.

This was as music to my ears, and off I started for home in double-quick time, thrilled with emotions of joy at the prospect of realizing my long-cherished hopes on the one hand, and with grave misgivings on the other lest my parents should refuse their consent. However, after carefully and fully weighing the matter, my parents gave their written consent, probably the more readily because my age might be the occasion of my rejection, and I might after all have to remain at home. At any rate, father gave me money with which to return from Springfield in the event of my failure to pass.

In giving his consent my father said: "Will, you can go if they accept you to carry a gun in the ranks, but if you are to act in the capacity of a clerk or waiter you can come home and wait on us."

The eventful day of our departure came, with the affecting scenes of the last farewell. Mother and sisters gave the parting kiss, and a mother's Christian advice was tearfully given. The weather was very cold, but amid the excitement of the parting scenes I forgot my overcoat, and, rather than repeat those trying experiences, I was going to take the trip of fourteen miles across the country to Winchester, Ill., where we were to join other recruits, without it; but one of my young friends having a horse close at hand, sprang into the saddle, rode over to my home, and brought it to me, and so off we started.

On arriving at Winchester we met with a hearty reception by the ladies and citizens generally of the city, and found in waiting a royal supper for the recruits who were coming in from various directions. The bountiful supper and the kind and generous entertainment accorded us in their homes by these patriotic citizens were greatly appreciated by the boys, and indicated the general willingness and desire to help in every possible way those who volunteered in our country's cause.

From Winchester we were taken to Jacksonville, Ill., and there carefully examined. So many of us being quite young, the examination was made all the more rigid. Here we were required to hop around the long hall in which the examination occurred, first on the right foot and then on the left, as rapidly as we could, and then to run around it twice at the top of our speed—a gait, by the way, which was not so very slow. The minute examination of eyes, ears, teeth, and limbs made a deep impression on my mind, and had a tendency to create within me a feeling of uneasiness lest, after all, I should not be accepted.

However, I was found to be of requisite height, and physically sound in every way; but now came the greatest barrier of all, my age. This emergency, though, I had clearly foreseen. I fully understood that while eighteen years was the legal age for acceptance as a soldier, yet with the parents' written consent, which I had obtained, a boy seventeen years of age would be accepted if otherwise admissible.

When the dignified, spectacled surgeon came to question me as to my age I straightened myself up so as to look as tall as possible, and determined to confront this emergency. Although a great admirer of George Washington, for the time I seemed to lose sight of the little hatchet story, and I so represented my age that a discrepancy of two years is to-day found between my enlisting age, as shown by my discharge papers, and my actual age, as shown by the old family Bible at home.

At this juncture the examining surgeon eyed me closely, and said: "You young rascal, you're sound enough," and then shaking his head added, "but I don't know so well about your age, judging from your appearance;" however, the point was not further pressed, and I was ordered to the side of the room with the boys who were accepted.

But while my sudden and not altogether creditable leap in age cleared my way to the enticing fields of military glory, it also led me to sufferings and exposures most severe, and resulted in shattered health for all my subsequent life.

Our next transfer was to Springfield, Ill., where, after another rigid examination, I found myself, with many others, finally accepted. Having now run the gauntlet of several rigid trials, I was proud of the fact that I was at last a soldier, and should in reality exchange my Lincoln torch for one of "Uncle Sam's" glistening Enfield rifles.

The question as to which branch of the service I should enter was decided before I left home, several considerations leading to the final conclusion. The infantry, cavalry, and gunboat service each had special attractions for me.

The gunboat service was the most fascinating to me because of my familiarity with the water. I could swim like a duck, and was as much at home in a boat as on land. In the absence of a boat it was nothing unusual for me to swim a great distance carrying a line in my teeth when seining, or to perform similar feats. But I liked my freedom so well that the confinement of the gunboat service decided me against it.

There were some very special attractions to me in the cavalry service. I was very fond of horseback riding, which I had often enjoyed on my Uncle White's horses and mules; besides, my cousin, Sam White, was a member of the Second Illinois Cavalry, and nothing would have suited me better than to join him; but my experiences with uncle's horses and mules had impressed me quite unfavorably.

When riding Joe, a little brown mule, at full speed he was almost sure to stumble, and often I would find myself suddenly thrown under him, and I would be compelled to extricate myself as best I could; Rube, an old raw-boned roan horse, Uncle John's buggy nag, not kept for beauty so much as for reliability, had a fashion, when ridden into the river for water, of plunging his head in up to his ears, and then, while vigorously shaking the water out of them, I found it difficult to stick on him with both hands clinging to his mane and my short legs tightly clutching to his bony sides; Pete, a little round bodied bay mule, was full of tricks, and threw every man or boy that ever mounted him. He was my forlorn hope.

I never wanted to ride him unless it was my only chance, for after working a half hour to get on him I had no assurance of more than a few rods ride, to be followed, perhaps, by a half day's chase in catching him. So these unfavorable exploits at horsemanship decided me against joining my Cousin Sam in the cavalry service. Besides, my enjoyable hunting expeditions, the long tramps with gun that I could take, the heavy loads of game I could carry, and the great fatigue I was capable of enduring, led me to believe I was better fitted for the marches and fatigues of the infantry service, and so I decided.

CHAPTER II.

Uniformed.

AFTER our second and final examination at Springfield we were marched out and up the street two or three blocks to a large government storeroom, where we drew our equipments.

On entering the room, which I had noticed had no sign to indicate "Uncle Sam" was doing business there, we found there were no counters nor shelves, but in lieu of these was a row of long tables on each side loaded down with soldier uniforms, etc. Each table contained but one kind of article, excepting the one where we drew plate, cup, knife, fork, and spoon, where all these were handed out on the plate. Behind each one of the tables stood a blue-coated clerk, with book in hand, doing a general credit business, requiring no references, and asking only for our names. This was so very different from the manner our home merchants conducted their business I was impressed that " Uncle Sam " was very reckless in the management of this store.

After each of us received his knapsack, canteen, and haversack, and its belongings, we drew the following articles of clothing: two pairs of gray woolen socks, one pair of heavy sewed brogans, two pairs of heavy drilling drawers, one pair of light blue woolen pants, one each dark blue woolen blouse, dress coat, and cap, one light blue woolen overcoat with cape, two gray woolen shirts, and one pair of gray woolen blankets with the large letters U. S. woven in the center of each. All coats and caps were supplied with the regulation brass button, surmounted with the king of birds, which just suited my boyish vanity. As I had already provided myself with a pair of high top boots with which to wade through the Confederacy, I drew no shoes.

"Uncle Sam" wrapped no goods and furnished no paper nor twine. As we were hustled past the tables we were hastily sized up, and the articles previously mentioned were handed or tossed to us. No time was given for folding, and before we had reached the overcoat table the avalanche of accouterments, blankets, and clothing had us completely overloaded. Although I had up to this time been very anxious to get my wardrobe of blue, I was now very glad there was no more of it, for I was about to lose a part of what I had received. But we waddled along as best we could with our enormous loads, and as we did so we presented a comical appearance indeed.

Before being marched out of the room we were allowed time to pack, or try to pack, our knapsacks. Some of us had never so much as packed a valise, and now as this band of recruits was down on the floor, each trying to pack his cart load of government clothing, together with his two large army blankets, in his knapsack, it made a very ludicrous scene.

The fact is, we could get but a portion of our new

wardrobe in our knapsacks, and when the order to march was given we gathered the rest up in our arms.

By this time it was nearly dark, and we were marched out to Camp Yates, a distance of some two miles, through a deep snow. Although it was very cold, yet our heavy, bunglesome loads and exercise in wading through the deep snow warmed us up to fever heat and caused us to perspire freely.

We arrived in camp just at dark, and were assigned quarters in wedge tents, which were supplied with a liberal amount of straw. After getting inside the tents we threw down our loads, unslung our knapsacks, and soon found ourselves chilled to the marrow, and with chattering teeth. Having no lights or fuel, we wrapped ourselves in our blankets, which were our only protection against freezing.

We were soon notified that supper was ready for us in the barracks, distant about a hundred yards, but the weather having suddenly turned bitterly cold, the wind howling and shrieking furiously outside, we decided to spend our first night in camp supperless rather than face the terrible blizzard.

We had just come from pleasant homes with their warm suppers and comfortable feather beds, and this seemed like a decidedly cool reception by "Uncle Sam;" however, it did not chill our young ardor, but it did make us want to get South, away from the fierce clutch of the ice king.

The officers had not anticipated this sudden cold wave, or we should have been better provided for. The night was simply terrible. I was awake a good portion of it rubbing my nose, ears, hands, and toes, trying to keep them from freezing. I had previously read *Washington and His Generals*, and during my rubbing exercise, trying to keep warm, I reviewed Valley Forge and his freezing men, and it was a serious question in my mind if we were not going to have a duplicate of it at Camp Yates with frost-bitten boys.

The first day of January, 1864, is memorable for the severity of its cold in that latitude. On that morning, when the time for roll call came, the mercury was twelve or fifteen degrees below zero. We were all badly frost-bitten. My nose, ears, toes, forehead, and finger ends were frozen. As soon as our situation was known by those in charge of us we were moved into one of the large barracks; but before those of us who had boots could go we were compelled to wait until the camp guards could thaw them out, for they were frozen so hard we could not get them on.

After getting thawed out, which was about 9 A. M., we were marched to the dining room barracks for breakfast, but, on arriving, we found the victuals so frozen we were compelled to take them to the stove in the other barracks and thaw them out. Our breakfast was served on long tables in tin dishes, and each ration consisted of a half loaf of baker's bread, one pint of coffee, a plate of boiled beans, and about six ounces of meat, now known by the tame and modest name of bacon, all of which were frozen solid except the coffee, and the ice was an inch thick on that.

Being of an observing turn of mind, I noted a few

peculiarities about this dining room, different from the one I was accustomed to at home. In the first place they had neglected to spread the cloths on the table; there was also a noticeable absence of chairs, so that guests were expected to eat standing; and, although I had had no supper, and breakfast was quite late, and I was consequently as hungry as a bear with keen scent, yet I could smell no victuals, so I could but note the contrast between this breakfast and the savory meal which was presided over that morning by my little black-eyed mother at home, where, if I could have been present, I would have had a whiff of hot buckwheat cakes, smoked sausage, and the delicious aroma of boiling coffee.

This first night's lodging and breakfast at "Uncle Sam's" expense, amid these disagreeable conditions, put our patriotism to as severe a test as any we met until we entered Andersonville Prison.

The large barracks we were in were of but one thickness of inch boards, and contained but one large stove, and that for some unaccountable reason, unless it was to prevent its being upset, was in one end instead of the center, so that but few could get near to it at a time, while the rest were compelled to resort to the most vigorous exercise, such as jumping, wrestling, etc., in order to keep from freezing when out from under their blankets.

We were kept here but three days, when, the weather having sufficiently moderated, we were marched to Camp Butler, a distance of some six miles.

At Camp Yates we had packed our citizen's clothes

and expressed them home, and donned our suits of blue, which seemed to lighten our hearts as well as our knapsacks, and, although our toes were frost-bitten and sore, yet we stood this tramp to Camp Butler quite well.

Here the barracks were better and the weather had moderated, so that we were quite comfortable, except from the stinging and burning of our frost-bitten parts.

These barracks were one hundred feet long, and contained a double row of bunks on each side. Here we indulged in our first letter writing. Tin plates resting upon our knees were our writing desks, and as we sat with our feet dangling over the edge of our bunks the room had the appearance of an immense bluebird house, with part of the birds on their perches and part on the floor, and all having a merry time.

Here, drawn up in line outside the barracks, with uncovered heads and uplifted right hands, we were sworn into the service "for three years, or during the war." Myself and comrades were assigned to Company K, Fourteenth Regiment, Illinois Volunteers, Infantry.

We were then marched to the paymaster's quarters, where each man received three hundred dollars bounty in new crisp greenbacks. This looked like another piece of reckless business management on the part of "Uncle Sam," giving a lot of young fellows so much money in advance on a contract, before they had hardly commenced the job, which rather impressed me that it must be a ticklish piece of business, and that he was very anxious to have it finished.

Fifteen dollars was the most money I ever had of my own at any one time before, and this amount of bright new bills looked like an immense sum to me; but as I knew my parents were in moderate circumstances only, and, as I knew, keenly felt the absence of their only boy in more ways than one, before my bounty was given to me I had fully made up my mind what I would do with it. Twenty dollars went into my left trousers pocket, and the rest, a roll of two hundred and eighty dollars, into my right pocket; and with my hand on this latter amount I went directly to the express office, where for an hour in the great crowd I clutched my roll before I could exchange it for an express receipt, which I immediately inclosed in my first letter home. A number of the boys did the same, but many of them kept all they got. The twenty dollars I got changed, and, when I returned to the barracks, secreted the most of it in my underclothing for safe keeping.

On my return to the barracks I found there a lively trading scene. The sharpers were there in full force with trays and baskets full of knives, combs, pocket-books, revolvers, watches and chains, and all manner of pinch-back jewelry, and brass and silver-plated letters and numbers for soldier caps. Each trader was surrounded by a group of recruits, eager to exchange their new greenbacks for the sharper's trash, and when the curtain dropped on the scene some of the young blue-coats were loaded down with one or two revolvers each, and supporting a watch and chain and other jewelry in proportion.

As for myself, I purchased a silver-plated laurel

wreath, about two inches in diameter, and a silver-plated company letter, K, and State letters, Illinois, and the number of my regiment, 14, which were all placed on top of my cap, the letters and the numbers all going within the wreath, and all appearing very neat, and, as I thought at that time, giving a very important finish to my uniform; though, for reasons which will appear later on, I did not keep them very long.

CHAPTER III.

OFF FOR THE WAR.

WE were kept at Camp Butler but a few days only, waiting until transports, which had been much delayed by heavy ice in the Ohio and Mississippi Rivers, could arrive at Cairo, Ill., to take us South.

About January 9, 1864, we boarded a train, were placed in good passenger coaches, went to Decatur, Ill., and thence to Cairo. "Uncle Sam" still indulged in his extravagance by furnishing free lunch and calling for no tickets; but he was heading us southward, and knew what he was about.

After a jolly ride on the cars we arrived at Cairo in due time, and were immediately marched to the wharf on the Ohio River side of the city. There we found several transports in waiting.

We embarked on the large government steamer *City of Alton*. On looking around I could see no difference between this and the beautiful Illinois River side-wheel steamers with which I was familiar, excepting the arrangements for the protection of the pilot. It looked as if a very large boiler had been cut in two crosswise and a piece seven or eight feet long set on end in the pilot house and then split down on opposite sides, so that the pilot and his wheel were inclosed within the two halves. This formed an excellent protection for the pilot in his exposed position to the bullets of bushwhackers and bands of guerillas, which infested the country along the Mississippi River south of Cairo.

We embarked without display; indeed, we simply walked in over the old-fashioned stage plank, and without even a colored porter to assist us with our baggage, or to offer to check it when once aboard.

The steamer's decks were packed with recruits and government stores; indeed, she was loaded to the guards, and sometimes the waves would dash over them. My chum Hardin and I had quarters 'midship on the boiler deck.

After we were assigned quarters, and were fairly settled, the captain waited until there was a suitable opening in the heavy floating ice, which almost covered the surface of the river, so that he could back the steamer out and turn its prow Dixieward. Then the bell struck, the machinery started, the stage planks were drawn in, the hawser turned loose, and soon the steamer glided out into the turbulent, ice-fettered waters of the Ohio, and as the vessel's prow swung around to the South our backs were turned on home and loved ones. From hundreds of young lips came the words, "Farewell, Illinois," "Farewell, old Sucker State!"

We then began to realize that we had burned the bridges behind us. A little tinge of homesickness came stealing over us, and we could but wonder if our feet would ever again press the soil of the

"Prairie State," and our eyes ever behold again the dear ones left behind, or whether we should be sacrificed to swell the numbers of unmarked graves beneath the magnolia and the pine.

Passing the Cairo point, and from the Ohio into the "Father of Waters," those serious reflections were soon banished by the novelty of seeing three States at once without knowing exactly which one we were in.

By the time our steamer was under full headway the sun had set, and the already chilly air became more piercing, until it was freezing cold. Hardin and I looked in through the glass of the front cabin door, but "Uncle Sam" had begun to change his tactics a little, and now no soldiers, except officers and some old veterans, who were the steamer's guards, were allowed inside the cabin. A guard was stationed at the cabin entrance, which was as good as saying, "No recruits need apply."

As Hardin and I peered through the glass door we could see a large red-hot coal stove surrounded by military officers and veterans, who were smoking, chatting, and having a comfortable, jolly time of it. We could also see a long stretch of tables being spread with white cloths, preparatory for the evening meal, all presenting a very inviting picture, as viewed from our chilly standpoint, and which made us eager to get inside.

Hardin and I both had a good knowledge of steamboats, how they were officered, and the duties of each, so we decided the steward was the man for us to see in order to obtain more comfortable quarters; accordingly, we hunted him out and proposed our plan to him, which was to work in the cook house or cabin for board and lodging on our trip down the river.

This, however, he speedily rejected, as he had more help and applicants than he could use; however, he informed us there was one empty stateroom which he thought we could get by paying four dollars each to Memphis, which was as far as this transport was chartered to go. He also offered to see the clerk and endeavor to procure the room for us if we desired. The amount mentioned did not include meals, but we told him to do the best he could for us. He soon returned with the cheering word that he had succeeded. So, after securing our tickets, we got our traps and moved in, and were soon chatting with the comfortable group around the blazing fire.

From this more genial point of view, as we looked out, we beheld quite a different scene from the one we had looked in upon. Peering through the same glass door through which we had made our attractive observations could be seen the grinning faces, blue noses, and chattering teeth of our less fortunate comrades. Although the dividing wall which separated the "ins" and the "outs" was but a thin plate of glass, yet there was a vast difference in their condition, which we were now fully prepared to appreciate.

Our stateroom was near the center of the cabin, so that when the table was set we were brought into close proximity to the large silver urn of hot coffee. By little courtesies, in the shape of cigars, sandwiched now and then with ten cent pieces, we soon succeeded in getting into the good graces of the head waiter, who had an eye to business. In this way our plain empty tin pint cups every meal, before the tables were cleared, found their way to the more noble polished silver urn, and returned to us with its warm congratulations and pressing invitation to call again, which, as if fearing to insult its gracious highness, they never failed to do.

Through the same subtle medium hot rolls, beefsteak, potatoes, and other delicacies found the avenue the tin cups traveled, and each meal marched in and took position on our bright tin plates; indeed, we fared quite sumptuously in our private apartments.

With the boys outside it was quite different. Government rations—coffee, sugar, bacon, and hardtack—were issued to them. They had no means for cooking except at the fires under the boilers, or by bribing the cook to boil their pails of coffee on his galley stove. Besides, they had the cold to contend with, the hard deck to sleep on, and, having no checks, their baggage to look after; and, the baggage being so great in quantity, and all of the same pattern, it was no easy matter to distinguish that belonging to one recruit from any of the rest. To relieve the situation somewhat in this matter small squads were formed, their baggage was thrown together, and they took turns in keeping guard over it.

The tickets Hardin and I received answered as passes to let us out and in the cabin, and these we frequently loaned to the boys who were outside so that they could go in and get warm by the stove while we amused ourselves viewing the passing sights, towns, gunboats, etc.

In passing gunboats we were invariably required to

slacken speed and report whence we were from and whither bound. I recall one very dark night when it was thought dangerous to advance on account of the heavy ice. We landed and remained all night under cover of a gunboat which was anchored out in the stream. Steam was kept up all night; officers were at their posts, and to prevent an attack on the land side of the steamer videttes were placed well out in the woods to give the alarm in case of approaching danger. The night passed quietly, however, and we were not molested.

Reaching Memphis, Tenn., we landed at a large wharf-boat at the foot of the levee, and disembarked. Of course, Hardin and I had to give up our comfortable quarters on the elegant steamer. Before we did so, however, the old waiter, who seemed to take quite a fancy to us, gave us a supply of good things for our haversacks, and, all things considered, we felt we had received full value for the four dollars we had paid for our tickets and the little extras we had given the waiter.

From some of the old soldiers we met with inside the cabin we had learned some points about packing knapsacks and rolling up blankets army fashion. Had we not had an excess of woolen goods beyond what old soldiers ever thought of carrying we might have gone ashore at Memphis with trim knapsacks. This we were ambitious to do, for with cumbersome bundles, together with our smooth faces, we were certain to be recognized as raw recruits, a distinction which we very much disliked. Yet the old soldiers seemed to take malicious delight in calling us raw recruits, and often, to exasperate us the more, would add: "Do your mothers know you're out."

After landing we bade adieu to some of the steamer's guards we had become acquainted with on the trip, walked over the stage plank and the wharf-boat to the shore, not to find free 'busses with drivers eager to take us to the best hotels, but for a plunge, under a heavy load, into Memphis mud, ankle deep, on a march to Fort Pickens, some two miles out on the river bluff, there to wait for transports to take us to Vicksburg, Miss.

Here we were assigned quarters in tents, and had to wait only three days, and, on account of the deep mud, we were heartily glad we did not have to wait longer.

While here we had our first sight of Confederate soldiers. Some twenty or more of them one day rode out on the opposite side of the river, a half mile or more distant. While they were halted on the river bank watching us climb up and down the high, steep, and slippery bank after water, a gunboat anchored out in the river threw a shell which exploded about twenty-five feet immediately above their heads, and which sent them pell-mell back from the river out of sight; nor did they ever appear again.

Here the blue-coats from Camp Butler, edging their way southward, began to meet the spring bluebirds winging their way northward. They were on our direct line of travel, and we boys wondered if any of them were the ones we had seen at home, and, if so, why we might not whisper to them a little message for the dear ones there.

CHAPTER IV.

Joining My Regiment.

THE evening of our third day at Fort Pickens our down-river transport steamed into port. We at once received orders to pack up. This was a welcome order, for we were only too glad of the opportunity to get away from the sticky mud of the Memphis region.

Arriving at the wharf we found a very large stern-wheel transport, provisioned for Vicksburg, awaiting us, and we were immediately marched aboard.

Hardin and I again found ourselves with quarters on the boiler deck, and before we were fairly settled the cable was drawn in, the captain signaled the pilot, and out backed the steamer into the swift, muddy stream, and amid the gathering shades of evening we were soon under full head of steam for Vicksburg, with Memphis lost to view.

The last of the old waiter's good things had by this time disappeared, and, finding that we could not get quarters inside the cabin without paying an exorbitant price, and the weather being much warmer than when we left Cairo, and our pocket-books being somewhat depleted, with no pay-day close in view, my chum and I decided to accept the situation, draw our plain rations, and take care of them in true soldier fashion.

It was about 9 p. m. before we could get a chance at the fire below so as to boil coffee and broil bacon, which, with hard-tack, made up our evening meal. While partaking of this army repast I thought I could understand why the old examining surgeons scrutinized our molars so very minutely. No unsound tooth would have been half a match for that hard-tack, while false ones would have been utterly useless. We afterward found out that it was a good thing that it was so hard, for, carried as it had to be in the large government wagons, often over rough corduroy roads, soda crackers and cream and butter wafers would soon have been ground to powder. So the absence of shortening in the "tack" kept it fresh much longer, and made it hard so that it would stand rough traveling.

Supper over—the dishes not washed, but simply wiped out with paper and put away in our individual oil-cloth cupboards—we proceeded to prepare for the night's lodging. In the absence of a black walnut bedstead and woven wire springs we substituted the steamer's deck.

Our first mattress was genuine wool, but only the thickness of a government blanket. The second one, also, was wool in the shape of our dress- and overcoats, smoothly spread. Then came the first sheet, not of white muslin just from the laundry, but another wool blanket. Our remaining two blankets answered for top sheet and spread. Our knapsacks were laid together for bolster, and our blouses and pantaloons were folded and laid on top of these for pillows.

When completed we found ourselves in possession of an average soldier's bed while on board a transport. But, notwithstanding our fine woolen double mattress, about an hour at a time was as long as we could quietly rest, when we found it necessary to "spoon" to the right or to the left, and thus change position to prevent the eagles on our brass buttons in our upper mattress from gouging holes in our youthful and tender anatomy.

Our bed, however, had several good features. No burglar could hide under it. In case we rolled out we did not have far to drop, and the floor being about as soft as our bed it would not wake us up. Then, when once awake in the morning we were decidedly glad of the opportunity of getting up without waiting for some one to pull us out. It was therefore strongly conducive to early rising—a very good feature for soldier boys and others.

One morning, about 4 o'clock, when steaming around a bend in the river some fifty miles north of Helena, Ark., we were suddenly wakened from our peaceful slumbers by a terrible crash that made our stanch steamer tremble like a leaf from stem to stern. Our boat had collided with another large transport coming around the bend from the south. Both steamers were under full headway. Each had given the proper signal, but the stubborn pilots were old enemies, as we afterward learned, and neither would give an inch to the right or left, so the two steamers madly plunged into each other like two infuriated beasts. The shock threw down everyone standing, and those who were not already up immediately arose and began to plan for their safety.

If the worst should come, Hardin and I decided to jerk off the headboard of our bed—the two outside cabin shutters just back of our bolster—and jump into the river with them and use them as life floats with which to reach the shore, and very glad I was that I knew how to swim.

Day was just dawning in the east, and very fortunate indeed it was for our huge antagonist, which received decidedly the worst of the fierce encounter. It was also fortunate that the channel at this point ran close to the shore. With her bow badly stove in the unfortunate steamer slowly backed off in a sinking condition, and barely had time to reach the shore on the Arkansas side, when she sank.

As the other boat did not blow up or catch fire, and there was a town from which aid could be obtained, after seeing all safely landed our transport steamed slowly and cautiously ahead, the proud champion of the duel, but with fifteen or twenty feet of her lower forward deck on the starboard side torn away, and a large hole stove in the hull within six inches of the water line.

The hole was temporarily patched by the boat carpenter. This enabled us to reach Helena, the nearest government post, which we did about 3 P. M. that same day. Here, our transport being considered unsafe, we were landed to await another. The post commander, not having anticipated our detention, had no preparations in the way of tents or other shelter for our accommodation, consequently some of us were quartered in a brick church. We were requested not to injure or mar the building or any of its furnishings.

and guards were placed to see that the order was obeyed—an unnecessary precaution, for, young and wild as we were, we had been brought up to respect the house of God.

On entering the building Hardin and I, knowing there would be some open floor space within the altar, made a bee-line for that locality, and immediately staked out our claim by spreading a blanket on the floor. This gave us the best sleeping accommodations the building afforded. We remained there three or four days, did all our cooking outside of the building, and left it in quite as good condition as we had often seen churches in the North the morning after a festival or oyster supper.

Marching back to the river, we embarked on our third and last transport on our voyage to Vicksburg. From here on we met gunboats much more frequently. The mariners seemed to take great delight in trying to torment us raw recruits by depicting some great calamity that was likely to befall us, telling us of torpedoes that were ready to blow us into "smithereens" if there was not some skillful piloting done. They insisted that Vicksburg had been retaken by the Johnnies, and that on nearing that point we were very likely to be captured or blown up. Their favorite story, however, was to the effect that a large Confederate force had been seen a day or two before a few miles below with a battery, which at that time, perhaps, was lying in ambush for us. But as we had as late and reliable news from Vicksburg as it was possible for them to have, fully assuring us that our flag was still floating in triumph there, these marine yarns amused us.

While *en route* from Helena to Vicksburg we could frequently see, especially on the west side of the river, where large plantation residences had been burned, the two tall chimneys of each standing with lower and upper fireplace intact, which seemed to serve the purpose of head and foot stones of the resting-place of the ashes of the cremated mansions. Or, when seen, especially on the low, black bottom lands of Louisiana, they reminded us of the obelisks along the Nile, standing as silent monuments of great events.

We learned that these buildings were not nearly all fired by Union soldiers, but that their proud owners often set the torch to their own homes to prevent them from falling into Federal hands.

Our trip from Cairo down was quite tedious, making us all glad to get on *terra firma* once more. Arriving at Vicksburg one bright, sunny morning the latter part of January, 1864, we soon disembarked and were marched up into the city, and halted near the famous courthouse, which, during the memorable siege, had been the target for a hundred Union guns. The many large, ragged holes in the courthouse bore ample evidence of the good marksmanship of the Union cannoneers. But high above these rough, cannon-pierced breaches, and still on above the apex of the cupola, we beheld an inspiring sight. There in the fresh morning breeze proudly and triumphantly waved the grand old starry banner.

We were to accompany a provision train to our regimental camp, some twelve miles to the east of the city; but learning we were not to start for an hour or two, we concluded we would take a hasty glance at some of the sights. Our ramble soon brought us into a large artillery park, where we hastily inspected over a hundred guns of different sizes and patterns, together with their deadly projectiles. Our attention was especially drawn to one piece of ordnance, a small brass two-pound cannon, mounted on a very light and graceful carriage, to be run by hand. The piece was highly polished and the carriage newly painted and freshly varnished, indicating that it was somebody's pet, and that we were not its only admirers. Boy-like, I could not keep my hands off it, and found it ran as lightly as an ordinary hand-cart. What a gun, thought I, for the Fourth of July! Or what a battery four of them would make with six Shetland ponies to each, and with battery boys all nicely uniformed! And what boy would not have been proud to be captain of such a battery?

Passing on from the park, with its then silent and harmless implements of war, and taking a last look at its boy-bewitching beauty, we were soon diving in and darting out of the many bomb-proof tunnels that honeycombed the Vicksburg hills, and which had been used by the Confederate soldiers and beleaguered citizens as places of safety. These hills have incorporated in their composition enough clay to make them tenacious and cohesive, and thus to render them susceptible of being tunneled without caving in. So the Johnnies found these tunnels their safest places of retreat during the bombardment.

Before quitting our rapid ramble we visited the camp of the Eighth Illinois Infantry on the outskirts of the city. There we found old friends and acquaintances from Naples, Ill., who were occupying some of the deserted works the boys in gray had so stubbornly defended and so reluctantly given up.

There we spent but a few moments, delivered some messages from home to the boys, and on double-quick time went back to the courthouse. Arriving there almost out of breath, we found the boys had already received orders to move, and were preparing to start.

We immediately got into our soldier harness, and were soon in the long moving column of heavily loaded white-covered wagons and rollicsome recruits heading eastward out of the city. The road, much traveled and deep cut, up hill and down, through a rough country, led us through both the Confederate and Federal works which were used during the siege, and some of which were in close speaking distance to each other.

We arrived at camp about dusk. Although a short march, yet, as it was my first at carrying accouterments, I found myself quite weary, and experienced much pain from my frost-bitten feet. I immediately joined my regiment, where I found, much to my surprise, Nic Fulks, a young man who at one time worked for my father, and Dan Haskell, a young farmer from near Naples, with whom I was well acquainted and who was one of the regimental color-bearers. As soon as they learned I was in the squad of recruits they hunted me up and escorted me to the log cabin their mess were occupying, where I was introduced in good shape to seven other old soldiers of the mess, and to Jack, the colored cook, an escaped Mississippi slave about seventeen years old.

The mess were all grown men, and when Dan and Nic entered the cabin with me they said: "Boys, here is a youngster from our town in Illinois. His father and he are both friends of ours, and if there are no objections we want to take him into our mess."

No one dissenting, I was at once adopted into their army home by these nine big bronzed brothers in arms who afterward shielded me in many ways as much as if I had been their own younger brother; and I have always looked upon that evening's reception by that old mess as one of the most fortunate events and brightest spots in my checkered army experience. Besides being congenial, and possessing sterling soldierly qualities, in this mess we had two noncommissioned officers, Sergeant William Close, and Dan Haskell, the regimental color-sergeant; and in every respect it was equal to any in the company.

My chum, Hardin Abrams, was also fortunate in getting into Orderly Sergeant Henry Stall's mess. But, strange as it may seem, intimate friends as we were at home Hardin and I never messed together after reaching our regiment. Indeed, it was often the case with soldier boys that their warmest friends after reaching their regiments were those whom they never met before. However, Hardin and I made up for our separation by many pleasant visits to each other's mess.

CHAPTER V.

Camp Life.

THERE not being cabins enough to shelter all, some of the less fortunate recruits had to mess together in tents which were far less comfortable than the cabins, which had two rows of bunks across one end and a capacious stick and clay fireplace at the other end.

It was dark when I first entered our cabin, but a cheery pine-knot fire on the hearth, where Jack was preparing supper, illuminated the room so I could see every nook and cranny in it. This was an ideal place for winter quarters. The cracks between the pine logs of which the cabin was constructed were well chinked and daubed with clay. Along the sides of the cabin were numerous pegs, upon which we hung our muskets, accouterments, and our clothing. The floor was hard and clean swept. Our broom was made of a bundle of small cane stems with the leaves on. On one side of the cabin was a door swinging on wooden hinges, and having a wooden latch, while on the opposite side was a wooden window or shutter. The clapboard roof, which was exposed inside, was held in place by heavy poles.

The furniture consisted of a good-sized mess table

made of boards, a slab bench for each side of it, and for extra seats there were several homemade stools. A few cracker-boxes resting on their sides, one on top of the other, with openings in front, made a very respectable looking and quite a convenient cupboard, which, with our broom, completed our cabin's furnishings.

Tired and hungry as I was when I first entered, it struck me as being a very cosy nest. As soon as I got my heavy knapsack off, and the introduction was over, and I had taken a good wash, Jack had the supper ready and up, and we surrounded the table.

For supper we had the regulation beans and bacon, desiccate potatoes, 'tack dry and 'tack fried, and, as I was mpany, some pickles which one of the boys had dodged out to the sutler's and bought, with some apple-butter for dessert. The coffee—the like of which, it seems to me, has never been imported since the sixties—cleared with cold water, and which I drank without "trimmings," was simply superb.

The brilliant pine knot illumination, together with the relishable repast, was very enjoyable. It seemed to me as if the cabin, the cook, and these genial comrades were all conspiring to make me feel welcome; and, as I have before observed, that evening's reception by these old soldiers was one of the brightest experiences in all my army life.

When taps sounded for lights to be put out I was a little curious to know where Jack was going to sleep. The cabin afforded no loft for his bed, and there appeared to be nothing but the bunks for the mess. Finally, I saw him down on his knees in front of one of the lower bunks, which were about two and a half feet from the floor, unrolling a large bundle, which, to my great relief, proved to be his bed; and before I had finished bathing my sore and swollen feet, and was ready to retire, Jack was snugly stowed away under the bunks, snoring a heavy sub-bass, utterly oblivious of mess pans and kettles and of all culinary cares.

Before retiring, however, he, like all good domestics, made some preparations for the morning meal, which I watched quite closely, but did not fully understand until breakfast time.

He first took a large heavy sheet-iron mess pan and placed in it a lot of hard-tack, set it on the floor, and then took the butt end of a musket cleanly wiped off with his dish-cloth, and, holding the pan securely between his feet, gave the 'tack a vigorous pounding. When the crackers were sufficiently pulverized to suit him he poured some water in the pan, placed a cover over it, and set it on the hearth to soak until morning.

When I lay down in our bunk for the night with Nick I found it was filled up at least six inches deep with soft grass and leaves which were covered over with a blanket, the edges of which were tucked under to hold them in place.

I needed no rocking in this luxurious army couch after my day's march to put me to sleep, and very soon, securing a guide book from old Morpheus, I silently went marching through the mysterious land of dreams, and when reveille sounded in the morning it seemed as if I had but just gotten into bed, and had just begun my explorations through the enchanting country.

On awaking one of the first things to meet my drowsy gaze in the firelighted room was Jack with a musket apparently trying to pound out what appeared to me to be the bottom of the mess pan which contained the crackers he had prepared the evening before. But my keen scent was not long in making the discovery that he was grinding coffee, and I observed that he had a tall sheet-iron mess kettle between his feet this time instead of the mess pan.

When we went out to roll call it was barely light enough for the orderly sergeant to see to read the names of the soldier boys. Several, I noticed, were but half dressed. One big fellow was wrapped up in a blanket like an Indian chief. This, of course, would not answer so well for close inspection or dress parade, but the Fourteenth was an old regiment that had seen much hard fighting and had passed its day of rigid discipline, so that the big soldier's Indian toilet only created a hearty laugh instead of eliciting a reprimand.

We new recruits now, for the first time, had our names placed on the company roll. This put us in a position for duty and for receiving our guns. As we had now been in the service over a month without either we had begun to feel somewhat like poor boys on the Fourth of July without any fireworks, and were very eager to obtain our pieces.

At breakfast the reason for Jack's manipulations with the hard-tack the evening before with musket and water was made plain. The operation had produced a hard-tack batter, and that morning I tried my first army slap-jacks, a pastry which we ate with melted sugar sirup, which Jack had prepared with the surplus sugar not required for our coffee. Thus prepared and eaten they were quite palatable—about fourth cousins to buckwheat cakes, as they seemed to me, and a dish which I afterward found with monotonous frequency on our army bill of fare.

Breakfast over, accompanied by Nic Fulks I took a survey of the camp. I found it to be quite large and pleasant, situated on rolling ground in a forest of stately pine, oak, and beech trees, through which threaded several small streams of clear water. Numerous long, broad streets had been cut through, which were heavily flanked on either side by substantial log cabins. On the outskirts of this improvised Yankee city were many clusters of white tents and corrals of white covered army wagons, which formed a pretty fringe to the picturesque scene.

The camp this bright January morning presented an animated picture. Over the different headquarters in the balmy breeze gracefully floated the starry banner. Here and there on the clean drill grounds, in bright blue garb, were regiments and battalions, with their polished guns gleaming in the sunlight, on dress parade and inspection. Handsomely mounted orderlies dashed hither and thither with their orders. The sharp reports of the rifles of the returning pickets could be heard on the outskirts of the camp as they came off duty. These were replaced by fresh details under sergeants and corporals with guns at right shoulder shift and carrying well-filled canteens and haversacks, who gayly tramped past us as they went out to their posts. Dozens of squads of awkward recruits, under corporals who seemed disposed to assume brigadier airs, were seen awkwardly taking their limbs through the difficult evolutions of the drill. The inspiring roll of fife and drum, the clear notes of the cornet in the brigade brass bands, rendering martial airs, filled the clear morning air with thrilling music.

Along the pretty moss-covered banks of the clear, pebbly, winding brooks, and everywhere under the stately giants of the forest, could be seen the bright camp fires with their blue smoke lazily curling heavenward, while around them were gathered hundreds of merry plantation Negroes busily engaged washing and hanging out clothes, singing their comic plantation songs, and chanting their weird melodies.

In the cavalry camps and artillery parks could be heard the shrill bugle blasts and neighing of horses, and in the corrals the braying of mules, while the steady ring of the blacksmith's anvil in the busy camp that winter morning clearly portended an early move for a vigorous spring campaign.

This whole scene made a lively military camp panorama which fully met my highest expectations of army camp life, and was well calculated to thrill the average boy with a spirit of purest patriotism, and with wild delight.

As for myself, fresh from my home and the matter-of-fact experiences of everyday life, this fascinating scene filled me with electric enthusiasm. Shouting being out of order, the best I could do was to give vent to my pent up emotions by some lively whistling, which, as I thought, must have astonished the birds in the boughs above my head.

During our stroll Nic introduced me to the officers and men of our company. As Captain Strong, who enlisted us, never returned to the regiment, our company was under the command of its first lieutenant, John Kirkman, of Winchester, Ill.

The first colonel of our regiment was John M. Palmer, afterward major-general; but at the time of which I write it was commanded by Colonel Hall. B. F. Stephenson, after whom the G. A. R. Post of Springfield, Ill., is named, was our surgeon, and Rev. W. J. Rutledge, one of the pioneer ministers of the Illinois Conference, Methodist Episcopal Church, was chaplain of our regiment at that time.

Our regiment belonged to the Second Brigade, Fourth Division, Seventeenth Army Corps, which was commanded by the highly esteemed Major-General James H. McPherson.

On the afternoon of this first day, after reaching our regiment, we recruits drew our much-coveted Enfield rifles and accouterments, and we were at once put at hard drilling under a competent drillmaster, Corporal John Platner, a medium-sized, swarthy-complexioned, heavy-muscled young man, with the agility of a cat. Sometimes, when touched off with a spark of impatient, nervous energy occasioned by some recruit's awkward motions, this officer would call the squad's attention, and while we stood at parade rest would treat us to an exhibition of Hardee's Tactics with his scrupulously clean and highly polished rifle, which

Armed and Accoutered.
From a War-time Photograph.

for skillful maneuvering was simply astonishing; and at such times his rapid movements were performed with the admirable precision of machinery.

During these drills we also had some target practice, so that we might become familiar with our guns, and we soon learned how even a good-looking army rifle could kick. At this time our ammunition was buck and ball—a round ounce ball in a paper cartridge with three large buckshot secured to it. This made a heavy charge, and, if one did not hug his gun tightly to his shoulder when firing, the piece was liable to almost knock him down. Having to bite off the end of these tough paper cartridges before loading fully demonstrated to us the wisdom of the old examining surgeon's rigid refusal to accept any recruit who was minus a good set of incisors.

Our life in this delightful camp with its comfortable quarters, however, was soon to be brought to a close, and we were transferred to other scenes, for we had been enlisted for an important work, which must be done even though it should be at the sacrifice of all ease and comfort.

CHAPTER VI.

ON TO CAMP COCRAN.

WE had been kept busy at hard drilling but a few days when orders came for us to pack up and march over to Camp Cocran, which was situated some five or six miles distant on the bluffs near the crossing of the Big Black River, where General Sherman was concentrating his army for his famous raid across the state to Meridian.

Although we recruits had but fairly got settled with our regiment in its snug quarters, yet the order was not unwelcome, for we were all eager for adventure.

When the order was received immediately the entire camp became a scene of lively commotion. Long stacks of arms soon appeared in the streets as if by magic in front of the different quarters. Suspended from their fixed bayonets were swung the soldiers' broad leather belts with well-filled cartridge and cap boxes attached. Beside these hung haversacks in whose depths our fingers so often fumbled among tin plates, knives and forks, and spoons for the stray crumb of cracker. Touching these in intimate relations swung friendly canteens freshly filled from the bubbling brook. On the ground around and underneath each stack of guns were great piles of knapsacks and rolls of army blankets, the latter with their two ends tied together forming a woolen sash to be swung over their owners' shoulders.

With their personal effects packed and out of the way, the dwellers in tents drew the stakes, when ropes immediately slackened, the small white houses collapsed, fell to the ground, were quickly spread out, and, with poles placed within them, were soon rolled up, securely bound, and made ready to load.

The loud crack of the teamster's long, limber blacksnake was now heard cutting the morning air, and soon appeared at the end of the streets six pairs of long, erect-eared mules to each white-covered army wagon, shying and dodging to right and left at the smoldering camp fires and the heaps of black camp kettles and pans. Halting every few rods along the streets, the tents were quickly loaded. In the space between these and the wagon-bows at the top the colored cooks stowed away their cooking utensils, and when all were in place, and draw-strings to the covers were fastened, drivers spoke cheerily to their teams, tugs straightened, and at once the heavily loaded wagons rolled out into the roads and took their places in the moving train.

The command of company officers to "Fall in" is given; the roll of drums and blasts of bugles are heard; belts with cartridge-boxes are hurriedly buckled on; strong arms hastily slip through knapsack, canteen, and haversack straps; old and young heads bob through snug rolls of army blankets; brown hands grasp burnished rifles; color-bearers slip the oilcloth cases from the bright standards and unfurl them to the breeze; regimental officers gayly gallop to the head of their columns; companies double quick into line, and dress on the colors; the colonel's stentorian voice calls, "Attention, battalion! Forward! March!" and we are off. The drum and fife corps, marching at the head of the first platoon just in rear of regimental mounted officers, strikes up the lively strains of the old but ever-inspiring "Yankee Doodle;" in even ranks and steady steps—tramp, tramp, tramp—resound the boys' heavy brogans, keeping time to the lively tune; forty or fifty fun-loving colored cooks, old and young, bring up the rear of each regiment, and the camp is deserted, its beautiful white-fringed borders having vanished like mist before a brisk breeze.

At home, when moving, we would take the house furniture and leave the house, but in the army we took the house and left the furniture. As we fell in line and cast a glance back over the lately tented field the eye rested on naught beneath the towering trees of the forest save a broad expanse and wilderness of uncanny soldier beds, benches, tables, and cupboards, white wreaths of smoke from the dying camp fires were curling heavenward, and groups of colored refugees were chasing through the abandoned quarters picking up anything of possible value to them that the boys had overlooked or had thrown away.

Up to this time I had not been in line with my company except at the morning roll call, and now, as I obeyed Lieutenant Kirkman's command to fall in line, and sprang into position with the old regiment headed for the heart of the Confederacy, fully armed and equipped and instructed in the art of biting off a cartridge and ramming it home with my iron ramrod, I fully recognized my importance as a soldier; and as I dressed on the glorious colors carried by one of my own mess, and kept step to the music beside my bunkmate, Nic, my boyish pride soared to dizzy heights which it had never reached before, and certainly has not since attained.*

Camp Cocran was reached about 11 A. M., and with but slight fatigue.

The novelty of this my first march with my regiment, together with the stirring music which the numerous bands discoursed, so fascinated and absorbed my thoughts that, although I marched under a very heavy load, I scarcely noticed the burden, and when ordered to halt and stack arms I felt almost as fresh as when I started, and also realized that among music's many charms it possesses none more marked than in lessening a soldier's heavy burdens.

We were ordered to halt and stack arms near a large brick mansion which was used as the general's headquarters, and which stood in the center of an old abandoned plantation, the rail fencing of which had done duty in boiling coffee for General Grant's men.

The weather had changed during our march, and it

---

*In Memorial Hall in the State House at Springfield, Ill., may be seen the two identical flags under whose bright folds we boys slept, marched, fought, and saw our comrades die, and at the foot of these flag staffs, on the floor of the glass flag case. along with the photographs of some of my comrades, you will find one of the author in his wheel chair.

was now threatening rain, which made us eager to get up our shelters, and gather some bedding before the leaves should get wet.

The different quarters were soon marked out and tents unloaded, we receiving two for our mess, and in almost as short a time as the white cottages had collapsed at Camp Cowen they were up, stiff and taut, at Camp Cocran.

While some of our mess were employed putting up the tents and ditching around them, others started with blankets and axes on double quick time for the woods in search of bedding and furniture material, while Jack went in the same direction for wood and water with which to prepare dinner. Moss and leaves were found near the camp, also forks and poles for table and bed legs, and for crosspieces, but nothing suitable was found for bed bottoms or for table top.

Nic, Sergeant Close, and myself, while following a good sized stream, about a half mile from camp, were suddenly halted by pickets stationed near the edge of a large cane brake, which was so dense that it was impenetrable except along paths which were worn through by animals running at large. The cane was from fifteen to twenty feet high. This was what we were looking for, and, selecting the sizes suitable for our purposes, we cut it down and into proper lengths for our beds and tables, and in suitable quantities, until it required several trips for ourselves and others of our mess to carry it to camp.

After getting in we wove a sheet or mattress of the cane, single thickness, compactly, with a cross piece two feet from each end, and wide enough to cover the head and foot crosspieces of our bed, and to extend up each side six inches. The sides were secured by fastening them to the forks, which were left long enough for that purpose. Our knapsacks held the bedding in at the head, while a chunk of wood served for that purpose at the foot. The tables were made in like manner, minus the sides.

The canes used for the beds were about one and a fourth inches in diameter, and those for the tables about three fourths of an inch in diameter, and we used such quantities as to seem rather extravagant on good fishing pole stock.

I expect that John Chinaman and his funny little Japanese cousin would have shaken their heads, squinted their almond eyes, and considered " Melican solger man's" bamboo work rather crude, but it nevertheless made decidedly the best spring bed I ever slept on while in the army.

Our small wedge tents, thanks to Yankee ingenuity, had a yard-wide piece of old tent cloth sewed all around the bottom, which converted them into quite roomy wall tents, so that we could have our beds well up from the ground. There not being sufficient room inside our tents for the tables, this piece of dining room furniture had to be set up in the street just in front of our tents.

Before we had completed our furniture the rain came down in torrents, and the weather turned so cool we very much missed our cheery fireplaces in the log cabins. But none of us missed them so much as did Jack, who while cooking at such times had to put on an oilcloth blanket and get out in the rain, which persisted in putting out his green wood fire, and so tried his patience that his ebony countenance became more clouded, often, than was the sky above us. Of course, in such weather we ate our meals in our tents. Camp Cocran was much larger than Camp Cowen. The weather soon cleared up, but remained cool, and the brief time we remained here was improved by us recruits in hard drilling.

Here I found an uncle in the Seventy-sixth Illinois Regiment, Volunteer Infantry. They had been camped here for some time, and were quite comfortably situated, having good stick and clay fireplace chimneys, many of which were topped off with open-ended pork barrels; but as we knew we were to remain but a few days we did not indulge in this luxury. The entire camp was subjected to a general inspection of men, arms, ammunition, and everything pertaining to a soldier's campaigning outfit.

New clothing and shoes were issued, questionable cartridges were thrown away, and our boxes supplied with fresh ones. Men who were ailing attended the sick call, were examined by the surgeons, and, if not considered able to withstand the fatigue of a long march, were ordered to remain in camp and look after the tents and surplus clothing and baggage that should be dispensed with in order to put our army in light marching trim.

As to my own personal wardrobe, my heavy double blanket was cut in twain; my overcoat, dresscoat, and one blanket were left in camp. I drew an oilcloth blanket having a slit in the center, so that I could put my head through it when marching in the rain, in place of the one left. The old mess advised me to throw away my heavy boots before starting, and draw a pair of sewed brogans instead. But I said, "No, sir!" That was asking *too* much. Hadn't I had those ten dollar boots made on purpose to wear to the war, and with which to march through the Confederacy? So, notwithstanding all their arguments and persuasions, to my sore grief in the future, as the reader will learn, I stuck to my high-top boots.

I believe it was previously mentioned that I did not retain my company letter and regimental numbers on my cap very long. On reaching my regiment I soon noticed that the veterans had no distinguishing marks on their hats, and Nic advised me not to put them on the new hat which I had drawn and was now wearing in place of my cap, telling me that they might trap me, or reveal my identity if I should be discovered while engaged in some foraging expedition. So I concluded to dispense with them. But I could not dispose of my pretty ornaments to anyone. Even Jack refused to take them as a gift, saying: "Look hea, Massa Will, Jack's gwine on to dat ere raid, too, an' dis young nigger dun war no 'stinguishin' mark on his pusson, needer."

CHAPTER VII.

OFF FOR THE MERIDIAN RAID.

ON the first of February General Sherman arrived from Memphis. On the third, with light hearts, we broke camp and marched out under flying colors, leaving all tents and extra baggage behind. The day was bright. We headed east and crossed the Big Black River in the forenoon on pontoon bridges just north of the burned Jackson and Vicksburg Railroad bridge.

Here the army was halted for a few hours on an open plateau of bottom land for the purpose of issuing to the command three days' rations, and for the different organizations to be allotted their respective positions in the future line of march.

Our regiment was among the first to cross, and halted well to the east and center of the plateau. Glancing back westward we could see crossing the pontoons and filing in right and left on the open ground acres and acres of the boys in blue, with their gun-barrels glistening in the sun; well mounted cavalry troops, with their yellow-striped jackets and rattling sabers; batteries of Parrott and howitzer guns drawn by superb horses, with their gay riders in uniforms trimmed in red; and an immense train of white-topped ambulance, medicine, ammunition, and provision wagons drawn by well-kept and newly shod mules. The view was entirely unobstructed by tent or tree, and was a typical army scene.

Soon the entire command was busily engaged in drawing rations. Infantry, cavalry, and artillery sergeants with squads of men were seen crossing and recrossing each other's track, going in all directions from the provision wagons to their companies, with boxes of hard-tack on their shoulders, sides of bacon on their heads, and with large camp kettles filled with roasted coffee, sugar, salt, and hard soap.

On arriving at their companies boxes and vessels containing rations were placed on the ground; crackerboxes were soon pried open by the orderlies with a bayonet, or their covers knocked off with borrowed wagon hammers, and their contents then issued in mess pans for the different messes. When in camp the rations were turned over to the mess cooks, but on the march they were subdivided and issued to the several members of the mess, each soldier taking care of his own.

At once twenty thousand soldier boys were seen on their knees on Mississippi soil, not, indeed, to pay homage to "King Cotton," but in devotion to some of "Uncle Sam's" swine brisket and hard-tack, coffee, etc., all busily occupied in packing them away in their haversacks.

Before starting Nic had helped me make three small sacks out of oilcloth in which to put my coffee, sugar, and salt; and had provided me with a piece eight or ten inches square in which to wrap my bacon, and a small piece for my soap, which was carried in my knapsack. This oilcloth I found an excellent protection for my rations. Recruits who were not thus provided soon found they had a bad mix of provisions in their haversacks, for with their rations wrapped in paper they were soon softened by the bacon grease, and the swinging, jolting motion given the haversacks caused the flinty hard-tack to grind and thoroughly mix with their other contents. All such unfortunate recruits were soon easily distinguishable by a large grease-spot on the left hip of their blue breeches.

The three days' rations I received were in excess of the room in my haversack. Nic, however, kindly aided me by suggesting that I put the surplus 'tack in my knapsack, and to be very particular in packing it so as not to leave any corners to protrude out in any way, or they would gouge or chafe me. He also instructed me to secure and pack away twelve or fifteen pieces that others might leave, if I should find them. Some, even of the old veterans, would not undertake to carry so much, but depended on begging or foraging for a fresh supply if their rations ran short before another issue.

After rations were packed we filled our canteens with fresh water, Nic cautioning me to keep mine well corked, informing me that if it should leak and soak its woolen cover and my trousers the two rubbing together would chafe and scald me. This I found excellent advice, for afterward, when marching, I often saw soldier boys who had not taken this precaution with their right limbs rubbed raw from this canteen friction.

As none but loaded wagons were to accompany us, the empty ones, from which our first three days' rations were supplied, returned to Vicksburg. This was our last opportunity, therefore, before moving on to get letters started on the way to the dear ones at home. Such occasions the boys never failed to improve. Accordingly, knapsacks were quickly opened, paper, envelopes, and the little round wooden-cased inkstands taken out and opened, and with the white sheets of paper spread on cracker-boxes, drumheads, cartridge-boxes, artillery caissons, or anything we could substitute for a writing desk, brown soldier hands hastily jotted down a few lines something like the following:

"We have just crossed Black River. Are starting on a raid under General Sherman with twenty thousand troops; have three days' rations in our haversacks, and will be accompanied by a large provision, and ammunition train. Expect to be gone some time. Do not be uneasy or worry if you should fail to hear from us often. "Uncle Billy" [the soldiers' pet name for General Sherman] will bring us through all right. We are well and in good spirits, and will write the first opportunity we have to mail a letter.

"Yours affectionately,

"———."

"P. S.—Have orders to move in ten minutes. Good-bye to all. God bless and keep you."

"N. B.—Direct to Vicksburg, and put in some postage stamps. *Hurrah for the Union!*

"——— ———."

I can vouch for the above being about the purport and tenor of thousands of letters the old wagons carried back to Vicksburg that day.

There was one important item of interest, however, to both sender and receiver that I can as certainly vouch they did not contain, and that was our point of destination. It was very clear to us where we had been when we got back, but at that time this desirable piece of information seemed to be lodged under the crown of "Uncle Billy's" hat, and he was not at all inclined to be communicative on the subject. But the army seemed to have unlimited confidence in their general, as well as he in them, so there was no complaining. However, there were a great many conjectures and surmises concerning our objective point. Many seemed to think we were going to Mobile, Ala., to operate with our fleet in the capture of that city. Others thought we were going to the eastern part of the State to destroy railroads. But all was mere guesswork, and since reading General Sherman's memoirs I doubt if any beside himself knew our destination at the time, not even Generals McPherson and Hurlbut, who commanded the right and left columns of the expedition.

When we received the order to be ready to march in ten minutes letters were cut short, and fixtures were hurriedly stowed in our knapsacks. One man for each mess, or perhaps for a whole company, took our letters to the wagons which were to carry the mail to Vicksburg.

Before starting, I noticed Generals Sherman and McPherson seated on their horses, surrounded by a group of officers and orderlies, critically examining with their field glasses a heavy body of timber in our front through which we were to pass. Soon an orderly galloped from the group in the direction of a cavalry regiment, and that body at once dashed out in front of us. They, however, met but a small reconnoitering cavalry force of the enemy, which fell back after a few shots were exchanged at long range.

We moved out without deployment in compact columns, so that the Confederate cavalry would have but slight chance to dash in on us and get away.

General Sherman did not always burn all the bridges behind him. When his command was safely across on the east side of the Big Black, and the wagon train that was to return to Vicksburg had recrossed to the west side, the canvas pontoons on which we crossed were taken out of the river, collapsed, folded up, and loaded on the wagons with their wooden frames, stringers, floors, etc., together with their rope tackle, the whole outfit making no small train of itself.

The rear of our column had not advanced more than two or three miles from the river when the Confederate cavalry appeared behind us, completely cutting us off from our base of supplies, and causing us to depend for food upon the region through which we passed. But while they soon surrounded us on all sides, their force was not sufficiently strong to retard our progress longer than to give us time to rebuild bridges and remove obstructions placed in our way, while those behind us served as a spur to assist our rear guard in urging our stragglers forward.

Our cavalry was employed the most of the time in

our front, carefully feeling our way, but never getting very far beyond supporting distance of our infantry and artillery. Our cavalry force, but one thousand two hundred strong, was under Colonel E. F. Winslow. This was deemed sufficient for all practical purposes on our march. But a cavalry force of ten thousand men, under General W. S. Smith, had been ordered by General Sherman to start from Memphis on the first of February and march directly to Meridian and join us there. For some reason, however, they failed to start until the eleventh, and were headed off and defeated by General Forest, and so never reached us.

We had proceeded but four or five miles on our march when we were ordered to halt and stack arms, and were given some thirty minutes for dinner. Before starting those who were not already supplied with quart buckets provided themselves with such made out of fruit or oyster cans with wire bails. For some reason unknown to me these were called "blickers." While on the march their rattle made quite a din, yet their utility and unquestioned right in a campaigner's outfit were fully demonstrated, for by their aid, with a supply of water and wood, the soldier could have a cup of boiling coffee in a few minutes' time, which soldiers always prized. If we halted a dozen times a day, that often could be seen hundreds of men boiling coffee; and if ordered to fall in line before it was drunk it was carried along and sipped out of the blickers or emptied into canteens and drunk out of them.

On halting we would break ranks, unsling our

knapsacks, secure wood for fire, and while this was getting under way our roasted coffee was ground in our blickers with the butt ends of our bayonets and was soon in readiness for use. While our coffee was heating we would broil a slice of bacon by holding it over the fire on a forked stick, holding a cracker underneath to catch the dripping grease.

These three luxuries made up the common bill of fare for a marching column. But this was frequently enlarged from the poultry yards, smokehouses, potato patches, and sheep, cattle, and swine herds of the enemy through whose land we were marching; and often did our boys regale themselves with choice milk and sirup and honey on this expedition.

On this march all of the colored cooks did not go with us. Our Jack, who was along, only helped with breakfast and supper; the midday meal was prepared individually. As he was not sworn into the service of course he could draw no rations, clothing, or pay. These our mess provided for by dividing our rations into eleven portions instead of ten, giving him one of them. Besides giving him one dollar each per month to do our cooking and washing, we also provided him with clothing from our cast-off garments. In this way thousands of colored army cooks who were not sworn into the service were provided for.

When on the march these cooks were not required to keep in ranks, and having no guns or accouterments to carry, they could, and often did, lighten our burdens. Jack often kept several regiments in advance of us when we were not ourselves in the front.

and on making a discovery of some good water he would rush back after our canteens, and by the time we came up would have them ready for us freshly filled.

Sometimes when our regiment was well toward the rear of the marching column, or was acting as rear guard, our regimental wagons carrying our cooking utensils would get into camp an hour or so in advance of us. On such occasions Jack would go in with them, and by the time we reached camp, which was frequently after dark, we would find our faithful cook seated on a pile of rails or wood which he had gathered, with mess pan and camp kettle on the ground beside him, filled with water, waiting for us, ready to prepare supper as soon as he could learn where we would bivouac.

CHAPTER VIII.

On the March Through Jackson.

THE first day out our brigade marched near the head of the column, so that Jack had no opportunity of going in advance of us to make preparations. As it was dark when we reached camp several of us assisted him in getting wood and water. A number of regiments were in advance of us, and already had their fires started and suppers under way. The black pine smoke from these camp fires was very dense and blinding, and, at times, made it difficult to see or step without stumbling over some object or running into some person.

Dan, the tall color-sergeant, and I, while going in search of some water, had to pass through where several of these regiments were camped. In trying to keep up with Dan's long strides in the blinding smoke I had the misfortune to come in contact with a pile of knapsacks, tumbled headlong over them with my camp kettles and canteens, and, losing my balance, caught my toe under the end of one of a pair of long rails that were occupied by a happy party of steaming coffee blickers and sputtering frying pans, which, judging from their savory smell, were about ready to be taken from the fire. These were surrounded by ten or a dozen hungry, impatient Iowa soldiers. My unceremonious appearance on the scene at this juncture threw one of the rails out of place and upset the kettle party into the fire, nearly putting it out. The infuriated Iowans instantly sprang to their feet amid the stifling smoke, and wildly shrieked for vengeance. I gathered myself and tinware up as quickly as possible, and took to my heels, but got several more tumbles before I considered myself at a safe distance from the fierce Iowa blizzard that was on my track. My safe escape was only made possible by the extra smoke I had caused by upsetting the coffee and the protection of the old sergeant in my rear.

When we returned with the water, for which we had to go nearly a quarter of a mile, the rest of the mess had some rails collected for fuel and for sideboards to our beds. The cheery fire was blazing, and on both sides of it, with foot ends next the fire, were our camping couches, all ready to receive those who should occupy them. These couches consisted of two good-sized rails laid parallel to each other on the ground, about the width of a blanket apart, with the space between filled up with leaves and a kind of long grass that grew in that section. Over these were spread the oilcloth and woolen blankets, while knapsacks were used for pillows.

Each member of the mess contributed his share of coffee and bacon for the evening meal, and Jack did the cooking. During the repast, as we reviewed the events of the day, the Johnnies came in for their share of praise for having cut and ricked up such a lot of fine dry wood for us.

The early February air was crisp and frosty, and when I snuggled under our blankets beside Nic it was quite late, and he was sound asleep, as were most of the boys, except a few colored cooks, who were carrying water and making preparations for an early breakfast. The fires had all died out, and a slight breeze had swept aside the dark canopy of smoke by which the camp had been enveloped.

The night was perfectly clear, and over head, through the branches of the tall tree-tops, peered the old man out of the silvery moon, as if to guard us in our slumbers. Around him shone myriads of brilliant gems, as if so many angel-lighted lamps swung in space from heaven's blue-vaulted dome. Their light revealed the forms of thousands of brave men stretched prone upon the ground, wrapped in their blankets, and dreaming, perchance, of their far-away homes and loved ones.

This being my first night in camp on the open field, the novelty of the scene and the many thoughts which went flitting through my mind drove sleep from my eyes until near midnight. All was quiet, except the heavy breathing and snoring of sleeping soldiers, the deep hush only broken now and then by the loud braying of some hungry government mule and the "who-who-who, who, who, who?" of some inquisitive Mississippi owl, as if desiring to know what strange creature was disturbing the stillness of the night.

These midnight confusions and new surroundings, together with the fact that we were now in the enemy's country, cut off entirely from friends, led me in my reflections back to the dear old home-circle, and to the school I had left; and I could but contrast my surroundings now with what they were before, when Hardin and I were seated behind a badly carved desk in the old schoolhouse at Naples, and I thought how strangely "Uncle Sam" had let me down and out, first, from a snug cabin to a tent, and from the latter to open camp, with no protecting shelter.

The next morning we were up bright and early, and slipped out of camp just at dawn. The day was most charming, just cool enough for comfortable marching, though the roads were very dusty on account of the heavy travel. We had not proceeded more than two miles when we marched through the camp the Johnnies had occupied the night previous.

We marched fifteen miles that day. Before noon, however, my heavy boots, which were a little loose, were giving me intense pain. They had blistered my feet some the day before, but I had made no mention of it. I knew of several others with badly blistered feet who were in the ambulances, but my boyish pride would not submit to that, and when I reached camp that night I was suffering great agony, and knew I must have relief from some source, or not be able to march the next day, which would require a ride in an ambulance, or expose me to capture, to either of which I was strictly opposed.

When we got into camp, therefore, and settled, I unburdened my trouble to Nic with many misgivings. He looked at me with a kind of "I told you so" expression, which was rather humiliating to me, and said, "We will attend to them after supper."

When supper was over, with a piece of resin soap in hand, I accompanied him to a brook, where he helped me pull my boots off—no easy task, for after reaching camp my feet had swollen badly. A thorough bathing, however, gave me great relief, but I found it necessary, wearing my cumbersome boots, to keep up this practice every few nights, which became rather monotonous during our three hundred miles' march.

During this day's march wagon loads of new dresscoats, overcoats, and blankets were thrown away by recruits, who had thought they knew better what was needed on a march of this kind than did the commanding officers or the old soldiers, and, in many instances, I saw the latter and the colored cooks exchanging their old worn blankets for good new ones, and the colored brethren their badly worn coats for bright new ones. Jack, on this occasion, provided himself with both a new coat and blanket.

During the day we passed by a plantation which belonged to Jefferson Davis, the President of the Southern Confederacy. The fences were all gone, and I heard some one remark that "Old Jeff" would have to get "Uncle Abe" to come down and split him some rails before he could put in his spring crop. "Uncle Abe" was the soldier's name for President Lincoln, the old-time "rail splitter."

On the sixth we drove the Confederates through and beyond Jackson, crossed Pearl River on the pontoons, and camped some two miles to the east of the city for the night.

As we passed through some of the principal business streets of the city I saw some of the "boys in blue" coming out of stores with boxes of tobacco and cigars, neither of which had any attractions for me. But I thought I should like to patronize a Southern shoe store, and broke ranks to do my shopping, but failed to find any.

We had now reached the third day of our march, and, just as Nic had predicted, men were seen begging rations. Our mess had plenty of rations for supper, but as the provision wagons were late getting in it was midnight before many others had anything to eat.

Having now reached a point farther east from Vicksburg than any of the Union forces had ever penetrated to before the scenes were in marked contrast to those of the region we had passed through. Thus far the territory traversed seemed to be almost deserted, both towns and country presenting many blackened ruins, houseless chimneys, and fenceless fields. Now we were entering a rich cotton-growing district which had been hitherto unmolested by the Yankees.

The planters had fine residences and large plantations well stocked with Negroes, horses, mules, cattle, hogs, sheep, etc. We found full corn cribs, sweet potato banks, and large amounts of cotton which had not been shipped or disposed of on account of the blockades. But on our approach the whites appeared to become panic-stricken, and many deserted their homes, leaving them in possession of their former slaves.

Unlike these whites, the freedmen were in great

ecstacies of joy at this turning point in their history, and, hailing "Massa Sherman" and his soldiers as their deliverers, they bade adieu to the old plantations, and, male and female, old and young, flocked to us by the thousands. They came from the hill-tops and from the plains in their flight for freedom. They could be seen hurrying toward us across the broad fields and along the highways some on foot, carrying huge bundles on their heads or shoulders; others riding, and hauling their possessions in various kinds of vehicles, from an old single ox cart to a fine family barouche. Indeed, I saw several joining the caravan with loaded wheelbarrows, and it was no uncommon thing to see an old "aunty" with a half-dozen little bareheaded, half-naked children driving along the road in the rear of the column in a fine carriage, she dressed up in some "ob de white folks' finery," wanting to make a "'specutable 'pearance" when she should meet "Massa Sherman," while just behind her would be the old uncle, walking, and leading an old plantation mule with its head stuck out of a huge mountain of clothing, bedding, provisions, etc.

To one venerable-looking old black man, dressed in an indescribable suit of cotton patchwork, whose white wool was seen peeping out of the crown of an old straw hat, and whose toes were protruding from a pair of well-worn shoes, laced up with cotton strings, I said:

"How do you do, uncle?"

"O, bress de Lawd, I'se berry well, tank you!"

"Where are you going?" I asked.

"O, bress Massa Linkum, child, I'se gwine whar Massa Sherman an yous are all gwine."

These crude plantation specimens in nature's dusky uniforms, so oddly dressed, now ecstatic with inexpressible joy at their deliverance from a life of bondage, and eagerly endeavoring by grotesque speech, song, grimace, and gesture to set forth their great gratitude to the "Lawd" and "Massa Linkum" for their gracious deliverance, presented a spectacle at times so touching and pathetic as to stir the tender emotions of the brawniest soldier in blue, and at others so truly comical as to cause our aching sides to test our broad belts while convulsed with laughter.

On our route as far as Jackson the battle-scarred and devastated country would not have kept one good healthy pilferer in chickens, and the old soldiers, who had marched and fought over this ground, seemed to know it, and made no effort to improve our plain bill of fare by foraging. But the night we crossed Pearl River Dan and several of my mess declared their intention to have something to eat besides bacon and "'tack," if it was to be found within five miles of the camp. Accordingly, after supper, as color-bearers carry no guns, Dan borrowed one of ours, and, with two others, fully equipped with cartridge boxes, haversacks, and canteens, started, saying, "We do not expect to return before midnight."

When reveille broke the stillness of the following frosty morning the blue dome above us was still spangled with thousands of twinkling luminaries, and as we gathered around our camp fire, wrapped in our blankets, to dispatch our early breakfast, old Sol had not yet dispelled the morning twilight.

The foraging expedition of Dan and his comrades was a decided success, and, as the result, Jack gave us a breakfast of delicious boiled turkey and sweet potatoes and honey, in addition to our usual fare.

This being the first fowl or fresh meat of any kind I had tasted since reaching my regiment, I can assure my readers it was decidedly toothsome, although it was simply boiled in clear water, seasoned with salt and pepper, destitute of any brown basting, and having no delicious oyster dressing.

CHAPTER IX.

THE SKIRMISH.

WE had barely finished storing away the remains of our turkey in our haversacks when we were ordered to "fall in, and take arms."

We passed along over the dusty road at a good pace without any noteworthy event until we reached Brandon, then a good-sized village, which we entered just as the sun was gathering its fading rays behind the tree-tops in our rear. Here we found the depot of the Jackson and Selma Railroad, several large warehouses, and wharves stored with cotton bales, all in flames.

As we entered one street the intense heat caused by the fiery wrath of the old white King, now being offered as a burnt sacrifice on the altar of the "Lost Cause," was unbearable, so that we were compelled to halt, about face, retreat, and take another street before we could pass his fiery majesty.

After going into camp in a piece of timber which skirted the town two of our mess, Jim Howel's "bunkie," and Nic, my "bunkie," were detailed for picket duty. This naturally threw Jim and I together for the night. We at once took our blankets, and went in search of material for our beds. Coming across quite a large hole, filled with leaves, at the foot of an uprooted tree, we proceeded to fill our blankets. During the operation the toe of Jim's brogan struck something on the bottom of the hole, which produced a metallic sound. Instantly we both dropped to our knees and began clawing vigorously among the leaves, and soon reached a tin box about six inches wide and deep, and some ten inches in length. As it was too dark to read, we struck a match and set fire to some leaves. By the aid of this light we opened the unlocked box, which had a hinged lid with clasp fastening, and found it full of deeds, Confederate bonds, and five thousand dollars in Confederate money. We kept the money, and afterward Jim realized five cents on the dollar for some of his at a bank in Vicksburg. I was not so fortunate with mine. We also kept several bonds as relics, one of which, on the State of Arkansas, I have yet, which I would be pleased to cash at its face value, twenty dollars.

When through examining the contents we took a deed, and with pencil wrote these words on its back in bold hand: "Small favors thankfully received, large ones in proportion," and signed it, "Yankee Soldiers." We then carefully returned all to the box except what I have mentioned, placed the deed on top of the other articles with the inscription up; then, in the gathering darkness, by the light of the leafy fire, we safely returned the little casket to its shallow grave at the foot of the old forest giant, covered it with a thick blanket of withered leaves, trampled out the fire, and started for camp.

As we stole away through the darkness of the night, with our blankets filled with soft bedding material, and with our bogus booty, Jim remarked that the man who hid that box must have been foolish or frightened, as he had left it exposed to three destructive agencies, namely, Yankees, fire, and water. He also stated that while he would not care to be near enough to hear what the "Johnnie" would say when he should resurrect and open the box, believing it would not be complimentary either to us or our Yankee government, yet he would very much like to have a good photograph, picturing his position and physiognomy when he should first detect the loss of his Confederate scrip and read our Yankee inscription. Poor Jim was a brave soldier and one of the handsomest young men I ever saw. After his time in our regiment expired he returned home, reenlisted in another regiment, and was killed before Mobile.

After our evening meal was over I visited the town to take in the sights by the illumination of the still burning cotton. Among other scenes that interested me was a crowd of soldiers busily engaged with long sharp pointed poles punching up a large bed of coals. I noticed, as I approached nearer, that sometimes when they drew their poles out of the long mound of coals there were some dark objects sticking on the ends of them about the size of my two fists or even larger. Those engaged in this enterprise seemed much interested in it. On reaching the place I found they were gathered around the smoldering ruins of a warehouse in which several hundred bushels of sweet potatoes had been stored, which were now well baked, but the fire was yet burning so fiercely there was no possible way of obtaining the potatoes without the aid of these long potato forks, and the men in high glee were spearing for Mississippi yams, of which I soon obtained a haversack full myself.

An old Jersey soldier, who loaned me his yam spear after getting all he could carry, said he had dug a great many clams in his day and had been at many New England clambakes, but this Mississippi yambake, while it was very hot digging, beat the biggest clambake he was ever at, and he should have to write to his friends about it.

The next morning it fell to the lot of our brigade to march at the head of our column, and as usual, when we had proceeded but a mile or so, we passed through the camp the Johnnies had occupied the night before.

About 3 P. M., just as the head of the long blue column was surmounting the crest of a low range of wooded hills in our front, sharp firing was heard in that direction, and soon a force of our cavalry appeared on the brow of the hill and came dashing down the road toward us to report the trouble.

Immediately we were halted, and ordered to one side of the road to make room for a battery to pass to the front. Instantly four brass howitzers, each drawn by six strong horses, come flying by on the dead run, making the very ground to tremble beneath their thundering tread. They swiftly ascended the wooded crest, deployed to the right, and, rapidly swinging around until the cannon faced the enemy, were at once unlimbered, and more quickly than it can be related were belching forth smoke, flame, and shell.

I had never seen anything of this kind before, and, judging by the way the Johnnies had been retreating before us, I began to fear I never would. Being so close to where the battery was going into action, I got permission (at least I think I got it), and ran to the top of the hill, a little to the left of the battery, arriving there just in time to see them open fire on some dismounted Confederate cavalry who had taken position in the center of an open piece of ground behind two rail fences, and in a large cotton gin and other small buildings.

The guns were fired by volley. The first four shells, flying and screaming through the air over their heads and over the roof of the gin, passed beyond and burst harmlessly. Two shells of the second round struck the ground and exploded a few rods in front of the fence. One hit the fence, burst, and sent the old rails flying in the air and a group of Confederates scampering to the rear. The fourth went crashing through the barricaded side of the gin house, and in an instant came a terrible roar and crash, the shingles and sheathing flew off of the roof, smoke poured out, and the panic-stricken Johnnies rushed out of the building like bees from a disturbed beehive. Hastily they vaulted into their saddles and rode out of the range of the shells, which were now bursting at their heels, as rapidly as their four-footed friends could carry them. They were only some five or six hundred yards distant when the battery opened fire, and a number of them must have been killed or wounded, especially from the shell which exploded in the crowded gin-house, but I never learned the exact casualties. When our battery boys had dislodged the Confederates from the position from which they expected to open fire upon our infantry we moved on past the position as if nothing had occurred.

That evening, our brigade being in the lead, we bivouacked early, about an hour before sundown, in a wooded ravine opposite a large deserted plantation, the residence of which was in flames. As soon as we had stacked arms and could unsling our knapsacks we made a move toward the premises for rails and to secure something for our mess kettles if possible. When I reached there, out of breath, I found I was too late for anything but rails, but glancing through the smoke I caught a glimpse of a large family Bible lying on a center table near the middle of the room. I had no desire to take the book for myself; but not wishing to see it and the family record it contained destroyed, my boyish impulse was to save it for its owner's sake. Acting upon this impulse, I instantly sprang into the room, secured it, and just escaped as the roof and timbers fell in.

The Bible weighed ten or twelve pounds, and when I had caught my breath, collected my thoughts, and began to look around for some safe, dry place to leave it, I found the out-buildings had caught fire from the main one, so there seemed to be no hiding place for it. I then began to realize that I had a larger contract on hand than I had bargained for, and if it had been any other book I should have left it on the ground. But now that I had it in my possession I felt in a measure responsible for it, and finally decided to carry it to camp and leave it at some house the next day, where the owner would probably find it.

Reaching camp with it under one arm, with a rail on my opposite shoulder, I was chided by my comrades for "stealing a Bible," and all were urgent to learn the text I had selected to preach from that night. My explanation of motives for securing it only seemed to make matters worse. But notwithstanding these gibes I stuck to the Bible, and the next day I left it at a house about three miles from the place where I obtained it.

CHAPTER X.

THE BATTLE.

ABOUT 3 P. M., the 9th of February, just as we entered some wooded hills, the serenity of the sunny afternoon was suddenly broken by the loud roll and rattle of musketry, and the deep, heavy thunder of artillery in our immediate front. Our advance, which was but a few yards ahead of us, had encountered a line of Confederate infantry and artillery, which was posted on the crest of a range of hills that ran across our front.

Instantly I observed the old soldiers scan each other's faces as if attempting to divine the meaning of this sudden demonstration. Nic, turning to me with a determined expression of countenance I had never seen him wear before, said, "Will, there is a battle on hand and we are in for it. Stick by me." I made no reply, but had already decided I would try to do that very thing. Never had I seen so serious an expression on the faces of men as those old soldiers wore when that battle storm burst upon us. Its suddenness and fury were as the coming of a mighty cyclone unannounced except by a terrific roar and peal after peal of thunder from a clear sky. It was enough to terrify the bravest hearted, and the intense nervous strain of the instant was enough to age one by years. However, as I glanced up into those brave, rigid faces I could read in their firm expression, as clearly as if cut by sculptor's chisel, a determination to "do or die," and this, naturally, strung my young nerves up as they would not have been had they betrayed the slightest trace of fear.

But the intensity of the moment's strain was at once relieved by our being ordered double quick to the front. As we went in we met a yellow-striped cavalry regiment coming out pell mell through the timber, the steel-clad hoofs of their flying chargers cracking the brush beneath them as they leaped over logs, gullies, and brush heaps.

These scampering cavalry appeared to nettle some of our old infantry men, and as they passed by I heard one remark that he had never seen a dead cavalry man yet, and another said, "My kingdom for a 'hoss.'"

We had proceeded but a short distance when we began to meet stragglers and Negro cooks—chaff which the fierce tempest was driving to the rear. Then we came upon the dead and wounded. The first wounded man I saw was a Confederate sitting against a tree near the roadside, who was shot through the body. As we passed a rough recruit in our company rudely asked this man "how far it was a mile ahead." To which the wounded Confederate replied, "Three lengths of an infernal fool; if you don't believe it lie down and measure it yourself." Upon this we gave the poor wretch a hearty cheer which must have done him good, while at the same time it was a deserved rebuke to the unfeeling recruit.

THE BATTLE.

As we emerged from the timber into an open field on the hilltop we were met by a tornado of hot iron and leaden hail. The "ping," "whiz," "zip," and deadly thud of the minie balls were heard on every side. Solid shot and deadly shell went flying through the air, hatefully hissing and screeching as they burst over our heads or tore up the earth beneath our feet. As this terrific storm broke upon us, and we hurried through the smoke and dust to our position, I noticed in passing many dead and wounded. Indeed, it seemed strange that any could possibly escape unhurt. One poor fellow in blue uniform lay in a pool of blood at the foot of a large gate-post with his head as completely severed as if it had been taken off with a cleaver.

At this juncture a six-gun battery of brass howitzers dashed past, drawn by thirty-six powerful gray horses with distended nostrils, flashing eyes, and flowing manes, causing the hilltop to tremble under their heavy tread; and as their red-striped, blue-jacketed riders urged them to the top of their speed with whip and spur, every tug was pulled taut, and every nerve and muscle strained to its utmost. Their object was to gain a coveted position in our front, commanding a view of an opposite hilltop crowned by Confederate artillery which was now dealing death and destruction to our lines.

Arriving and deploying, each six-horse team wheeled its chariot of fire into position with the motion and velocity of a whirlwind; fearless riders sprang from the backs of their foam-flecked, fiery steeds; guns were unlimbered, caissons thrown open, brave battery boys rushed with bomb and ball to cannon's mouth, and with rapid rammer strokes crowded the iron feed down their brazen throats; pieces were quickly trained, lanyards drawn, and instantly their rigid lips of brass responded with the deadly language of the lightning flash and thunderbolt in mad defiance to the fierce tongues of fire, smoke, shell, and solid shot of the enemy's guns; and as our regiment right-wheeled into position on the hillside below them for their support the deafening roar and terrible shock seemed to rock the whole mound beneath us. Here the missiles of death, like a fierce meteoric shower, screaming and bursting over our heads in rapid and crashing sounds, from the cross-fire of Union and Confederate guns, appeared to rend the heavens and earth asunder.

We received orders to halt instantly, followed by the command, "Load at will; load!" and as our men bit off the ends of paper cartridges and rammed them home, and adjusted percussion caps, the metallic ring and click of iron ramrods and heavy musket locks were barely heard above the din of battle.

While in this act two recruits near me were hit. Deb Deposter, just at my left, was struck in the hand by a minie-ball while capping his gun, but was too plucky to go to the rear. A cannon-ball caught the protruding corner of Pat Wood's knapsack, whirled him around about-face, double quick, leaving him with his back to the enemy. Somewhat puzzled at Pat's singular movement, I asked him what it meant; and, as he faced about to the front, with surprised look and blanched countenance, he said, "That ugly thing sthruck me roit in the back."

Our gallant old Colonel Hall at that time was in command of our brigade, and as we were loading he rode along well in our rear on a large roan horse, speaking words of cheer to our men. He ordered Major McNolty, who was in command, to have four men from each company, who were the least able to go into the engagement, detailed as stretcher bearers. When Lieutenant Kirkman of our company called for men it seemed to me, on account of my age and size, that every eye in the company was turned toward me, while I had several boys in mind that I thought would be sure to avail themselves of this opportunity to escape the dangerous part of the fray. But, to my surprise, and to the credit and honor of these brave boys, not one of them deserted the ranks. The four men who did volunteer for this special work were about as large as any in the company, and ranged in age from twenty-four to forty years. The one aged twenty-four was a big-fisted, pugnacious recruit, who was constantly making trouble with some one smaller than himself, and who had made repeated boasts that he was eager to smell gunpowder. When, therefore, I saw this bully of a fellow slip out of the ranks and skip off with long strides to the rear for a stretcher I concluded he had had his smell of gunpowder and was satisfied.

As soon as our guns were loaded we were ordered to lie down. Instantly every man in the long line of blue with glistening gunbarrels and flashing swords dropped to the ground as if the whole forest of muskets and men had been mowed down by a single volley from the Confederate guns.

This being my first experience in battle, I was somewhat surprised to find that the handsomely dressed commissioned officers in this line of flattened infantry appeared no more conspicuous than others, nor did they seem any more afraid of soiling their fine uniforms than did the plainest private in his old blouse. What was still more strange to the uninitiated, it was very perceptible also that these officers did not manifest any aversion to having a stump or a log to obstruct their view of the front. No objects of all our long line of blue were left standing, except the flags with their staffs driven in the ground, and a few mounted officers in our rear.

With heels uphill and head down, our position, while thus held in support of our battery, was anything but comfortable or composing, exposed, as we were, both to artillery and infantry fire which we could not return for the reason that our own men were in the midst of a fierce engagement but about seventy-five yards in advance of us. I am quite sure, however, that I never seemed to be so large in all my life before, for, as closely as I could hug the hill and contract my frame, my extremities seemed entirely too long and my back to hump up entirely too high. But, though unfavorably situated, in accordance with my practice of making a daily record of my experiences, I decided that I would be no more exposed with my eyes open, taking observations of the tragic scenes in the midst of which I found myself for record, than if I were to keep them closed.

Some one hundred and fifty yards to the rear, and a little to the left of our battery, on another eminence, seated on his horse and surrounded by a group of mounted officers, I saw General McPherson, with field-glass to his eyes, scanning the field in front. Just then a mounted orderly, as if on the wings of the wind, came dashing up to the group from the left. Immediately two others started, the one for the left and the other for the center where the battery was posted, and as they galloped away with orders their fleet-footed chargers appeared to spurn the very ground beneath them.

Posted in our rear at regular intervals, and parallel to the line of battle, between it and the group of officers, was the mounted signal corps with their different colored flags fluttering in the breeze.

The mound above us where our battery was posted was enveloped in smoke and flame; and as the guns belched forth their showers of heated metal they reminded me somewhat of a picture in my old school geography of a volcano in eruption.

Midway between the top and base of the eastern hillside our line, like a broad band of blue ribbon, lay stretched on the brown grass to the right and left as far as the eye could penetrate through the smoke. Below and between us and the opposite chain of hills ran a small creek, skirted on each side by heavy timber. In these dark woods a stubborn fight was in progress. The Confederates were on the side of the creek next to us, and it was a question whether they would force our lines back to our position, or our forces drive them across the stream. As shadowy forms quickly glided from tree to tree puffs of smoke were seen, and the sharp reports of rifles were heard, and the whole fronts of the long lines of the blue and the gray in the dark valley seemed ablaze with streams of fire from hot musket muzzles, and the roll and rattle of volley firing swept up and down the battling lines as if in loud tenor accompaniment to the heavy thundering bass of the artillery on the hilltops above us. Over and beyond the plume-crowned pines which stood in the valley, through the rifts in the sulphurous clouds, the eye caught frequent glimpses on the opposite hillside of the long lines of Confederate gray gripping tightly their polished steel, while massed in support of the smoke-curtained, cannon-crowned crest above, which in its wild grandeur of action appeared as a twin crater to ours.

While lying here listening to the din of battle which filled the air, and watching the grand spectacle before me, I took in several byplays of the battle.

Our major, at the time of this battle, had two very fine horses, one a beautiful dark chestnut sorrel mare, and the other a large handsome dapple gray horse. The two were almost inseparable. His hostler was a large rawboned old German named Peter. The afternoon of this engagement the major rode the gray, leaving the chestnut behind the hill in charge of the hostler. This separation did not seem to please either of the horses, as was clearly shown by their frantic actions, and, when the balls were flying thickest and shells were bursting loudest, the brave four-footed lady, eager to be beside her handsome mate, took the bit in her teeth, and, despite old Pete's efforts to restrain her, brought him on a flying charge over the hill to our position.

It should be noted that the day we started on this raid to Meridian Peter's three years' service lacked but three days of being out, and he seriously objected to starting. But the officers refused to excuse him, which made him very angry. That the mettlesome mare had unceremoniously taken him into the midst of danger after his term of service had expired now seemed to make him still more wrathy.

Then, as if this were not enough, and to exasperate Peter all the more, just as he appeared in sight a shell exploded in the air immediately in front of the flying chestnut, which caused her to rear and walk off on her hind feet, pawing the air as if striking at the impudent shell, with Peter clinging to her neck. This little comic act, introducing itself on the stage where the serious tragedy of actual war was being enacted, caused the spectators for a moment to lose sight of the dangers by which they were surrounded, and a loud ripple of mirth swept up and down the prostrate lines of blue, which finally gave vent to a roar of merriment as the men shouted, "Hold on, Pete, you only have three days more!" These tantalizing words caused the old German's beer-mug of wrath to fairly froth over, and, be it said to Peter's discredit, that on that trying occasion he used some very discourteous, emphatic language in broken English about the officers, the men, the mare, and the ugly shell.

About this time the major noticed the unnecessary danger the pair were placed in, and ordered Pete to dismount and lead his pet out of range of the enemy's guns. The last I saw of this excited pair before the curtain dropped on this act Peter was down on all fours, spread out in front of the mare like a big frog, vainly endeavoring to drag her up over the hill, while the stubborn beauty had her feet firmly planted, refusing to follow the old man's lead.

In striking contrast to this comic scene, but an instant later, and quicker than a flash, I saw three men of the Twelfth Wisconsin Regiment, just a few yards in front of me, violently hurled to the ground and into eternity by a deadly solid shot. At the time their regiment was in line and engaged, and as the ill-fated trio stood in a row, one behind the other, and on a gradual elevation, the cruel ball tore off the first man's head, the right shoulder of the one behind him, while the third victim was stricken in the breast, the ball tearing an ugly hole through his body. Then the death-dealing demon, as if to wipe its bloody sides on the dress of mother earth, struck in the dead grass a few feet in front of where I lay, and went bounding over our regiment as if in quest of more human gore.

While lying here below and between the opposing batteries I plainly saw several solid shot from the Confederate guns before they reached us; also many shells coming and going in mid air.

Soon after the three Wisconsin men mentioned were killed our right began to swing around the enemy's left flank. The gray lines in the timber wavered, and we received the welcome order, "Up, and forward!" Immediately the long lines of support sprang to their feet and went rushing, cheering, down the hill. We swept the Confederates through the timber, across the shallow creek, and, like a blue tidal wave, our line surged up and over the crest beyond, and just as the sun sank amid his amber glory the long lines of Confederate gray, inferior in numbers and beaten, hastily retreated and left the field to the victorious Union blue.

CHAPTER XI.

After the Battle.

THAT night we went into camp in a body of timber which skirted an old cotton field, about half a mile distant from where the battle took place. As Colonel Rogers, of the Fifteenth Illinois, our "twin regiment," known as such because it brigaded with us, was inspecting the picket line in our front, a Confederate sharpshooter posted in a clump of woods on the opposite side of the field, at least a quarter of a mile away, no doubt thinking the mounted officer a good target on which to try his skill, displayed his fine marksmanship by landing a bullet plump against the large brass buckle on the colonel's sword-belt. The shining eagle on the buckle impeded the flying missile, but the heavy thump it gave the colonel over the pit of his stomach caused him to reel and fall from his horse as if dead, and compelled him to forfeit a part of his dinner; otherwise he was uninjured.

As far as Morton, near where this engagement occurred, our command had marched on two separate roads running parallel with each other east and west, and from seven to ten miles apart. Hurlburt's, the Sixteenth Corps, occupied the left, while our corps, McPherson's, the Seventeenth, occupied the right, but at Morton the two formed a junction. On the 12th Hurlburt's Corps had the right of way, and at night bivouacked on a small stream three or four miles east of Decatur, while McPherson's, bringing up the rear, camped for the night on the outskirts of the town.

As usual, during the day there had been lively skirmishing at the front and on our flanks, with an occasional dash on our rear guard. Entering Decatur as the shadows of the tall pines were lengthening to their eastern limits, we came upon evidences of a cavalry dash upon Hurlburt's wagon train, the dusty road being strewn with dead and wounded mules, abandoned white-covered wagons riddled with bullets, besides a number of wounded soldiers and teamsters.

On entering the town we found General Sherman and staff, and learned that our commander had just run a very narrow escape from being captured by some Confederate cavalry. Had these Johnnies but known of the prize so nearly within their grasp it is presumable, judging from the situation, they would, to the certain mortification of the general, consternation of the command, and the great pleasure of the captors, have galloped off with "Uncle Billy," a feat which forever after would have rendered them famous.

It seems, as was his custom, that General Sherman that day rode along with the advance corps, and as the Sixteenth Corps passed through the town he decided to halt there, with his staff, for the night with the Seventeeth Corps, the head of whose column was some four miles behind the rear of the Sixteenth. To make this undertaking safe he detached an infantry regiment from Hurlburt's command to guard the crossroads of the town until the head of our column should come in sight. He and staff then went to a large log house and made arrangements with the hostess for supper, had their horses unsaddled and tied to the fence, and went inside to await the preparation of the meal. Feeling fatigued, the general lay down on a bed and fell asleep. Presently the colonel of the regiment detailed as guard, espying a cloud of dust down the road in the direction of our corps, and being very eager to get into camp, took it for granted that it was occasioned by the head of our column, called in his pickets, and started with his regiment in the direction his corps had taken. This left General Sherman and staff wholly unprotected.

But the dust cloud the colonel had seen was occasioned by some straggling wagons of the Sixteenth Corps, and a light infantry support. When these arrived within pistol shot of the house where the general was, a body of Confederate cavalry that during the day had been hovering on the right flank of the Sixteenth Corps, discovering the exposed position of the wagons, struck them in the flank with the result mentioned on the previous page.

In the encounter some of the balls struck the house in which the general and his staff were located. On being awakened by this disturbance General Sherman started an officer on the run for the infantry regiment that had left him, and he and the rest of his staff and orderlies prepared to take refuge in an old corn crib near the house, and defend themselves as best they could. Fortunately, however, the officer soon overtook the regiment, returned on the run with it, and, deploying as they came, soon cleared the premises of the troublesome Johnnies, which, no doubt, saved the general and our nation from a great calamity.

That night, after getting into camp, Frank Durant, a seventeen-year-old recruit from Naples, while out foraging, trying to shoot a hog, managed in some awkward manner to wound himself with his revolver. The ball went through his left thigh about ten inches above the knee, just grazed the bone, and lodged next the skin on the opposite side from where it entered, whence the surgeon cut it out. It made an ugly wound, and, from its inflamed and swollen condition, must have been quite painful. But Frank was a gritty boy, and, notwithstanding that we had to march one hundred and seventy-five miles before reaching Vicksburg on our return from the long raid, yet he refused to ride in an ambulance a single step of the way, or to be excused from any duty.

At Decatur we destroyed a large amount of cotton and other stores, and on the morning of the 13th we were on our way bright and early, headed for Meridian. Our route lay through a rather low wooded country, interspersed with swamps and cotton plantations. Toward 10 A. M. the hitherto sunlit skies suddenly became overcast with dark, low-hanging clouds, and before noon the cold winter rain was coming down in torrents. Our leather cartridge boxes and oilcloth haversacks kept our ammunition and provisions dry, but as we trudged along the muddy roads with our heads poked through our rubber blankets, carrying our muskets under them, the heavy gusts of wind would catch our oilcloth coverings, fore and aft, and whirl them up over our heads so much that we became thoroughly drenched, and our woolen blankets saturated. My high-topped boots only seemed to serve as cisterns in catching the copious flow of cold rain-water from my oilcloth roof, and on becoming filled seemed as if they would glue me fast in the Mississippi mire.

As night approached we had a decided mix of men, horses, mules, and mud. The heavy ordnance train, provision wagons, artillery, and other heavy travel had cut the soil and mixed it up with the water on some portions of the road at least two feet deep. This "loblolly," if not the color, was about the consistency of flour paste or sticky starch, and the road presented the appearance of a long mud canal doing a heavy business, but having its tow-paths flooded, and every few rods a team with its craft sunk and stuck fast out in the middle of the channel. Wading around each of these government schooners thus stuck in the mud, in the pelting rain and knee deep in mud, were dozens of soldiers with long rails and poles trying to pry the wagons up and assist the faithful government mules with their heavy loads out of the almost fathomless mire.

This soil in places was quite peculiar, being a crust of solid ground about a foot deep resting on a seemingly bottomless abyss of soft black quicksand, the depths of which we were unable to fathom with our longest rails. A man walking over it would shake it for some distance around him, much like the shaking of rotten ice as persons skate over it, and after it became water-soaked horses and mules would cut through at every step and sink to their bodies, and wagons would sink to their hubs.

When we reached this portion of the road our engineers were not long in finding out that we would have to corduroy, and that in a hurry, or we would all be in danger of being swallowed up as Pharaoh and his hosts were in the Red Sea. So the pioneer corps was at once set to work with axes felling small timber and cutting it into proper lengths, and the infantry were put to carrying and placing it in proper position on the road. In doing this we would first put down long stringers lengthwise with the road on each side, to answer for mud sills on which to lay the cross-pieces, or floor, which were some eight or ten feet in length and were placed close together.

In some instances on passing over this corduroy road the heavy teams and wagons would sink the first floor, and often we would be compelled to lay two or three on top of each other before they would bear up the heavy travel. This was very laborious work, but the boys did it cheerfully.

Tall old Jim Scott—"Uncle Jimmie," as we all called him in honor of his whitening locks—known as the cupola of the company, being over six feet in height, as he stalked around in this ocean of mud looked much like a tall crane among a lot of little mud snipes. He and I, from our first acquaintance, were always on the best of terms, and cracked many a good joke together. That day, as we were waddling through the mud toward the wagons, carrying a length of heavy green sapling apiece, I thought I would have a little fun with " Uncle Jimmie," and so asked him if he did not think it a fine large day.

"Bedad," he replied, "everything is foine—the wither is foine, the country is foine, and it's a foine mud pie we're in; but, faith, had I thought 'Uncle Sam' would have been afther puttin' me to worruk buildin' a turnpoike for Jeff Davis, I'm blowed if I'd a 'listed atall, atall."

And "Uncle Jimmie" was not far out of the way, either, for while, of course, we were building the road for our own benefit for the time, I very much doubt if the Johnnies ever had so good a road through that country before, and it was certainly very much needed.

That night after getting into camp, wet, cold, and hungry, if the command was not covered with military honor it certainly was with Mississippi mud; and as soon as we were in and arms were stacked I was detailed for picket duty, and had to start off at once in the rain before we had time even to boil a cup of coffee or draw any rations.

Our squad of six men, besides a corporal, tramped about a mile before we reached the picket line, and then, just as it was growing quite dark, we were posted in the edge of a dense shallow swamp, where the water was about a foot deep. The reserve selected two large cypress logs on which to roost, and the vidette was posted about a hundred yards farther in the swamp on a very large cypress knee having the appearance of an oval-top stump about two feet high, with the bark grown over the top. The swamp itself was very dark, and by the time the vidette had gotten fairly perched upon the knee, and the reserve was strung out on the logs, the night was of inky blackness. So intense was the darkness that one of the boys at my side said to me, in a whisper, that a stack of black cats would make a shining light in comparison with it. In changing post, with the corporal for a guide, we could only stumble and grope our way, as if blind, among the trees and over the tangle of logs and cypress knees, and many were the fierce encounters we had with the great bunches of sharp-spiked palmetto standing as if posted as sturdy sentinels, with fixed bayonets, for the protection of their weird jungle home.

No lights were allowed on the picket line, and hence a fire to warm our drenched and chilled bodies or to cook by was out of the question entirely. I was as hungry as a gaunt wolf, and my poverty-stricken haversack contained nothing digestible but a very small slice of raw pickled pork, one hard-tack, a few stray grains of coffee, and some cracker crumbs. But these, after being washed down with a few draughts of swamp water, seemed to improve my condition a little.

When my turn came for vidette duty, and I was seated on the cypress knee, like a frog on a toadstool, with my feet hanging over in the water, from 10 P. M. until midnight, I was in constant dread that some old alligator would take me for a midnight lunch, and, being some one hundred yards away from the squad, I sat with fixed bayonet ready for his reception, and made frequent probings around my watery throne to assure myself that he was not there.

The season was too cold for the frogs to hold concerts, and the swamp was perfectly quiet with the exception of the rustling of leaves, the falling of rain, and the screeching and hooting of innumerable owls, which, from their impertinent and persistent inquiries, seemed bent on finding out who-who-who-who-who-who their Yankee callers were, even if it should take all night to do so. One inquisitive old fellow, with a heavy bass voice, perched in a tree not more than a hundred feet from where I sat on vidette, as if apprised of the fact that I could not talk back, put the question as to my identity so often and so loudly that it became very annoying, and made me fairly frantic for the privilege of breaking the monotony and responding to the midnight calls of his royal highness by making the old swamp ring with the discharge of my musket.

During the first part of the night I had only mastered the situation sufficiently to catch a few short naps, and put in the time, when not on vidette, trying various styles of riding the log, straddle, sidewise, and, finally, tailor fashion, with my knapsack on my lap for a pillow. When relieved from vidette I found myself so very tired, uncomfortable, and drowsy I was determined I would get some sleep, even though I should run the risk of a tumble into the water in order to get it. So I finally entered the land of dreams by stretching myself out on the log lengthwise on my stomach, lizard fashion, keeping all my accouterments on but my knapsack, which I placed under my head for a pillow, and my woolen and oilcloth blankets, which I managed by skillful manenvers to get spread over me in a way so that they formed a good roof for shedding the cold and pelting rain. Between my body and my hard, slippery bed I had nothing, except my knapsack, as mentioned, and my gun. The latter I kept dry by keeping it under my oilcloth roof and clamped to the log with my right arm and knee. The rest of the boys managed in about the same way, and had anyone not posted on Yankee "mud-sill" ingenious maneuvers chanced to get a glimpse of our dark forms as we lay stretched out on those old swamp logs that cold, rainy night, they might have been led to believe that "Uncle Sam" had enlisted and armed a squad of Mississippi alligators to do duty in his service while in the low lands of that country.

On being aroused in the early morning by the corporal to go into camp I found myself so stiff and unpliable from lying around and in the shape of the log that I could scarcely move a limb. The day and night's experience was enough to give the greenest old bullfrog in the swamp the ague and the toughest old alligator the rheumatism, and was twenty-four hours of the hardest service I experienced on the Meridian raid.

CHAPTER XII.

At Meridian.

ON reaching camp that damp, gloomy morning we found our regiment slinging knapsacks and taking arms preparing to move out with the marching column on the muddy road leading to Meridian. Our picket squad did not fall into line with them, but after receiving our rations from our comrades, who had drawn and taken care of them for us, we halted long enough to broil a liberal slice of bacon, and boil a quart of strong coffee apiece, and it was wonderful indeed what a warming, soothing, and limbering effect this hot repast, by a roaring hot fire, had on our collapsed stomachs, chilled bodies, and stiffened limbs.

The moving column was well under way by the time we had finished our frugal meal and were willing to pull out and leave our friendly camp fire, which made us feel so comfortable and was lightening our loads by drying out our water-soaked blankets and clothing, and it was 9 or 10 A. M. before we caught up with our regiment where they were halted in a lane, assisting the work of corduroying the road with rails from the fences which stood along its sides.

About this time the heavy mist of the morning

turned into a regular down-pour, giving us another cold drenching, and when we had finished our piece of work we pushed on through the mud and rain. Soon we reached the crossing of the Big Chunky River, a short distance west of Meridian. Here, finding the bridge destroyed, and there being no pontoons down, we went through the water, washed off some of the mud, and forded the swift, swollen stream. The cold, chocolate-colored water at the shallowest ford tickled us little fellows under the armpits, but we managed to keep our leather bustles and haversacks dry by carrying them over on our heads.

We marched into Meridian about noon, St. Valentine's Day, 1864, in a torrent of falling rain, all wet as an army of drowned rats. General Polk, a bishop of the Protestant Episcopal Church, had been in command of the place, and when we poked in, evidently not feeling prepared to give us a good warm reception, he backslid and Po(l)ked out in a hurry, and retreated in the direction of Demopolis, Ala., and very unkindly left us poor Yanks out in the cold winter rain to find shelter and entertain ourselves as best we could.

Our infantry forces were at once set to work destroying an arsenal, immense storehouses, and the Mobile and Ohio Railroad, north and south, and the Jackson and Selma Railroad, east and west, of Meridian.

Our regiment had barely halted near a large four-story frame hotel in the center of the town when puffs of smoke were seen and rifle shots were heard on all sides of the town. For the instant we supposed we were completely surrounded and were in for a hard fight. Men hurriedly snatched up their guns, expecting orders to fall in line of battle; but in a moment the wild excitement was abated. It appeared that some soldier on the outskirts of the town took a notion to try his wet gun to see if he could discharge it. The old musket performed all right, and its clear report on the heavy atmosphere gave his neighbor the fever to try his gun also, and the contagion seemed to spread rapidly from regiment to regiment, until pop, bang, rattle, and roar sounded all over the camp, and probably some fifteen or twenty thousand muskets were discharged within the space of five minutes. As the mysterious fusillade alarmed us for the instant it was no doubt startling to the few remaining inhabitants of the captured town.

When the little flurry was over I headed for what I took to be a large smokehouse in the rear of a dwelling, which, on entering, I found to be a detached kitchen, provided with all necessary paraphernalia used in cooking. But, to my boyish sorrow, I found it to be destitute of any provender. However, while fumbling among a lot of tin cans and bottles on a shelf above one of the side windows I fished out a pint flask filled with some kind of clear liquor, and not being a tippler myself, I was not quite sure what kind it was, and decided to take it to my mess and there have it sampled.

The first person I met on reaching the street was Uncle Jimmie Scott, who, like the rest of us, was very wet and chilly and looked somewhat dejected; but as he caught a glimpse of the flask in my hand his gloomy countenance brightened up a little, then clouded and drooped again, as he said: "Well, it's a bad fashion these Sacesh have of puttin' strichnine in whisky for the Yanks, an' ye's lucky, me by, ef ye's don't get pizened." After which, in a very paternal and solicitous manner he proffered to examine it for me. Believing if there was anything on earth "Uncle Jimmie" was a good judge of it was the article I had in my hand, thoughtlessly I handed it over to him, and before I had time for a second thought about what the tall, bony Irishman was up to, or he had time to find out whether there was any extra poison in it or not, he jerked out the cork, clasped the flask firmly in both hands, placed it to his lips, and, quickly turning his face and the bottom of the flask up toward the descending rain, he closed his eyes, and before I could prevent it by my many quick and vigorous jerks on his long arms he let the whole of its contents gurgle down his thirsty throat. The liquor, he afterward told me, was a very fine quality of old Kimmel whisky. I cared nothing for it myself, but some of my mess on that occasion were as mad as wet, chilly soldiers could well be, and gave "Uncle Jimmie" a severe tongue lashing, which, so far as I could discover, appeared to make him all the merrier, and to think the joke on them all the more enjoyable.

On reaching my mess farther down street I found them all seated around a ruddy camp fire in their oil-cloth blankets, busily engaged broiling bacon on the ends of their iron ramrods, and earnestly watching Jack's big mess kettle of steaming coffee, which was about ready to take off. I, too, soon had a slice of pork broiled, and joined them in the midday meal.

Just as we were washing the last of our toasted hardtack down with the hot coffee smoke and flames were seen to suddenly burst out of a dozen or more windows of the large hotel near us. The building being constructed of yellow pitch pine, the flames spread rapidly, making a very hot fire, and consumed it in a very few minutes. Our mess never knew who set it on fire, but as our regiment was halted nearest to it we got the credit for it. Having had orders against burning private property, as a punishment for the offense, as soon as the fire was over our regiment was marched a half mile out of town. The building was completely furnished, but wholly deserted except by cats and rats. These ran out of it into the streets, singed, mewing, and squealing, by the dozens, and were killed by the soldiers, which, while decidedly tough on the poor singed cats and rough on rats, furnished very lively sport for a few minutes, and was heartily engaged in by the old Yanks as well as the younger ones. None of the army of singed boarders escaped the slaughter, except two or three cats, which were not badly burned. After this episode hundreds of cold, water-soaked soldiers gathered around the big blaze to warm themselves and dry out their clothing and blankets.

Our command remained in Meridian and vicinity some five days awaiting the arrival of General W. S. Smith with his force of ten thousand cavalry from Memphis, who, as previously stated, failed in his attempt to join us.

During this stay our infantry were kept busily employed destroying the railroad tracks in all directions, while the cavalry were scouting as far to the northwest as Philadelphia, a distance of thirty-five or forty miles, feeling for General Smith and his troops.

While here we were more or less solicitous respecting our situation, for our command of twenty thousand had now penetrated into the enemy's country one hundred and fifty miles from its base of supplies, and were disappointed in our expectations of forming a junction with a strong cavalry force. To add to our anxiety, while we apprehended no danger from the west, the direction from which we had come, yet there remained three directions—north, south, and east—from which the Confederates could quite easily be concentrated on railroads entering Meridian.

The morning of the 15th of February, in company with a good portion of the Seventeenth Army Corps, we marched south along the Mobile and Ohio Railroad as far as Enterprise. Here the command was divided into working parties and guards, so that while some were at work tearing up the railroad track others were posted out some distance on each side of the track to prevent a surprise. Tools for this work had been brought along with us, or picked up at various stations along the way. When it came our regiment's turn to work, we little fellows, by common consent, were appointed firemen on the Mobile and Ohio Railroad, a position that I very much enjoyed, even though I had to walk and the pay was small.

In destroying the greater portion of this track whole regiments and brigades were strung out on one side of it, a man to each tie, who, after prying the ties up, took hold and turned the whole thing upside down, and then pried and knocked it to pieces with crowbars and sledge hammers. On some other portions of the track the outside spikes were first drawn and the rails rolled off at the ends of the ties, after which the ties were ricked up into wedge-shaped piles four or five feet high; the rails were then placed across the top tie so as to evenly balance, leaving just space enough between them for the flames to have a good sweep, and then we boy firemen had our sport in firing hundreds of ricks of pitch-pine ties, and watching the long, heavy iron rails bend to the ground from the heat. Then the men would take the rails and twist them into all manner of shapes, handling them with their heavy tongs, or wrap them around the trees as iron cravats, until the track of the old Mobile and Ohio Railroad had so many twists and turns in it that its best iron horse could not have followed it.

The second day, while engaged at this work, we had a light fall of snow, which added very much to the picturesqueness of the busy scene. At that point the road passed through a long avenue of tall, stately evergreen trees. On either side of it, as far as the eye could penetrate through the feathery flakes of falling snow, could be seen long stacks of guns and tall piles of knapsacks, which, together with the graceful evergreens and the ground around, were covered with a mantle of fleecy whiteness. In marked contrast with these, the roadbed itself was covered with thousands of busy bluecoats, whose uniforms were kept clear of the falling snow, as was also the roadbed, by the heat of the high-leaping flames from the burning ties. So there could be seen at once the red flames, the white snow, and the blue coats—our national colors, displayed as if in high carnival, with a lively crowbar accompaniment.

At Enterprise we burned a large amount of cotton and other stores. The morning after our first night there it was reported that General Sherman had been compelled to move his headquarters three times during the night previous on account of the fire which had been spread by the high winds.

Our brigade was camped that night just outside of the town on a bald knob commanding the place. The weather had now turned much colder, and in our exposed position we got the full benefit of the wintry blast. As night approached Company G of our regiment, composed entirely of Germans, for the purpose of protecting themselves against the piercing wind, all went down to the town with their blankets and returned with them full of cotton for beds, and no doubt sweetly slept and dreamed. Toward midnight, however, when all were sound asleep, and the wild winter gale was at its height, these beds caught fire from some flying sparks, and the flames spread rapidly from bed to bed and quickly consumed the whole field of combustible couches. Being awakened by the commotion, and peeping out from under my old gray blanket, I beheld such a scene of excited Dutchmen and heard such cartridge explosions as I had never seen or heard before. The contents of the cartridge boxes were snapping and popping like bunches of cannon crackers, while the Germans were jabbering and jumping out of their fiery beds and away from the cartridge explosions in a most lively manner.

CHAPTER XIII.

A Foraging Expedition.

ONE cold, gloomy morning, while camped on the elevation mentioned, from which we had a good view of the surrounding country for several miles, a boy belonging to another mess and myself, considering our camp life rather prosy, held a little council of war, and decided on a raid to a plantation which we could see some two miles away.

Before starting on the expedition we mapped out our route, which lay across fields and up several low wooded ravines. So, after slinging our canteens and haversacks, we strapped on our cartridge boxes, shouldered our guns, and descended from camp into the lower woodland. When about three fourths of a mile from camp we managed to run the guards where some of our boys were on picket by promising to return that way and divide if our raid should prove a success.

About 11 A. M., emerging from a ravine in a pasture near the residence we had started for, we cautiously crawled to the top of a ridge to take observations and form a plan of approach. Here we entered a clump of bushes, and climbed up two small trees, from whose leafy boughs we had a good view of the premises. We discovered that the large, snow white residence of the plantation stood on a beautiful elevation nestled among a clump of fine old shade trees, handsome evergreens, and neatly trimmed shrubbery; and surrounding this residence were so many white barns, outbuildings, and Negro cabins that the premises presented the appearance of a trim little country village.

As we peered out from our observatories in the tree, tops a Sabbath quiet seemed to pervade the little hamlet. At first sight none of the villagers appeared to be astir, though this did not disturb us so much as the total absence of any stock or poultry on the premises. We had come provided with a couple of sharp knives, and now it looked as if we should have no occasion to use them.

We had been in the trees but a short time, discussing the safest plan of approach and the way of escape in case trouble should occur, when, by a little closer scrutiny, through the trees surrounding the house we were rewarded with a glimpse of several blue coats and two white men dressed in citizen's clothes in a large garden which adjoined the door yard. This discovery assured us that the coast was clear, and we at once slid down to the ground, picked up our guns, emerged from the brush, and were soon in the garden with those whom we had discovered, surrounding one of a half dozen large potato banks that were filled with choice sweet potatoes. At the opening in this bank, on his knees, handing out potatoes to the four soldiers, was one of the citizens, a man about thirty-five years of age, dressed in a neat and clean suit of homespun, whom I took to be a rather intelligent hired man, and whom the other man addressed as Henry, telling him to give the gentlemen all they wanted. The four soldiers were standing quietly by, filling their haversacks and stuffing potatoes around inside of their blouses, until the quartet looked like as many puffy toads.

As we climbed over the fence and approached the party the proprietor, a tall, well-built, elderly gentleman, somewhat to our surprise, addressed us boys as gentlemen, and invited us to have some of his sweet potatoes, and as he lifted his broad-brimmed black hat to us we both saluted him in true military style and thanked him for his kind offer. This man had a clean shaven face, pleasant features, long white hair, and was dressed in a suit of black broadcloth. As we approached, and before I had secured any of the potatoes, he beckoned me to where he was standing, a little apart from the group, and invited me to go to the house with him and get something to eat. This I consented to do, for there was a certain noble look about him that completely captivated me and disarmed my suspicions.

When we started I had no idea of entering the house, but expected to stop at the kitchen or dining room door and take my victuals in my hand like a tramp. But as we came up to the back veranda he halted in front of the door of the large dining room, and gave orders to have a dinner served for a gentleman and to send him word to the parlor when ready. He then entered a long hall, and as he did so I halted outside. When he noticed I was not following he stopped and seemed a trifle embarrassed, and then asked me if I would not go inside and wait until the servant should prepare my dinner. To this I replied I thought

I was not dressed properly to be seen in a gentleman's parlor. He said that would make no difference, as in my vocation I could not control my dress. Then I was rather nonplussed, for I was not thinking so much about my dress as I was about my gun. The latter I did not propose to let get out of my hands, and it seemed it would be a rude thing to carry it into the old planter's parlor, especially when he seemed so very hospitable with me.

At this juncture I made up my mind to return to my comrades and not to enter the house at all, and, turning on my heel to do so, he asked what the trouble was. I then frankly told him I did not want to carry my gun into his parlor or go in without it. This instead of displeasing only seemed to amuse him, and he said: "Come right in, young man, gun and all. It's the proper thing to do. I will take no exceptions to your rifle, and while the servant is preparing your dinner I wish to have a little conversation with you." I then followed him through the long hall into the fine large parlor at the front of the house, where he seated me in an upholstered rocking-chair in front of a cheerful fire in an elegant open fireplace, the rich mantel of which was elaborately covered with bric-a-brac.

We had been seated in the comfortable room but about ten minutes when I heard rapidly approaching hoof-strokes, and turning to look out the window I noticed for the first time that the blinds were all closed, and that the light in the room was produced by the bright pine-knot fire on the hearth. I then began to fear I was entrapped, and asked my host what it all meant. He seemed somewhat agitated, and replied that he did not know, but would go to the front door and see, expressing a hope that there would be no trouble. As he started I did also, and he had but barely reached the door when I heard a loud knock, and voices outside both at the front and rear of the house. Seeing that we were hemmed in, I decided to return to the parlor and await developments. In an instant the front door was thrown open, and I heard some one on the veranda ask the proprietor if he was the man of the house, and if there were any more men inside. To this he replied in the affirmative, stating that there was one servant and a soldier within. The command was then given for the sergeant to take two men and go in and arrest the soldier, at the same time ordering the planter to point the soldier out. The planter entered the parlor door smilingly, which I could not quite understand. Hearing the sound of the rattling of sabers and the cocking of revolvers in the hall, my hair fairly stood on end, for I thought I should certainly be roughly handled if captured as a forager in a Confederate parlor.

But my fears were soon quieted when I saw three Yankee dragoons enter, though with drawn revolvers, who on seeing my diminutive size and blue uniform lowered their revolvers and burst out in a roar of laughter. They had entered the room expecting to arrest a Confederate soldier, and found a Yankee boy recruit instead. This also explained the old planter's smile, which, while mystifying to me, was doubly significant. In the first place, having invited me in to enjoy his hospitality, I do not believe he wanted me captured in his house by the Confederates; besides, having no love for the Yankees, by not making known the kind of a soldier he was entertaining, it gave him an excellent opportunity to get a good joke on a Yankee officer, which he succeeded in doing admirably.

When the three cavalrymen returned to the veranda without a captive, I heard the officer ask them where their prisoner was, to which they replied: "O, pshaw! Cap., it's only one of our boys in there." In a moment the three soldiers returned, and a large cavalry captain with them. As they came in I stood up and saluted the officer, who, without returning my salute, demanded in an angry tone to know what I was doing out there two miles from camp by myself. To this I replied that I had been invited in to dinner, and was only waiting for it to be served, and that my comrades were out in the garden getting some sweet potatoes. This he did not seem to credit, and roared out that it was false, that there was not a Union soldier on the place when they came up, except myself, and that it was hardly likely that a Southern gentleman would invite such a specimen as I into his parlor to wait for dinner. This led me to surmise that my comrades, when they heard the approach of this cavalry squad, suspecting they were Confederates, had fled, and that really I was the only Union soldier left on the premises.

As I stood there before the officer on the beautiful soft carpet, and caught a life-size view of myself in a large mirror, I confess I could not blame the officer for doubting my veracity, for as I viewed myself from head to foot, standing with my old musket at parade rest, my soiled blouse stuck inside my dirty pantaloons, the bottoms of which were tucked into the tops of my coarse boots, I, too, thought I was an unprepossessing looking specimen for a gentleman to invite into his parlor for any purpose, much less to await the preparation of a sumptuous dinner. But I told the captain I could prove the truth of my assertions. However, he would not listen to this, and had one of the men take my gun, placed me under arrest, and marched me outside. As we went out, however, I saw the planter in the hall with several soldiers standing near the parlor door, where he had been listening to our conversation. Presently he came out and called the officer to his side, and when the latter returned to the squad where he had me under guard, he said: "As you are but a boy, and I have no extra horse for you to ride, I will release you."

I told him I was much obliged to him, but to please let me get some of the potatoes.

"Be in a hurry," he said, "and get away from here, for we are going to start in a few minutes."

Returning to the garden, I once more found Henry, who, as he helped me load up, told me he was a slave, and that he was going to run off that night and come into our lines. I now for the first time detected a slight tinge of mulatto blood in him, and a few days afterward I saw him in the Negro corral and learned from him that my comrades, on hearing the approach of horsemen, ran off before they knew who they were. He also informed me that the Negroes and stock belonging to the plantation had been run off on the approach of our army, the old "massa" only remaining behind with a few servants because of the sickness and inability of the old "mistress" to be moved.

After filling my haversack with potatoes, and stuffing so many inside of my blouse that I could barely climb over the garden fence, I started, and as I balanced on its top whitewashed plank I caught a sight which fairly made my blood boil in my veins. There on the back porch was the cavalry captain being escorted into the dining room by the planter to devour my dinner.

When about half way to camp, while in an open field, following a deep ravine looking for some good place at which to cross it, I noticed some cavalry in a lane where I thought they could see me. Not being certain whether they were Union or Confederate, I became much excited and eager to cross the ravine so that I could reach some timber where I would be obscured. I presently came to a place about six feet wide and seven feet deep, the banks being perpendicular. Throwing my haversack and canteen across the ravine, with a run and a jump I landed safely by them, but with such a sudden stop that my big load of potatoes jerked the short tail of my blouse from my trousers and dumped them all on the ground. This placed me in a more serious predicament than ever, for I was almost afraid to take time to readjust my blouse and pick up the potatoes; but rather than lose them I decided to try it, keeping an eye on the cavalry while at work. To my great relief, however, the cavalry squad turned into a lane leading in an opposite direction and soon passed out of sight.

Entering the timber, I became confused as to directions, and twice I came out near the place where I had entered. After a while I was halted by some one in a clump of small pines. From the peculiar tone of his voice I was unable to tell to which army he belonged, and all I could see was about a foot of the muzzle end of a musket pointing toward me. This so startled me than when the guard gave his challenge: "Halt! Who comes there?" I scarcely knew how to reply, but said, presently, in a tremulous voice: "A friend with sweet potatoes."

The guard then said: "Advance with your 'taters!'"

Obeying the order, I was delighted to find I had been halted by a big, good-natured Indiana volunteer, who as I came up said he had been listening to me crack brush for some time. Then, laughing, he added: "Well, youngster, you have got 'em bad, very bad. It's about the worst case of sweet pertaters I ever saw. Looks like they're about ready to break out all over you."

When I told him they had back where I had jumped the ravine the big Hoosier fairly roared with laughter. As I started for camp I handed him two good-sized potatoes for passing me in, and as I left him he said: "Say, you young rooster, if you are out there after any more 'taters' 'twix' this and mornin', remember they are legal tender for the countersign at old Indiana's post."

When I arrived in camp my mess were more pleased to see me than my potatoes, for the boy who went with me had returned several hours before and reported me as captured by Confederate cavalry.

CHAPTER XIV.

Our Return March.

WE remained at Meridian and vicinity to hear from General Smith until the morning of the 20th of February, and during the time completely destroyed the railroads around that junction. Getting no tidings concerning General Smith, our entire command, the Sixteenth and Seventeenth Corps, started back, heading toward Canton, Miss., arriving there on the 26th.

The second morning on our return trip, while in the skirmish line, as I passed through the front door yard of a large plantation, lying in the path, midway between the front gate and veranda, I saw two dead cavalry boys in blue, side by side, in pools of blood, their bodies yet quite warm. The reports of the shots by which they were killed we had heard but a few moments before as we were approaching the house. As I passed through the yard one of the Union generals and staff rode in, and as they did so a woman came running out of the front door wringing her hands, and going up to where the general was viewing the dead cavalrymen, she wildly cried: "O, I shall die! I shall die!"

To this the general replied: "No, madam, I don't

think you will die just yet. But here are two of our boys who have been killed by shots fired from that house," and added: "You had better go back into the house, and I will see that our men do you no harm."

The killing of these boys in this yard seemed a very cruel thing, but, as they considered us invaders, I suppose those who did the shooting believed they were doing it in defense of this home. They undoubtedly looked upon us about as did the inmates of those unfortunate Ohio homes which were along the line of Morgan's raid, or those of Pennsylvania who unfortunately fell in the line of march of Lee's invading army.

That night, just after dusk, we went into camp in a sheltering timber by the side of an old field which was inclosed by a rail fence. Early the next morning we noticed twelve or fifteen horses on the opposite side of the inclosure about a quarter of a mile distant. A dozen or more of our boys, suspecting no danger, started across to capture them, but just as two of them had caught and mounted a horse apiece hundreds of us who were watching saw the squad fired into by some dismounted Confederate cavalry. During the night they had evidently set and baited a nice little trap for the purpose of catching us by turning their horses loose in the field, securing two of them near the fence to keep the others from straying away, very cleverly secreting themselves in some brush just in the edge of the timber near by, and there waiting for the Yanks.

As the puffs of smoke arose from the Johnnies' carbines I heard an old soldier remark that he thought all the time that the situation over there looked suspicious, and that he wasn't hankering after any horses that morning. Then as I jumped up from the fire to get a better view a feeling of faintness came over me, for two or three of our company boys were in the squad, and I was afraid they would be left over there. Indeed, in the fusillade several of our men were wounded, but, luckily, all managed to escape, and came in on a lively run, most of them minus their hats, the two on the captured horses not much in advance of those on foot.

To even up with the Johnnies for this sharp trick, while we were finishing our morning meal a six-gun battery was brought up and masked in some timber and underbrush near the edge of the field. Then, after our brigade had breakfasted, we shouldered arms, fell in line, were marched to the rear of the battery, and there in easy supporting distance were ordered to lie down and keep perfectly quiet, while the bands were taken forward playing national airs as though leading a marching column.

It was between 9 and 10 A. M. before the silence of our little "mum" party was broken, when a brigade of gray-coated cavalry came out of the timber on the opposite side of the field, and, after they had opened the fence, rode through, formed into line of battle, and then advanced across the field toward our position on a sharp gallop, their every move after entering the inclosure being in plain view. In the crisp morning air their horses were quite frisky, and it was indeed a pretty sight as the long line of prancing blacks and bays, sorrels and grays, dressing on the colors, with noses in line, their long manes gracefully flowing in the morning breeze, came gayly sweeping across the opening toward us, their riders meanwhile wholly oblivious of the terrible storm of destruction that awaited them.

They were allowed to approach to within about one hundred and seventy-five yards of us, when the battery men quickly ran the six howitzers out from their ambush, and opened on them with grape and canister and shell. The rapidity of this fire seemed as a continuous roar of thunder, and was most deadly in its effects, mowing down great gaps of both horses and men.

The Johnnies were so completely surprised and panic-stricken that they never returned a shot, but wheeled and flew back for the shelter of the timber on the dead run, not a few of them on foot, while a number of horses in the stampede were without riders, the flying stirrups of their empty saddles apparently acting as spurs to rush them on. Several of the riderless chargers, led by a large gray with the blood running down from his right shoulder, came galloping into our lines, and were captured.

The projected shells continued to explode at the heels and over the heads of the retreating Confederates until their last man and horse, except the dead and wounded, were out of sight. The position of our infantry on this occasion would have enabled them to deliver a sweeping fire in connection with the battery, which would have almost annihilated that cavalry command, but we never fired a gun. Why the fire was withheld I never knew, but attribute it to the humanity of some officer, who thought we had fully squared accounts with the Johnnies.

That afternoon, as we were marching along on the dusty road, all tired and somewhat chafed in spirit from the extra effort required in overtaking our command, the first man to the right, just in front of me, while dodging under a low limb which hung over the road, struck me a hard blow on the top of my head with his gun barrel. While dodging under the same limb myself my gun barrel gave a surly man behind me a heavy thump on his pate, and while I was cogitating about the carelessness of the man whose gun had struck me this fellow administered to me a fearfully hard kick. This greatly enraged me, for, being attacked both in front and rear, my combative energy got the best of me, and, springing from the ranks, as the surly man, who had not only hurt me but had grossly insulted my boyish pride as well, came from under the limb I dealt him a blow with the butt end of my gun that fairly staggered him. There might have been an inglorious fight if my comrades had not interfered in time.

The afternoon of the 26th, when within two or three miles of Canton, we passed a rail inclosure containing fifty or sixty dead mules, which the Confederates had shot to prevent their falling into our hands.

After entering Canton quite late in the evening, in company with Nic, my bunk mate, Mose and George Langley, of our mess, and six other men of our company, I started out on a foraging expedition. Arriving at the picket line just a little after dusk, my messmates induced me, much against my own wish, to return to camp and assist the rest of the boys and Jack to prepare some good beds. So I returned, while they went on what proved to be, alas, a fatal trip. All nine of them were captured that night, and seven out of the nine afterward perished in Andersonville prison, brave, generous-hearted Nic among them. He now sleeps beneath the moaning pines in the National Cemetery, where that frightful prison-pen once stood. To me it was like losing an older brother or a father, and henceforth my army life must be deprived of the wise counsel and the brotherly care of this noble soldier.

Returning to camp, I made a good bed for Nic and myself out of straw from a stack near by. I sat up quite late waiting for his return, and during the night I was awake a number of times, and felt over on his side of the bed to see if he had not returned. But when reveille sounded it found me still alone. Jumping up, I hastily dressed myself, went to roll-call, and there found that all nine of the men I had started with the night before were missing. This cast a gloom of sadness over the entire company, for they were all good men, old and tried soldiers, and the loss was a heavy blow on all of us.

On the 27th of February General Sherman left us and started for Vicksburg, escorted by Winslow's Cavalry, arriving there the following day. The remainder of the command was left under the senior major-general, Hurlburt, with orders to remain at Canton and vicinity until the 3d of March. While there we destroyed the railroad, which was also cut below at Jackson, and both north and south of Canton. Here we captured a large quantity of rolling stock, among which were twenty-seven locomotives, which were all demolished and burned, excepting the bells.

The second day while here, as I was passing a large residence on the outskirts of the town I heard low, muffled brays that greatly puzzled me. A wagon train was passing at the time, and several of the donkeys belonging to it were braying. I soon made up my mind, however, that the subdued braying I heard did not come from them, and I appointed myself a committee of one on investigation. Going to the barn attached to the premises, I made a careful search, not leaving until I had examined the loft and every bin. Finding no donkeys there, I then visited several other barns on the same alley, with like results. Then returning to the premises first visited, I found the house locked up and deserted. I carefully examined all the outbuildings, but no donkeys were to be found. I then tried the outside cellar door at the rear of the residence. This was also securely locked, but I succeeded in getting it open, and as the light shone in through the dark hole I was greeted by the loud braying of a span of large bay mules, which stuck their big heads and long ears into the doorway, evidently pleased at the prospect of being liberated from their dungeon.

The cellar doorway opening had been dug back some distance so as to let the mules in, and the excavation then filled up, and the windows had been carefully darkened. Within the cellar the donkeys had access to feed and water sufficient to keep them during a siege of several days, and if we had camped in the town but one night, or the mules had not answered the bray of the donkeys in the passing train, it is likely their owner would have had the pleasure of resurrecting them himself, and of chuckling over the way he had beaten the Yanks.

As soon as I discovered them I called to some passing soldiers, who helped me get them out, and "Uncle Sam's" quartermaster was soon in possession of an extra span of fine large mules at the expense of the Confederacy. Such things were considered a part of our work, and I mention it that the boys and girls of to-day may know of these veritable incidents of the great Civil War that the writers of history books never think of mentioning.

We remained at Canton until the morning of the 3d of March, when we all took up the line of march leisurely toward Vicksburg, arriving at our old camp on the bluffs west of the Big Black River on the afternoon of the 6th.

As we crossed the quivering canvas pontoons that spanned the muddy stream we completed a successful raid of three hundred miles into the very heart of the Confederacy, during which we had been entirely cut off from our base of supplies for thirty-one days. Our generals had demonstrated by this time that in so far as our army subsisted on supplies obtained in the country through which we were passing our government was that much the gainer, and the enemy correspondingly crippled, which was considered a better method of bringing them to terms than the sacrifice of human lives.

Pen cannot describe the hilarity of the boys of our command upon that memorable occasion. On approaching the river every flag was flung to the breeze; every band in the victorious command, over twenty in number, was playing lively national airs. At Canton our teamsters had taken the bells from the twenty-seven captured locomotives and brought them along, and these were all swung on their wagons and were ringing; twenty thousand bronzed warriors, carrying their hats and caps aloft on the muzzle of their guns, were lustily singing, "John Brown's body lies a moldering in the ground," while thousands of "contrabands," following the marching column, now getting their first taste of freedom, joined heartily in the chorus, "Glory, glory hallelujah," not a few of them audibly indulging in expressions of praise and prayer. Everything that lovely afternoon seemed to conspire to make a boy who had shared in the dangers and triumphs of the expedition join in the most enthusiastic demonstrations.

Thus ended Sherman's famous Meridian raid, which, no doubt, was an influential precedent, and a potent source of inspiration in his grander "march to the sea." By it the Confederacy in that section was so crippled that our command was no longer needed in that region, and so could be transferred to the Army of the Tennessee, as it soon was.

CHAPTER XV.

Again at Vicksburg.

THAT evening, when we got back to our old quarters and took possession of our tents and belongings, which we had left in charge of a few of our sick boys and some of the colored cooks, we found a large mail that had accumulated during our absence, and which was distributed to us. We also found newsboys in camp with the latest St. Louis, Chicago, and Cincinnati papers.

We were all eager to get our letters so as to hear from home and the outside world once more, and were quite anxious to learn what the rest of the Union army had accomplished during our absence. While the orderly was distributing our mail to us one comrade read aloud from a late paper for the benefit of the company. Among the important news thus read was an account of the passage of a bill by Congress by which the grade of lieutenant-general was restored, and that General Grant was to be promoted to that office, and placed in command of all the Union forces. Instantly our hats were taken off and thrown into the air, and three cheers and a tiger for General Grant were heartily given. When quiet was restored, down the column a little the comrade read:

"All is quiet on the Potomac." Then the Eastern army came in for a scoring, and more than a half dozen voices were heard to say: "You can bet your boots it won't be so quiet on the 'Pot-o-mack' when Grant gets over there."

These were about my sentiments too, but I could not help reverting in my own mind to the time before I enlisted, when I saw this quiet man busy in his unpretentious way around his little wedge tent at Naples, Ill., dressed in his plain blouse, with slouch hat, and looking almost as common as any man in his regiment, and how I then thought Governor Dick Yates had made a great mistake in placing such an unpretentious looking military man in command of a regiment.

Mail day furnished a scene by no means uncommon in army life. On receiving their mail almost all the soldiers would slip off by themselves, as if afraid lest their letters would contain some family secret. This, however, was not the real object of their seclusion. They knew that the bravest heart is often most tender, and were suspicious that their emotions might be betrayed by a trickling tear-drop, started by some loving word from home.

Although I was feeling quite jubilant there were several things during the distribution of this mail that greatly stirred my emotions, and unbidden tears would flow, as when my missing comrades' names were being called, and especially that of poor Nic, who had been my special friend and bunkmate. Two letters which I received, addressed in the familiar hand of my loving mother, warned me that I had better seek a secluded place for their perusal. Although as full of mischief and fun as a boy could be, and never sick or homesick while in the service until a prisoner, it was always wise for me thus to do if I did not wish to reveal my emotions when reading mother's letters. Often did I upbraid myself for giving way to my feelings at such times, foolishly, as I thought, for a soldier boy, and, although I would vow I would not be so foolish again, yet the very next time a letter would come from mother, the moment I caught a glimpse of the "Dear Willie," her pet name for her boy, the blinding tears would start into my eyes. One of the saddest things I witnessed during the distribution of army mail was when a homesick comrade's name would not be called. Every feature of his saddened countenance would show his great disappointment, but he was sure to receive expressions of sympathy from his more favored comrades.

During our long raid, although it was the first march of any consequence I had taken, and I was a tender recruit fresh from home, and was encumbered with my heavy boots, which at Meridian I had so badly burned while drying them that the soles and uppers had to be "whanged" together with strings, I never rode a step nor missed a duty on picket, or skirmish, or in battle. This so pleased the old mess that when we got back they gave me the title of " vet.," of which I was always as proud as the bravest brigadier of his brightest stars. This title, coming from these old soldiers, I felt fully repaid me for all my exposures and sufferings. And this new title made me all the more determined that my comrades should never catch me shirking or indulging in any weakness not becoming a veritable " vet."

The morning after we got back to our old quarters was devoted to letter writing. Besides writing one to my parents I wrote a long one to my schoolmates to be read to the school. In it I gave them a description of our raid. I also referred to a song we boys and girls sang at school, the chorus of which was:

> " So let the cannon boom as they will,
> We will be gay and happy still."

I remember telling them that that chorus was very well for boys and girls in the schoolroom, but on the battlefield I found I was not happy until the cannon ceased booming.

After the letter writing the rest of the day was devoted to a general wash-up. It was fortunate for us that the weather was pleasant, for the most of the command had to boil their trousers, the only sure means of death to a troublesome enemy that would sometimes invade them. To the lookers-on it was quite amusing to see large numbers who had but one pair clad in drilling underwear over boiling kettles, anxiously watching until their garments could be taken out and dried.

The pantaloons I drew at Springfield, Ill., were much too large for me; but after several trades I had a pair which fitted me around my waist, but they were about four inches too short for me. As long as I wore them tucked in my boot-tops this made no difference; but my boots having worn out, I was now wearing a pair of brogans I had picked up, and it did make a big difference. After boiling my trousers I waited around in the sun two or three hours for them to dry, and when I got into them I found they had shrunk several inches, and the gap between them and my shoe-tops was greater than ever. Stooping over to take hold of the bottom of my trouser legs to draw them down so as to form a junction with the top of my socks, they crawled up my limbs still farther, and I failed to get them inside my sock legs so as to tie them down. However, I finally got out of the dilemma by sewing a piece of cloth on the bottom of each trouser leg. This was not very scientifically done, and when completed looked as if I had been trying to ornament them with a couple of large flaring flounces, which the boys said made them look like a combination of petticoats and trousers. In a few days, however, I drew a new pair and threw this unsatisfactory combination away. These new ones were also much too large for me, but I soon got the regimental tailor to cut them down to fit me, and having drawn a new hat and pair of brogans, and had my blouse and other clothing washed up and my hair cut, I made quite a respectable looking soldier boy.

We were but fairly settled in our old camp when we were ordered to march into Vicksburg, whence we were to be transferred to the Army of the Tennessee. Arriving in the city one very warm morning, we were at once marched down under the shadeless river bluffs to await the arrival of a transport that was expected at any time. A strong camp guard was thrown around our regiment to prevent our straying off and being away when the boat should arrive.

After waiting several hours in the broiling sun with no steamer in sight, a number of us boys became restless and wanted to go up in the city, but we could get no passes. The most of the officers had already gone, and this made us all the more eager to go. So some twenty or thirty of us held a council and decided we would try it. Selecting a good place at which to pass the guards between the beats of two good-natured soldier boys who, we were quite sure, would not shoot or use their bayonets on us, we got into a rollicksome game of leapfrog, and when these two sentinels were walking in opposite directions our entire squad quickly leapfrogged out between them. They appeared to take no notice of us, and we were soon up in the city having a good time, although compelled to dodge the officers.

While in the city I saw a newly enlisted regiment of colored soldiers drilling which was made up of the green plantation Negroes whom we had picked up on the raid. They all seemed fond of martial music and of their display. They put on all sorts of comical airs. Dressed in brand new suits of bright blue, with polished shoes, white gloves, burnished guns, shiny brass buttons and shoulder-guards, together with large black-plumed hats trimmed with cord and tassels and pinned up at one side, and bearing their company and regimental letters and numbers, they made a gorgeous sight that was amusing to those who had learned that glitter and show doesn't amount to much in the hardships of real army experiences.

Passing a building on one of the principal streets

of the city in which I noticed a number of soldiers seated around tables, I glanced up at the sign, and read, "U. S. Christian Commission Rooms." Never having been in one of these buildings, I thought I would enter and see what was going on, and did so. Most of the soldiers who were there were reading or writing. Behind the counters were several ladies who gave the boys paper and envelopes, on the left upper corner of which were the words, "From the U. S. Christian Commission." A number of other useful articles were on the shelves, such as rolls of white bandages, socks, underwear, sheets, pocket and needle books, jellies, pickles, jams, and other good things to eat.

As I entered the room with my hands thrust into my penniless pockets, and my new hat cocked to one side, I noticed a mischievous looking young lady, some twenty or more years of age, I judge, behind one of the counters near the door, who seemed to eye me quite closely. As I walked by I also took a pretty good look at her, for I believed her rosy cheeks, black, sparkling eyes, and clean white apron were those of a Yankee lass, and if so she was the first Northern girl I had seen since coming to "Dixie."

After I had been in the room a few moments I leisurely sauntered down to near the center of it, where there was an elderly lady, who at once engaged me in conversation. While thus engaged the young lady made it in her way to walk down to us to ask the other lady some question. Then turning to me, she said: "My soldier boy, you have a button off your blouse, can't I sew it on for you?" Supposing she meant for me to take my blouse off so that she could sew the button on, I felt rather awkward, for I didn't see how I could very well do that, as I was wearing it belted inside my pantaloons as an overshirt. Hesitating a moment, I then blushingly said : " I—I—I thank you very much, but I—I guess not." Both ladies must have surmised my thoughts, for they glanced at each other in a significant way and smiled, which rather plagued me, and, seeing my embarrassment, they tried to turn it off by asking me if there was not something else they could do for me. I had a fondness for red raspberry jam, of which I saw they had a supply, but knowing it was only intended for the sick I would not ask for any. Not seeing anything else I thought it would be proper to ask for except writing material, I said : " If you please, I will take a sheet of paper and an envelope."

While the elderly lady was getting these for me the younger one asked me if I had a housewife, which so puzzled me I could hardly believe my ears. Blushing again, I said : " A wh—a—t ?" " A housewife," she repeated. " Wouldn't you like a neat little housewife to help you do your sewing and darning?" By this time the room seemed exceedingly warm to me, and the ladies were apparently almost dying with suppressed mirth. I thought myself rather young to be wanting a housewife, and that the girl was getting rather forward for a stranger. But remembering the hard time I had experienced piecing down my old pantaloon legs, and not wishing to be entirely " bluffed," I finally summoned courage sufficient to gasp out : " I—I—I believe I should like one," but was rather confused in my own mind as to what kind of one she was going to offer me. She then laughingly said: "You shall have the very best looking one in the room." However, instead of making me an offer of her own hand she handed out to me a very pretty needle-case well supplied with sewing and darning needles and pins, and having several pockets filled with yarn, skeins of black linen thread, and buttons. That neat little housewife I have to-day in a cabinet among other choice war relics.

After thanking the ladies for these articles they had so kindly given me, I seated myself at a table near the door, where I could hear a boat if one should whistle, and proceeded to write a letter.

The upper blouse button that the young lady wished to sew on for me was one that Jack had pounded off when washing my blouse by beating it over a log with a paddle, the way the colored people in the army had of washing. I had my letter but fairly begun when, glancing up, I saw standing by my side, equipped with a brass button, needle, and thread, the owner of the black eyes and white apron. The persistent girl then said, playfully: "Now I have you, and if you don't sit still like a good boy and let me sew this button on I will bayonet you with my big needle." Seeing I was cornered, I surrendered with as good a grace as possible, but all the time wondering if I had gotten my neck and ears clean when I washed in the muddy water of the river, just before starting up town.

By the time she was ready to clip the thread with a pair of scissors which hung by her side we had become pretty well acquainted, and by way of apology in case I had failed in getting my neck and ears clean I ventured the remark that we had a very dusty march that morning coming in from Black River. She asked me if I had a mother, to which I replied in the affirmative. "I suppose," she said, "you are writing her a nice letter, and will tell her all about the Christian Commission."

"No," I said, "I am writing a letter to a widow."

"Has she any boys in your company who can't write?" she inquired.

"No ma'am," I replied; "I have been corresponding with her ever since I enlisted, and the correspondence is getting very interesting."

"What! You writing love letters to a widow lady?"

"Yes, ma'am," I said, "but only for the fun of it."

This seemed to disgust her, and she said: "I had a better opinion of you than that, and if your mother knew it she would be ashamed of you, and I am for her."

Seeing she was going to snap off the thread of our conversation about as suddenly as she had clipped the sewing thread with her scissors, I said: "I don't see anything so very wicked or so much to be ashamed of in a boy writing love letters for a comrade who can't write, especially when I don't charge him anything for it."

I now had the satisfaction of seeing somebody else embarrassed besides myself, and the young lady made about as poor an "out" of apologizing for her severity on me as I had in refusing to have a button sewed on, or in accepting a needle-case. But she wound up our conversation by saying: "You are a bad boy, anyhow, for leading me into a trap of that kind."

About this time the whistles of several boats were heard, the advance of the fleet that was coming to transport our command up the river to Cairo, Ill. This cut our conversation off. Quickly folding my partially written letter, I slipped it into the envelope, and both into my pocket, tipped my hat, and was off on a run for the wharf, arriving there just as my regiment was slinging knapsacks preparing to embark on one of the transports.

As we boys all got in on time none of us were punished further than a slight reprimand for being absent without leave.

CHAPTER XVI.

OFF FOR A NEW FIELD.

WHEN fairly quartered on the steamer she was soon out into the river and under way headed for Cairo, Ill. I improved this opportunity and finished the letter I had begun for my old comrade while in the U. S. Christian Commission Rooms. This man was a widower of about forty-five, and enlisted at the same time I did. He belonged to another mess, and neither he nor the widow with whom he was corresponding could write. She was about his age, and the correspondence was occasioned by her presenting to him a white linen handkerchief just as he was starting for the army. As a mark of his appreciation of this gift and esteem for the giver he never used the handkerchief, but kept it unsoiled by carrying it in his knapsack folded in several thicknesses of paper inclosed within a piece of oilcloth wrapping. After we joined our regiment he noticed that I wrote letters for several of the boys, and requested me to do the same for him.

About this stage of affairs, as I remarked to the young lady in the Christian Commission Rooms at Vicksburg, the correspondence, as a result of the handkerchief episode, was getting very interesting.

The widow had changed scribes, evidently, and I judged from the handwriting and the tone of the letters he was receiving that her present amanuensis must be some lively young girl about my age, and the way we two youngsters were warming up those two old hearts was indeed amusing.

Having now become accustomed to roughing it, and the weather being milder, our trip up the majestic "Father of Waters" was much more pleasant than the down trip had been.

We passed Memphis and Fort Pillow a few days after the merciless massacre at the latter place, and arrived at Cairo the 28th of April, this time to find it very rainy and the snow and ice displaced by oceans of mud and water, the city being partially inundated by the swollen rivers.

Notwithstanding this disagreeable state of affairs it seemed very pleasant to touch toes with the old Sucker State once more, where we were nearer our friends and had a good chance for our lives if we were fortunate enough not to get drowned.

After disembarking we were marched out to an elevation in the north part of the city alongside the track of the Illinois Central Railroad. Here we were quartered in some tents having bunks raised above the ground about two feet. The second morning after taking possession of these quarters, on awaking, we found the water had flooded our tents and was up to within three or four inches of our bunks and still rising. When this discovery was made we quickly jumped out into the muddy liquid, gathered up our effects, and waded out to still higher ground, leaving the flooded tents for the catfish and turtles, as they did not belong to us.

In this movement for self-preservation every man acted for himself and without orders, and in it I got separated from my old mess for several days. This was occasioned by myself and five other boys taking up quarters in a large hollow sycamore log, which was about fifty feet long, and which some former and higher flood had lodged against the railroad embankment, where it was held from rolling into the waters below by several limbs on its lower side. The railroad at that point served the purpose of a levee, and the water at that time on the side where the log lay was up to within a few feet of it. Our regiment was quartered on the opposite side of the track from the water, and was protected from it by the roadbed, and was sheltered by some tents made out of oilcloth blankets.

On reaching the log we found it to be nothing but a shell, having an opening about four and a half feet in diameter at the butt end. We explored the interior of it with a candle to see that there were no snakes or other objectionable inhabitants in it, and discovered that twenty-five feet back from the mouth the opening was still some four feet across, and as the rain was pouring down in torrents we were not long in deciding that this tubular hotel would suit us. We accordingly took up our abode in it, and, despite the continued rain, spent a very pleasant week under its friendly roof. We drove pegs into the inside walls, upon which we hung our guns and other accouterments. We also made some good beds out of hay that we foraged. These were sufficiently roomy so that we could sleep two in a bed, thus requiring three beds for the six of us.

One of the best things, however, about our novel house was the front porch, where we cooked with ourselves and fires well protected from the rain. This we made by chopping away five or six feet of the lower side of the shell at the entrance, leaving the upper half to project over for a roof. The end of the log extending in beyond our beds we used as a storehouse and woodshed. At night we lighted our rooms with candles, using our bayonets stuck into the log for candlesticks. And here in our dry, cosy nest, as we "listened to the patter of the soft rain overhead," we had a fine place for army boys, where we could sleep soundly at night, and at other times open our knapsacks, take out our old letters and read them, look at the pictures of friends, examine our little trinkets, write letters, and darn our socks and mend our clothes, assisted by our "neat little housewife."

There were two contingencies, however, that somewhat disturbed our otherwise complacent minds while occupying this log hotel, especially at night time. One was the possibility of the rising flood reaching our tenement, and the other was the possibility that the heavy jarring of the many passing trains might cause the limbs by which it was supported to give way and let us roll down into the turbulent waters. But, escaping these two calamities, I found it decidedly more pleasant sleeping within this log on a dark stormy night than I had found it on the top of that old log in the alligator swamp down in Mississippi.

Just after the Meridian raid General McPherson

assumed command of the Army of the Tennessee. This left one army corps without a commander. General Frank P. Blair, then a member of Congress, by request of General Sherman, resigned his seat in that body, came West, and by appointment assumed command of the Seventeenth Army Corps. Our division, Crocker's, and Leggett's of this corps rendezvoused at Cairo some two weeks, awaiting the return of the reenlisted men of the Second Division, who were at home on veteran furlough.

We broke camp about the 15th of May, 1864, and marched down through rain and mud and water to the fleet which was in waiting for us on the Ohio River side of the city. There we embarked for Clifton, Tenn., which is situated on the Tennessee River in one of the southern counties of that State, a point on our route to the Army of the Tennessee, which had now started on the famous Atlanta campaign and was in the field near Huntsville, Ala.

Our regiment boarded the side-wheel steamer *Illinois*, a large freight transport, the largest river craft I had ever seen. The most of us were quartered on the boiler deck, which had but a small cabin in the center of it for the accommodation of the boat's officers. The remainder of the floor space was left free for all kinds of freight. On this deck we found a small space fore and aft occupied by cannon. In the surrounding space, except that occupied by our guns, was a fringe of white-topped provision, ordnance, ambulance, and medicine wagons, which were standing jammed up against each other side by side, and with their hind wheels backed up against the outside rail or guard. The tongues of these vehicles were all stuck up in the air as stiff, straight, and noncommunicative as an officer of the regular army. As these silent tongues interposed no objections we were soon crowded into the wagons and under them out of the rain.

We were to take a large drove of cattle to the front, and our boat had its full complement on the lower deck of bawling cattle, squealing horses, and braying mules, which, together with their kicking and stamping, strongly suggested the ancient confusion of Babel, if not in kind, at least in degree. The hull of our transport was loaded with ammunition, provisions, etc., as was also the space not otherwise occupied on both decks. As we took up our quarters amid this mass of animate and inanimate freight, with the rain descending in torrents and the vast floods of angry waters surging in maddened fury, as if bent on the destruction of all things unsheltered, to my young mind there were strong suggestions of the deluge, with its terrible destruction, and of Noah's ark, with its securely protected occupants.

When the entire fleet was loaded bells were rung, hawsers were cast off, and soon we were on our way up the Ohio with an escort of two gunboats in our front and one in our rear, and as we passed by Cairo all the flags of our large fleet were flying, whistles were blowing, bells ringing, bands playing their liveliest national airs, all conspiring to stir a boy's patriotic spirit to the highest pitch, and make him feel proud that he was on board of one of those government transports headed for the front. I was not yet sixteen, was well and hearty, had seen just enough of military life to make me eager for more, and, being fond of the water and of adventure, this lively trip along with this large war fleet up the broad Ohio and the deep, clear, winding Tennessee was to me one of ravishing delight.

We entered the mouth of the Tennessee, at Paducah, Ky., the evening of the first day, and the following day we passed the historical Fort Henry, then dismantled and deserted.

The second day burst upon us clear and bright. A lovely May morning it was, with all nature wearing her brightest charms, causing us all to feel gay and happy. The flowers were in bloom. In the graceful overhanging boughs the thrushes and mating mockers were warbling their sweetest notes, while farther up the cedar-covered rocky cliffs could be heard the plaintive sound of cooing doves. Men sang of home and love while our bands played their softest, sweetest melodies; and, as I gave ear that mild, rosy May morning to strains of "Home, Sweet Home," so tenderly discoursed by military bands and sweetly sung by boys in blue, I could scarcely realize that I was being borne again to scenes of angry war; and when the touching chorus of the song was reached my soul, echoing its tender sentiment, almost yearned for a glimpse of the old fireside and the loved ones gathered there. That morning we saw a company of Confederates lying along a ravine near the river watching our passing fleet. They were in plain view and easy range from the upper decks, but, like ourselves, appeared peaceably inclined, as if enchanted by the day's dreamy sweetness and enamored by music's gentle charms. So we simply exchanged a good look at each other, reserving our fire for some future fray.

On this transport, as usual, there was no chance for us to get any cooking done except about the fires under the boilers, or by bribing the cook to set a kettle or a pan on his stove for us. While at dinner that day regaling ourselves on dry crackers, broiled bacon, and strong coffee, secretly wishing we had a good kettle of bean soup, the steamer's cook, as if divining our thoughts, helped us out of our difficulty by setting a very large pan of baked beans and bacon out to cool on the deck just outside of the cook room door. This cook room, unlike any other that I ever saw, was on the same deck and under the same roof that the officers' cabin was. This threw our company and the baked beans and bacon in close proximity; nor was it long until our relations grew more intimate, for no sooner had the fat colored cook turned his back than the big square pan, containing not less than a peck of beans and eight or ten pounds of bacon, started on a lively sliding journey under the wagons, and nearly all of our company got a share of its contents, and baked fingers as well, along with the sport it gave us.

When the cook reported his loss search was made for the missing pan and its contents, but before the searching party had reached our company the booty had been divided, safely hidden, and the big pan was resting on the bottom of the river. We kept an eye on that door for more beans, but none ever appeared again. We felt grateful, however, to the cook for what we did get, though it never seemed quite convenient for us to thank him.

CHAPTER XVII.

Our March to Rome, Georgia.

ARRIVING at Clifton, Tenn., about the 18th of May, we disembarked, ascended the rocky, cedar-covered hills, and remained there two days waiting for the fleet to discharge its freight and for the lading of the wagon trains. We then started east for Pulaski, Tenn., having in charge a large drove of cattle. Our route lay through a sparsely settled country made picturesque by several clear streams meandering among its tree-clad hills.

Our first day out from Clifton our animals, soldiers, and especially General Blair, being quite fresh, we made a long and hard march. It seemed to us that the general was especially bent on getting to the front as if to make up for lost time while he was in Washington, and as if he was afraid the Johnnies would all be killed before we should reach the scene of battle, and his trip West thus prove a failure.

During our first night on this march General Crocker's headquarters were in a large plantation residence on the outskirts of our camp, about half a mile distant from where our regiment bivouacked. That night found us all much fatigued from our long march, but, notwithstanding this, after supper a boy whom we had nicknamed "Pigeon" and I, having noticed some fifteen or twenty head of cattle near General Crocker's headquarters as we passed by, decided we would make a foraging tour and capture fresh meat if possible. These cattle belonged to the plantation, had been driven into the yard, and were protected by a guard at the front gate.

That night a curtain of white, billowy clouds was thrown over the blue sky, partially veiling the moon. The night, however, was sufficiently bright to enable one to outline good sized objects at quite a distance. Reconnoitering the premises under cover of a row of shade trees which stood in front of the house, we discovered a gate near one of the corners of the house that opened from the back door-yard into a large orchard. Waiting until all the lights about the premises had disappeared, and until we thought all were asleep but the guard, we climbed over the fence and then crawled along in the shade of the trees and shrubbery to the orchard gate and propped it open. With both guns in charge I was stationed, flat on my stomach, near the gate, so as to head off one or two of the cattle into the orchard when Pigeon should drive them up, for we were sure of getting caught if we should undertake to butcher one in the yard, and the guard would miss them if we should drive them all out. The cattle were a mixed lot, ranging from sucking calves to work oxen. Pigeon was to get himself up into as near the shape of one of the calves as possible, and with his pockets full of pebbles (gathered from a gravel walk), which he was to use in place of a whip, he was to crawl out among the herd, pick out one or two, and drive them around toward the gate where I lay.

After chasing around on all fours for nearly an hour, using up several pocketfuls of pebbles, he finally succeeded in separating from the rest of the herd an old crumpled-horned cow and her yearling heifer calf, and then drove them toward the gate, through which we soon succeeded in chasing them into the orchard, the old cow as she passed through throwing up her tail and heels into the night air as if trying to brush a mosquito off of the old man in the moon. Shutting the gates, we shook hands, declaring the yearling was our meat, and then started in hot pursuit. Knowing if we should shoot we would arouse the camp, we decided that we would drive the cow and heifer to one of the remote corners of the inclosure and there slay the calf with our bayonets. So after fixing bayonets and removing the caps from our guns we were off for our prey. But the cattle took shelter in a wilderness of old peach trees and blackberry bushes in the back part of the orchard, so that we found it impossible to corner the heifer and stab it with our bayonets. Failing in this, we then left our guns in a secure place, and obtained a supply of brickbats from a pile of bricks we had discovered near the center of the orchard, and again took up our pursuit. Finding the cattle, we tried to knock the heifer down with our bats. About the third or fourth attempt, when I was some fifteen feet in front of the heifer, and Pigeon was just to the right and a little to the rear of her, he said: "Now, 'Vet.,' you have a good chance, blaze away." Whereupon I blazed; but instead of killing the calf the bat, after striking her right shoulder, glanced off and hit Pigeon just below the belt, nearly collapsing him; and when I got up to where he was lying, my only hopes of his recovery were based on the character of the pet names he was lavishing on me and his questionable praise of my marksmanship.

This last effort was as near as we ever came to getting that fresh meat, for, after unbuckling Pigeon's belt and rubbing his stomach for half an hour, he was then but barely able to walk even with my assistance. However, while chasing around after the cattle we came across a sitting goose, and having failed to capture the heifer I proposed that before we should start to camp, leaving the guns with Pigeon, I would go and get the goose, which was agreed to. She was sitting at the root of a dead peach tree in some blackberry bushes. On reaching the place, so as not to frighten her away from the nest, I thought I would reach my hand in gently and seize her by the neck. But instead of being frightened, when I got my hand to within about six inches of her head the saucy thing nabbed it and well-nigh took a piece out of it; and as I jerked it back the briers gave it a fierce rake, so that in this first assault I had much the worst of the encounter. Seeing that the old goose was determined to "hold the fort," I decided to capture her panther fashion, by springing on top of the nest, briers and all, and grabbing her in the fall. But, O horrors! I found she was sitting on a nest of explosives, and when I dropped there were loud reports. The pungent, penetrating odor from these bombs almost took my breath. Fortunately, however, for me, as I dropped the old goose spread her wings, and thus protected my clothing from the most of this paralyzing perfume, and I was not long in extricating myself from the unpleasant situation, this time carrying off my prize. I soon had her killed and her feathers washed in a small branch which ran through the orchard.

Returning to Pigeon, we prepared to move. I slipped his cartridge-box on my belt to carry it for him, as his diaphragm was too sore to bear its weight. Then, with both guns and the goose on my left shoulder, assisting Pigeon with my right arm as much as I could, we made our way to camp, arriving there about midnight in a rather demoralized condition. After getting Pigeon into bed I woke Jack up, and we built up a fire and put the goose on to boil, after which Jack retired while I remained up for about two hours poulticing Pigeon's stomach with socks wrung out in hot water, and keeping up the fire under our goose kettle. Pigeon now being easier, and resting in the embrace of "nature's sweet restorer," I retired. On awakening the next morning Jack informed me that our mess, who had risen some time before, had pronounced the goose worthless and ordered him to throw it away. Thus ended the most unsatisfactory and fruitless foraging expedition I was ever engaged in.

Breaking camp that morning just a little after sunrise, we made a march of twenty miles before we bivouacked for the night, which brought us to within thirty miles of Pulaski. During the night a report reached camp that Wheeler's Confederate cavalry were threatening the railroad at that point. So the next morning we were on the move before sun up, and that day we tramped thirty miles, up hill and down over dusty roads, with our heavy loads, reaching Pulaski just at sunset almost fagged out. On our arrival at that point we found Wheeler was not there, but was expected to strike the road fifteen or twenty miles north. We were allowed but a few minutes to prepare and eat supper, when we were loaded in and on top of box cars, and there held until we should receive a dispatch that would inform us just where we would be wanted. Being very much crowded we could get no rest. Between ten and eleven o'clock, no word having been received, we were ordered out of the cars, and were soon under our blankets asleep. But we had not been in bed more than an hour when a telegram came, stating that Wheeler was heading for Elk River Railroad Bridge, some fifteen miles south of us.

We were soon up and on board the cars again to await orders. But again no orders were received, and toward morning we returned to camp and got, perhaps, two hours' sleep. Then came reveille, a hurried breakfast, and we were off for Elkton a short time after sunrise, and reached there about 3 P. M. the same day. There we were given over a day's rest waiting for the balance of our command to come up with the cattle we had left when we started on our chase after Wheeler.

The loss of nearly two nights' sleep, foraging and boarding and unboarding the cars, along with forced marches over hot and dusty roads, had me pretty well tuckered out when we reached Elkton; so as soon as we had halted and stacked arms I sought shelter from the rays of the scorching sun under a big gourd vine, like Jonah's, which covered a fence corner, and there I lay with my head on my knapsack fighting flies and dozing until the cool of the evening. Then going down to the Elk River I took a plunge in its cooling waters, and, after partaking of a supper of Jack's hot coffee, fried bacon, and some crackers, along with a delicious stew of green gourds, I retired, and the next morning awoke feeling much refreshed and ready for any demands the day might bring.

That afternoon the portion of our command having charge of the cattle overtook us. During the following night a heavy rain fell, which caused a sudden rise in the small river, making its current very swift. This made it very difficult to get our pontoons down so as to cross. During the next morning, after this was accomplished, and a part of the command was safely over, the quivering bridge, while it was filled from one end to the other with frightened cattle that were crowding and horning each other, broke in two near the center and instantly went to pieces. The boats, being secured by strong hawsers, swung around against either bank, but the cattle and other portions of the bridge, in a great tangle of heads, horns, stringers, and planks, were all quickly swept down the swollen stream. Many of the cattle were drowned, and others had their legs broken, the steep clay banks, made slippery by the late rains, making it difficult for any of them to get out.

It required several hours to gather up the bridge material and get the pontoon in condition to cross on. In the meantime we got a good supply of fresh beef by butchering the broken-legged steers, which was the first we had out of the drove we brought out with us from Cairo. The reason of this was that at that stage of the war the railroads over which Sherman's supplies were carried were being constantly torn up by the enemy, so that it was often exceedingly difficult for him to obtain needed provisions for his forces. Hence these four-footed, self-transporting supplies were not to be used until the very last moment, or in a case like the one mentioned, where the cattle were disabled from traveling.

After crossing to the south bank of the Elk River we headed for Athens, Ala., arriving there the next day about 10 A. M. The following morning reveille sounded early, and we were soon off trudging along in the red mire (the soil being red in that region) toward Huntsville, Ala., arriving at that pretty town with its shaded streets and fine large spring the next day about 11 A. M. There we remained several days reorganizing the command, for the time had now expired for which the Fifteenth Illinois Infantry and our regiment, the Fourteenth, had enlisted. These regiments were so much reduced in numbers from long and hard service, and from the failure of many of the men to reenlist, that they were now consolidated and were called the Veteran Battalion of the Fourteenth and Fifteenth Illinois Volunteers. My company letter was now changed from K to F, by which the new company, formed from the remnants of Companies I, C, and K, was known.

These changes were not at all agreeable to me, for they took from me several of my particular chums, who returned to their homes, among them big Dan, the color sergeant; besides, it left me with but two of the old mess and Jack, our cook, and so we had to organize a new mess. Also, there being a surplus of officers, some changes were made among them, which was, to say the least, unpleasant. The most prominent change among officials was that of Colonel Rodgers, of the Fifteenth. Being senior and ranking officer, he was given command of our battalion, so we had to part with gallant Colonel Hall of our regiment. Our first lieutenant, John Kirkman, who commanded our company, went home, and First Lieutenant Thomas A. Weisner, of Company D, was placed in charge of our new company. This change in our regimental and company officers we regretted simply because of the high esteem in which we held those taken from us. But we soon formed a strong attachment for our new officers, who were brave, kind-hearted, and generous men.

When our old comrades came to leave we found it hard to part with them, and my feelings were much wrought upon when I came to say "good-bye" to them, and especially so when I took big Dan's brawny hand in mine for the last time, and gave him a message to bear to the "dear ones at home."

At Huntsville I met with another sore trial. My old school and seat mate, Hardin Abrams, was taken sick with a fever, and we had to leave him there in a hospital, and I was separated from him during the remainder of my army life.

Thus my readers will see that the vicissitudes of army life brought many changes in companionship, often severing the strongest ties of friendships, which would naturally leave one, especially a boy so young as I, with feelings of lingering loneliness and sadness.

We remained at Huntsville but two or three days, when we broke camp and marched southwest to Decatur, Ala. Here we met a small force of Confederates, which we soon dislodged. Crossing the Tennessee River on pontoons, we started southeast through the mountains of northern Alabama toward Rome, Ga., a distance of one hundred and twenty-five miles, which, considering the heavy rains that were falling, and the condition of the roads, was accomplished in a remarkably short time.

Several nights during this forced march we did not go into camp until after midnight. This caused the soldiers to enter strong complaints against General Blair. On these wearisome night marches we were all too tired and jaded to talk much, and, except these occasional outbursts of complaint, some of them in emphatic and inelegant language, nothing was heard save the steady slushing tramp and clattering sound of the marching column, and an occasional sharp command to close up. But on we pressed until we reached our destination, the city of Rome, which we found in possession of the Union troops.

CHAPTER XVIII.

Guarding Railroad in Sherman's Rear.

THE Confederates, who had evacuated Rome but a short time before we arrived there, had thrown quantities of their stores into the Coosa River, and we found the Union troops engaged in fishing them out. As soon as we had halted and stacked arms we joined them in the sport. Being fond of the water, this was just to my liking, and in one of my dives I came up with a ten-pound caddy of good tobacco, a trophy which was much prized by those of my company who were users of the weed.

We remained at Rome but one night, when we broke camp and continued our march southeast through Kingston and on to Etowah, Ga., situated on the north bank of the Etowah River. Arriving there June 6, 1864, we found both wagon and railroad bridge destroyed. We were now in the immediate rear of the army of General Sherman, who was pressing his way onward to the siege and capture of Atlanta, the enemy sharply contesting every foot of ground.

We remained at Etowah two days, when, crossing the river on canvas pontoons, we proceeded southward through the Altoona Mountains to join Sherman's forces, whose cannon we could hear thundering around Ackworth, twelve miles away to the south of us.

While at Etowah we camped on the river bank in close proximity to a graveyard. The first night we were there we had a very heavy thunderstorm, the rain coming down in perfect torrents. About midnight, the ground being flooded to a depth of five or six inches, I awoke to find the water running in one of my ears, which would have occurred sooner but for the fact that my knapsack pillow had kept my head above the rising tide. Assuming a sitting position, I took a survey of the situation by nature's own majestic electric light, which at times was so vivid as almost to blind me; and having during the day noticed near the center of the cemetery a large tombstone, which, unlike its upright comrades, lay flat upon its six brick pillars some eighteen inches above the ground, I concluded this would make the dryest bed I could find. I gathered up my belongings, and by the aid of the flashing lightning succeeded in making my way out through the briers to the tombstone, though not without several tumbles on the way. I soon folded my water-soaked woolen blanket double and spread it on the marble couch, placed my knapsack at the head for a pillow, lay down and covered myself up head and ears with my rubber blanket, and, although a perfect deluge of water was falling, I was soon oblivious to the flood, which by this time gave this city of the dead the appearance of a small lake dotted over with white sails. On awaking the next morning, not having changed my position after lying down, I found upon my side which was next to the slab impressions of its name, dates, and poetry. It certainly proved the hardest bed I ever tried, and is the only one I slept on during the service which I am positive I could find now just where I left it.

On the 8th of June our command reached the little station of Altoona, which is situated at the foot of the Altoona Mountains at the southeast end of the famous Altoona Pass. Our brigade, the Second of the Fourth Division, Seventeenth Army Corps, numbering fifteen hundred men, was detached and set to work fortifying the pass as a secondary base of supplies, and I suppose as a place to fall back to in case of the defeat of our main army, the booming of whose artillery around Big Shanty, some twelve miles south, we could now hear.

Our camp was situated on the top of the mountain at the south side of the pass. Here we had an unobstructed view across the broken country to Kennesaw Mountain, eighteen miles southeast of us, where the Confederate forces under General Johnston were fortified. Our forces had crowded close up to the base of Kennesaw Mountain, and that night, when on picket duty, I could see their fuse shells in aerial flight, making their long and graceful curves from the base to the summit of old Kennesaw.

That day, the 11th of June, the first railroad train came thundering through the pass, the engineer and fireman making all the noise they possibly could with bell and whistle, and being greeted with such ringing shouts and cheers as only jubilant soldiers can give. This train was loaded with provisions, and, strange as it seemed to us, had crossed the Etowah River on a new bridge, where on the 8th, but three days previous, we were compelled to cross on pontoons, and at which time there were no signs of a bridge but the old stone abutments.

We were kept busy patrolling the railroad, guarding supplies, and building fortifications around Altoona during the last weeks of June and the early part of July. On the 14th of June the Confederate General Polk was killed by a shell from one of the Union guns —the same bishop-general who had retreated before us as we entered Meridian, Miss., a few months previous.

On the 27th of June the great assault on Kennesaw was made. The wounded from this engagement were sent back for us to care for, and came by the train load. I was detailed among others, and worked three days and nights helping put up hospital tents, make beds, and remove the wounded from the cars to them. These poor wounded men were torn up in all conceivable shapes, and their sufferings were indescribable. Many of them had had their limbs amputated at the field hospital before being placed on the cars, and as we carried them out some of them would cry with pain and bemoan the loss of their limbs, while others, more gritty, would laugh and joke as if they considered it a pleasure to lose a limb in defending the old flag. I remember one little fellow especially who was about my age. He had been shot in the head, an ounce ball having struck him in the right eye and passed out back of his ear. The second day after he was shot he was up and around watching us work.

The first day we were at this work a train load of wounded came in before we had the tents ready for them, and, as the train was in a hurry to return to the front for more, we carried the wounded off and placed them on the ground, and made them as comfortable as possible in the gracious shade of the pine and chestnut trees. While we were getting the tents up and the wounded into them a violent thunderstorm came up, and in some way one poor fellow was overlooked and left out in the storm. When taken out of the cars he was placed at the root of a tree on a soft cushion of leaves found in quite a large hole about six inches deep. He had been shot through the body, which left his back quite weak, and when carried out he was left sitting up against the tree for support; but in some way he fell over into the hole filled with water from the storm, and, being too weak to raise himself up, was drowned in this shallow pool. We placed him in a suitable grave lined with pine boughs, his body wrapped in his blanket, covered it with more of the evergreen boughs—fit emblems of immortality—and after filling up the grave penciled his name, company, and regiment on a piece of cracker box, and placed it in proper position for a head-board. Such was the common method of burial in such cases. Indeed, during all the time I was in the service I never saw anyone buried in a coffin. I will not attempt to describe the work of the surgeons there, with their merciless knives, saws, and probes, which I witnessed. The thought of it makes me shudder yet. But I saw two ministering angels moving around among the wounded tenderly, whom I remember with delight.

These were two women in clean, bright calico dresses, quickly passing from cot to cot with white bandages, cups of warm soup, and tins of lemonade; who, with warm, loyal hearts full of good cheer and loving sympathy, did far more toward reviving the spirits and inspiring the courage of the wounded than the surgeons with all their skill and professional implements.

After we were relieved from this hospital work I was detailed with others at one time to make an *abattis* down the mountain side in front of our rifle-pits. For this purpose acres and acres of timber were cut down as follows: Beginning at the lower line of the *abattis* with hundreds of axes, we would cut the trees half off on the upper side, and thus work our way up the mountain side until we reached the long line of rifle-pits; there we would cut the trees entirely off, felling them against those just below them, which in turn would fall against others still below them, and so on until the whole body of timber, acres in extent, would go down with a perfect crash as suddenly as if struck by the swoop of a cyclone, making a perfect tangle. This done, we would then go down the mountain to the lower edge of the *abattis* and work our way up again to the rifle-pits, this time sharpening all the branches of the trees. When completed this made a very formidable obstruction to an advancing foe.

On the 3d of July the Confederates relinquished their grip on Kenesaw, evacuated that natural stronghold, and also evacuated Marietta, and retreated to the south, taking a new position near the Chattahoochee River. This weakening of the Johnnies made us feel jubilant, and formed a very inspiriting topic of conversation for the Fourth of July.

The morning of the 4th, as I stood on the depot platform among a group of comrades, a train load of soldiers came in from the North. These were men returning from veteran furlough, and among them was my cousin, John K. White, of the Forty-first Illinois Infantry. He came direct from Naples, Ill., where my parents were living. He knew I was stationed at Altoona Pass, but I did not know where he was. Although he was a man grown and I but a mere lad, yet we were always more like brothers than cousins, and when we met that day he gave me a hug that nearly broke my ribs. It is needless to say that we had a most delightful visit during the day. He brought me many pleasant messages from dear ones as well as all the home news, while I gave him an account of my experiences since we separated at Vicksburg. The next day he went on to his regiment, which belonged to our division.

On the 6th or 7th of July we broke camp at Altoona, boarded a train, and went to Marietta. This pretty little town, nestled in the lap of old Kennesaw, with its shaded streets, brick stores, good churches, and neat dwellings, was one of the prettiest I saw anywhere in the South. We arrived there that afternoon, and the evening was employed in putting up our shelters.

The first thing I did the next morning after breakfast was to climb to the top of the mountain. It was a beautiful clear morning. As I ascended in company with several of my comrades we noticed that there was scarcely a square yard of ground but had been torn and plowed up with shells from the Union guns, thousands of fragments of which were scattered around over the ground, though some had never exploded. Trees were riddled and full of holes and dead boughs hung from every tree top. In some instances whole tree tops had been cut off by shot from our artillery. Behind nearly every log, stump, tree, and rock were great piles of paper from cartridges the Johnnies had bitten off.

Arriving at the summit, I climbed the very tallest tree I could find, and from its topmost branch cut a twig out of which to make a pen holder as a memento of the noted place. While on this lofty perch I enjoyed a beautiful view of the surrounding country, and off to the southeast, six or seven miles, I could make out the positions of the Union and Confederate forces by the smoke from their camp fires.

On the 10th I was detailed, with some fifty others, to bury the dead on the right of Little Kennesaw, about four miles distant. These were the Confederate slain, and had lain there in the summer sun and rains but partially covered ever since the assault on the 27th of June. The weather was exceedingly hot, and the piece of ground over which the dead were scattered was but about four or five acres in extent. There we found some two hundred of the slain, while millions of green flies swarmed about and on the rank blackberry bushes, now loaded with ripe fruit, but which we dared not eat. The stifling heat and sickening odor rendered the place and work almost unendurable. Pen cannot describe the ghastly sights which there met our eyes—too ghastly and sickening to attempt a portrayal. It required the best part of two days in which to accomplish this disagreeable task. No headboards could be placed at the graves to mark them, and no doubt many homes in the South mourned the death of these dear ones, never knowing of their place of burial.

Of the many I assisted in burying the case of one young man may claim special mention. His grave I might have marked if I had had the material with which to do it, for I obtained his name from a soiled letter which I took from his side pocket. It was a bright, cheery missive, full of expressions of love and words of encouragement from his betrothed. In it she had inclosed a small piece of pretty linsey which she had woven with her own hands for a new dress for herself. As we buried this young man I said, "Poor girl, poor boy!" and the cruelties of war seemed more bitter than ever.

The few days we were at Marietta we had rather an easy time of it. When off duty, in company with my cousin, Royal Moore, of Company I, One Hundred and Twenty-ninth Illinois Infantry, I engaged in the jewelry business. Indeed, we did quite a thriving business, manufacturing and selling and trading rings to the native whites and to the colored people. These rings we made out of metal percussion caps which we picked up on the mountain. These metal tubes were about the size and shape of a number ten or twelve cartridge such as is now used in shotguns. They were thicker, however, and had a thread cut around the outside of them by which they could be screwed into the shell, and which held them securely in place. These we contrived to unscrew with our bayonets. The metal of which they were made seemed to be a composition of copper and brass, and when rubbed up was about the color of Guinea gold. Out of these metal caps we would cut and make the rings with a broken saw and a file, and when made would brighten them up with a piece of blue woolen goods. When thus completed they were quite bright and attractive, and enabled us to get fancy war prices for them in cash, pies, milk, sweet potatoes, etc. But notwithstanding the business proved quite remunerative, I should not want to engage in it again unless I could get the enemy to unscrew the dangerous percussion caps from the unexploded shells.

While at Marietta we were ordered out early one morning to go to Resaca, Ga., by train to intercept Wheeler's cavalry, which was momentarily expected to strike the railroad at that point. We arrived about noon that day, and for two days scouted through the surrounding country, and finding no trace of them we returned to Marietta, arriving at camp about 10 P. M.

We had left a few sick and Negroes in charge of the camp, Jack among them, whom we soon awakened and asked if he had anything for us to eat, having eaten nothing since breakfast. Jack replied: "Ise got nuffin 'ceptin' coffee an' bacon, but if sum ob de mess starts a fire I'll see if I can't fin' suffin'." This was agreed to, and off he started, and in about half an hour returned carrying in his arms two dozen loaves of steaming hot baker's bread, which with our coffee and bacon made us a relishable supper. But Jack would never tell us where he obtained the bread, always replying when asked about it: "Don' ax Jack dat question. Jes ax if dar is any mo' whar dat come from."

One day while encamped at Marietta General John M. Palmer, our first colonel, made us a visit, and the hour among his old comrades was very pleasantly spent in reminiscences of previous campaigns. This was the last time we saw him during the war. Also it was while we were encamped here that General McPherson, our old corps commander, was killed, on July 22d, near Atlanta. The death of this gallant and greatly beloved officer cast a gloom over the whole army. How strange that our noble corps commander, who led us on the Meridian raid, and General Polk, who commanded the Confederate forces at the place at that time, had within a few days both fallen on Georgia soil and on battlefields but a few miles apart!

CHAPTER XIX.

Busy Behind Sherman.

ABOUT August 1 we were ordered back to Ackworth to guard the railroad over which Sherman was getting his supplies. We went by train, and when we arrived we took quarters in the depot and abandoned storehouses. Here we were kept on the go night and day, scouting and patrolling the railroad to prevent its being torn up or trains thrown off by the Johnnies.

This work was both arduous and dangerous, for the enemy seemed determined to capture or ditch all trains possible. The road in this section runs through a rough, broken country, which was then covered with brush and timber close up to the track, so that we were in constant danger of being ambushed as we patrolled it in small squads. Our beat was two and a half miles north to Altoona Creek Block House, and two and a half miles south to the point where we struck the northern line of the beat of the guard at Moon Station. It was fortunate for us that the enemy was more intent on injuring the railroad track and derailing trains than in firing at us. We were required to inspect the track carefully to see that the rails and everything were in place, and as we passed along many bright moonlight nights, especially when outside of our picket lines, we were wholly at the mercy of any lurking foe that might be lying in ambush.

Several times while we were stationed at Ackworth, during the month of August, trains were thrown off the track near the town, train guards were captured, and what provisions were wanted by the enemy were taken, the foe making good his escape before any force from town could reach the point of attack. Sometimes a guard would pass along entirely unmolested but a short time before a train would be wrecked, although the Johnnies must have been concealed in the thick brush beside the track as they passed.

One of their methods of throwing trains from the track was by the use of an iron shoe and a wooden wedge. One squad, consisting of Sergeant Thomas Cunningham and Privates Frank Durant, Charles Paine, Charles Harper, William and Peter Gross, and myself, all members of the same company, once captured an outfit of this kind. That day we started out immediately after an early breakfast supplied with a full day's rations. We were to relieve a squad in patrolling the road south of us toward Moon Station, and expected to meet them near the picket lines coming in to be relieved. Failing in this, suspecting something might be wrong, we continued on down the track, keeping a sharp lookout for the guards or a derailed train. Not seeing either, we did not halt until we reached the point where we should meet the guards from Moon Station. This was at the mouth of a deep cut where the road ran through a hill midway between the latter station and Ackworth. At this point, the northern extremity of the cut, the track comes out on a high roadbed, on the west side some forty or fifty feet high and very steep, while on the opposite side it was only four or five feet down to the level of the woodland, which was covered with a heavy growth of timber and brush close up to the roadbed. Near the north end of this cut there was quite a curve in the track, so that engineers on northbound trains could not see the end of the cut until within a few yards of it. This made it a very dangerous place, and one where we always expected trouble. Indeed, we sometimes kept a special squad of men there to watch and guard it.

Not finding the squad we expected and had gone to relieve, and hearing no response to our calls, and seeing nothing of the guard from Moon Station, after a brief consultation, no train being in hearing distance, Sergeant Cunningham decided we had better go to the south end of the cut and see if we could get any information from some natives who occupied a log hut which stood there, and then hasten back before any train should come along.

From a woman at this house we learned that no guards had been seen there since the evening before, that some Confederates had been there during the night, and that near daylight she had heard some firing and supposed the guards had been driven off or had gone to Moon Station for assistance. We then returned to the north end of the cut to secrete ourselves in the brush to guard the track until we should be relieved. After returning we halted on the track a few moments while discussing the situation. The sergeant then ordered us to take a position just east of the track in the brush, and as we proceeded to execute the order we heard a great rustling and crashing out in the thick brush not more than twenty feet from where we had been standing. This commotion was made by a squad of Johnnies who were there awaiting an opportunity to wreck a train. There were seven or eight of them, and our squad immediately fired at them, but they all escaped. We chased them for about a quarter of a mile, exchanging shots as we went, but decided it would be useless, in view of the density of the forest, to pursue them farther, and returned and took a position near the railroad track, secluded in the thicket. From the position these Johnnies occupied it is evident that each one of them might have picked his man and shot us down.

Soon after taking our position one of our boys found the iron shoe and the wooden wedge referred to secreted under some leaves. The iron shoe was made out of an old plowshare, having a groove in it so as to catch the flange of a car wheel and run it upon and over the rail. The wooden wedge was about eighteen inches long and four inches thick at the large end, and both had clamps with which to fasten them to the rails. The two were designed to be used on rails opposite each other, and could not have failed to accomplish their work.

Soon after finding these a train of twenty-five box cars came through the cut. The train was loaded with soldiers. Every car, both inside and on top, was full. Desiring to send some word into camp, we waved them down, and while halted we showed the trainmen these instruments of death. Their gratitude was unbounded for this timely discovery, which, they felt, had in all probability saved them from a horrible death. The shoe and wedge were sent to General Sherman, and our squad was officially complimented for our prompt action and sound judgment in guarding the dangerous position until relieved.

One dark night during the time we were encamped at Ackworth I was detailed, with some others, to drive the Johnnies from a train they had captured about a mile below town. When we reached the train we found that the Johnnies, after capturing the train, which was loaded with army stores, not being able to carry prisoners with them, held our men captive only while they were loading their horses with provisions, and then released them and rode off in the darkness with their booty.

At another time, while patrolling about a mile north of Ackworth, one day about noon we met a train going south which the Johnnies had tried to capture, but failed in the attempt. The train slowed up and the men told us of their encounter. On our way to the place we met a brakeman who had jumped from the train when the Johnnies were on the track trying to signal it to stop. He had been captured and every shred of clothing taken from him excepting a pair of white cotton drawers, and when we met him, trudging along bareheaded and in his tender bare feet over the hot road, he was decidedly the wrathiest railroader I ever saw. The Johnnies had also relieved him of a good watch and all his money, and the language he was using about them would be out of place here. He said they were not satisfied with what they had taken from him, but cursed him for not having on more clothing, as they had not obtained enough to go around.

While here we had flour issued to us instead of hard-tack. This we at first used in biscuits baked in Dutch ovens, but we soon discovered that we had good bakers in our battalion, and further investigation revealed the fact that we also had masons and tinners. Ascertaining this, it was but a few days until a brick building was torn down and the brick used in the construction of bake ovens and its tin roof converted into large bread pans. Then such baker's bread as we had issued to us I have never seen excelled.

During the first week in September Companies A and B of our battalion were ordered and marched to Big Shanty, ten miles south of Ackworth, to guard the railroad at that point; and our company, F, at the same time was ordered and went five miles south to Moon Station.

At Moon Station it so happened that my company relieved the company of which my cousin, John White, was a member—the cousin who spent the Fourth of July with me at Altoona Pass. When we relieved them my cousin's mess turned the shanty they occupied over to our mess together with its furniture. This was quite a favor to us, for we had a good deal of rainy weather while we were there. The shanty was a good one, having a board roof, good beds, and dry bedding, and, with the sides inclosed with our rubber blankets, we could keep dry despite the hardest rains.

Moon Station was a wood and water station midway between Altoona Pass and the Kennesaw Mountain, and was five miles south of Ackworth and five miles north of Big Shanty. It was guarded by a rail stockade having between forty and fifty loopholes. The garrison at this time comprised our company, numbering, all told, eighty officers and men and four Negro cooks.

During the month of September here, as previously at Ackworth, we were kept busy as beavers scouting and patrolling the railroad to prevent the enemy from ditching the trains and cutting the telegraph wires.

On one occasion I was called out in the night to go with a squad to the relief of a train that had been ditched near Big Shanty. Arriving at the scene of disaster, we found the engine and five cars in the ditch, and that all the trainmen had been captured and taken off but the engineer, and he was under his engine with a broken leg. He told us that when he saw the obstruction on the track, and knew his engine must go off, he threw his gold watch into the brush and jumped. While some dug him out others searched for his watch with torches, but failed to find it.

On another occasion I was called out early one morning, before the sun was up, to go to the relief of a captured train. This one was within a half mile of the one just mentioned. When we reached the train we found it had not been thrown from the track, but had been held up by an obstruction on the road, and that after the Confederate cavalry had captured all on board, and loaded their horses down with provisions, they had set the long train of box cars on fire. When we arrived there was nothing left of the train and its cargo but the iron, and along the middle of the track great piles of burning corn, oats, flour, beans, and coffee.

Toward the last of September the Johnnies grew bolder, at times riding up in squads and firing on our pickets, which, on account of our small numbers, were posted not more than two or three hundred yards from the stockade. One afternoon twelve of them, dressed in blue uniform, rode up and fired on an outpost south of the stockade, and made good their escape before our pickets knew who they were.

Matters kept growing worse with us until the 2d of October. That day Orderly Sergeant Ben Burch and a small squad of men, when returning from Big Shanty with a wagon load of provisions, were captured by Confederate cavalry. General Thomas's wagon train, several miles in length and well guarded, was passing north at the time, and, being between it and the railroad, this cavalry squad, evidently fearful lest they could not cut through the moving train encumbered with prisoners, held their captives but a short time and then released them, telling them they would call for them the next day.

Pat Woods, the Irish boy who was so suddenly turned around on the battlefield in Mississippi by a cannon ball, was in this captured squad, and was shot through the right wrist for talking sharply to one of the guards, and when shot he seemed about as much surprised as he was when the cannon ball spun him around, and said to the guard, "And sure, what did ye go and do that for?" Indeed, he kept up his impertinent remarks until the guards would probably have killed him had not Sergeant Burch interfered and put a stop to his talk. Pat was a brave boy, and after the close of the Civil War served with credit in the regular army, and died while in that service in the West.

That afternoon a squad of fifteen or sixteen of us, while out reconnoitering in the direction of Big Shanty, where we had heard some firing, came across Sergeant Burch and the men who had been captured with him. The sergeant deeming it dangerous to proceed further, we returned to camp and made our report. On our way in I bound Pat's wrist with my large red silk handkerchief which my mother presented to me the day I left home.

The evening of that day I was detailed for picket duty. It was very dark and rained nearly all night. My post was east from the stockade. The reserve were posted in some brush and timber on the west side of a small field, while I was near the center of the field behind a large stump. Crouched behind this stump under my rubber blanket from midnight until 2 A. M., by the aid of the frequent bright flashes of lightning I saw several squads of Confederates riding north on a road not over one hundred yards east of my position, but I deemed it unwise to fire at them. The next morning, after reaching camp, I found that others had seen some of the enemy during the night. This gave us no small degree of anxiety as to what the Johnnies had in view. At the time we supposed that Sherman's whole army was between us and the Confederate army, and that those whom we saw during the night were only some of Hood's cavalry sent out to damage the railroads and gather supplies. In reality, however, Hood had now started for Tennessee, and was running his whole army of thirty-five thousand men around north of Sherman to demolish the railroad track between Altoona Pass and Kennesaw Mountain, and to capture Sherman's base of supplies at Altoona Pass, some ten miles north of us, where he had collected the stores for his march to the sea.

Hood's move on the railroad at this time was undoubtedly a complete surprise to General Sherman, for at the time there were no Federal troops in the valley from Kennesaw to Altoona, a distance of some eighteen or nineteen miles, except our Veteran Battalion, six companies, numbering but between four and five hundred officers and men, while Altoona Pass at the time was garrisoned by only eight hundred and ninety officers and men. Companies A and B of our battalion, commanded by Captain Gillespie, were stationed at Big Shanty, the first station north of Kennesaw. Three other companies were at Ackworth, the first station south of Altoona, under command of Captain Crinion, I think. Our own company, F, numbering eighty-four officers and men, commanded by Captain Thomas A. Weisner, was at Moon Station, about midway between Big Shanty and Ackworth, near the center of the valley.

Such was the situation on the memorable morning of October 3, when our captain received this remarkable order: "Hold on as long as possible, and then surrender yourself and men on the best terms possible."

CHAPTER XX.

Battle of Moon Station and Capture.

AS the morning advanced heavy musketry firing was heard in the vicinity of Big Shanty. From this we were satisfied that trouble was brewing, but could not understand what it was. A train going south that morning with army stores was captured about two miles south of us, and our guards, who had skirted the timber along the track on their way to it, came near being captured as they approached.

The same day, between 1 and 2 P. M., a train load of cattle, heavily guarded, went south. This was soon followed by a train of army supplies. This latter train, however, returned in a short time, and as it backed into Moon Station we were informed that the cattle train had been captured and that this one had barely escaped the same fate, and as it could not get through to Big Shanty it would be taken back to Altoona Pass and there wait for orders. The cattle train had been captured less than a mile south of our post, and soon we heard the most terrible bellowing I ever listened to. The Johnnies had set fire to the train, which had on board not less than three hundred head of cattle, all of which were burned.

At Moon Station the railroad ran north and south

between two gently sloping hills. The track was on an embankment some five feet high. Our rude stockade stood on the east side of the railroad about fifty yards up the slope from the track, and was made out of chestnut rails, stood on end, with loopholes notched in them about four feet above the bottom of a ditch that was two feet deep and which ran around just inside the stockade. About twenty-five yards farther up the hill were our shanties. At the station there were no buildings except a log house which stood a little to the north and front of the stockade and about half way between it and the railroad east of the track, and a long woodshed and a large water tank which stood across the track almost opposite it. Both hillsides had been pretty well cleared of timber, yet on the west of the railroad a few scattering trees, stumps, and small patches of brush still remained. Some two hundred yards south of the stockade the road ran through a deep cut in a hill which was covered with a dense growth of brush and timber. At the northern end of this cut began the high grade before mentioned, which continued past the station. After the train referred to backed in from the south, about 2 P. M., no more patrols were sent out, and those that were out were held in the quarters as fast as they came in. The pickets, under command of Lieutenant Kieffer, were instructed when attacked to hold their posts as long as possible and then retreat to the stockade.

Every preparation for battle was made. A heavy square wooden box containing one thousand rounds of cartridges was carried into and placed near the center of the stockade, and opened so as to be of easy access to our men as supplies in our cartridge boxes should give out. Our Enfield rifles were carefully examined, put in order, loaded, and fresh caps put on.

We were now expecting the enemy to attack us at any moment. Our orders were to run for the stockade as soon as the pickets were driven in, and as far as possible to cover their retreat. As for myself, I was determined on getting into the stockade as quickly as anyone after we should learn the pickets were falling back. Knowing there were but a little over half enough loopholes for the company, I resolved, if possible, to have one of them, and to have one on the side next to the railroad if I could get it. With this in view I early strapped on my cartridge box, and held to my gun all the afternoon.

Our pickets were first fired upon about 2 P. M., and later at different times during the afternoon; but they held their ground until near dark. My mess, as did nearly all others that evening, took our guns with us when we went to supper. Our table, made of rough boards supported by stakes driven in the ground, stood in the alley back of our quarters. Between five and six o'clock in the evening, as we were standing around a half finished supper, with our guns leaning against the table by our sides, suddenly "whiz," "bang," "zip," rang the guns on the opposite hilltops, volley after volley. Our pickets, being attacked in force, were returning the fire and retreating down the hill toward the stockade at the top of their speed. Instantly knives, forks, cups, and spoons were dropped, and, seizing our guns, we made a wild rush for the stockade. I was among the first to enter, and never halted until my gun was run through a loophole near the center of the side of the stockade next to the railroad. Those of us who were in the quarters when the firing began had barely entered the stockade when the enemy opened on us from the opposite hilltop. Their first fire went wild, the balls whistling and singing at least thirty feet above our heads. But their guns were soon depressed to the right range, and then "spat," "spat," "thud," "thud," "thud," the leaden hail showered against the stockade and the clay embankment which was thrown up against it on the outside, causing the splinters to fly from the one and the mud from the other. I had barely gotten my rifle run through the loophole when those to my right and left began to fire. Just then an old soldier, who was evidently vexed at not getting a loophole, gave my right arm a vigorous jerk and yelled out: "Shoot, you young rascal, or give me that hole."

I was braced to receive the wicked kick of my gun and never turned, but hallooed back at the top of my voice: "I'll not give up this hole nor fire my gun until I see somebody to shoot at."

Just then a Johnnie broke cover from behind a tree, and, drawing a careful bead on him, I fired and quickly handed my gun back and received a loaded one in exchange. This kind of work was going on all around me, and our fire was so rapid and deadly that the enemy on the opposite hill where the attack first began soon retired behind the slope to devise some better way of approach on the stockade.

After our foe had retired from in front of my side

of the stockade, upon which all the first attack was made, with almost breathless suspense, and with eyes kindled with the fire of battle, we watched through the loopholes for his next appearance. But four or five minutes, however, of extreme suspense prevailed, when the boys on the south side of the stockade sang out: "Here they come! Give it to 'em!" and began a rapid fire. Above the din I could hear John Coats, Bill Clark, Jim Corey, Jule Eldred, and others yelling: "There goes one! There tumbles another! Give it to 'em, boys!"

All this time I was in a feverish state of excitement, standing with my loaded gun run out through the loophole ready to fire at the first Johnnie that might come in sight, but I could see none to fire at, for they were now pouring through the railroad cut south of us, and filing off to the left or west of the embankment too far to one side for me to see.

A brigade of gray coats, under command of General Reynolds, of Arkansas, came through the cut on the dead run; but while their speed was high it required several minutes for them to turn the corner and get down behind the railroad bank out of the range of a destructive fire from the south side of the stockade, and while they were turning this deadly angle many a brave Confederate fell.

As soon as they had all made their way through the cut there was an ominous lull for a few minutes, with none of the enemy in view except their dead and wounded. During this time Captain Wiesner, our gallant young commander, told us the Johnnies were working their way up to us behind the railroad embankment, for us to keep perfectly cool, and reserve our fire until they should show themselves, and then, taking good aim, to fire as rapidly as possible and make every shot count. At the time this command was given a brigade of fourteen or fifteen hundred determined Confederates were strung out behind the railroad embankment directly in front of us, while our numbers all told were but eighty-four. They were about fifty yards from the stockade—so close, indeed, that we could hear them talking and their officers giving orders.

Our captain's orders were obeyed to the letter, and our fire, ranging from the fifty yards in our immediate front to two hundred yards on either side of the stockade, with two loaded guns for each loophole, to start with, and two men to each to work them, told with most deadly effect. As rapidly as we fired and handed back our empty guns our comrades behind us had loaded ones ready for us to grab, and so rapidly did we thus load and fire at times during the evening's engagement that sometimes our smoking guns were so hot we could scarcely hold them. During this time the Confederates poured a heavy fire on the stockade from behind the railroad embankment, while we returned it with such execution that we held them in bay for nearly three hours. Firing then ceased for a short time, during which we could hear the Confederate officers as they were forming a storming party and gave orders preparatory to the charge. Hearing this we stood to our guns, hammers raised, and fingers to triggers. It was a moment of unspeakable suspense as we thus stood and peered through the loopholes over the long steel barrels of our trusty rifles.

breathlessly awaiting the desperate charge and the proper moment to press the death-dealing trigger. We had but a moment to wait when the enemy, maddened at their loss and our stubborn resistance, surged over the roadbed and made a wild rush up the hill with their peculiar yell. In this fifty yards of open slope we mowed them down like grain before the sickle, but with our most rapid and deadly fire we could not check them. On, on they swept up the hillside in the face of our leaden hail, a mad, resistless tide of gray, whose right and left striking the stockade, swept entirely around it, completely engulfing us in a seething mass of yelling Confederates. Four Confederate flags were soon waving over our stockade, and their smoking rifles thrust through our loopholes, and for a few moments our brave old company fought the desperate Johnnies under their stars and bars, at times our muskets locking horns with theirs in the same loopholes in a hand to hand contest.

About this time our captain was wounded in the right side; several others were slightly wounded, and two of our men were killed. The forty rounds of ammunition in our cartridge boxes were exhausted, and to my personal knowledge not over a handful of the thousand rounds in the large box remained. And now, with our ammunition exhausted, Confederate rifles blazing through the loopholes on all sides of the stockade, and surrounded by overwhelming numbers, Captain Wiesner, considering the morning's order to hold the position as long as possible had been fully obeyed, ordered us to cease firing, and throwing his black hat up in the air high above the stockade, shouted: "We surrender!" The enemy still continuing their fire, we clutched our guns, expecting an order to fix bayonets, and were just ready to obey it when they ceased firing and the desperate battle of Moon Station was ended.

At the time of the surrender Allen Crisp, one of the youngest boys in our company, was lying on the ground with a bullet hole through his body. Old Uncle Jimmie Scott, my Irish friend, the cupola of the company, had a shattered knee, from which he died. These, with our captain and several others but slightly wounded, were all of our men who were injured in the stockade, and I think none were wounded until the Johnnies got to our loopholes. We never knew the exact loss of the enemy in this engagement, but from what we could see around the stockade there must have been over one hundred killed and wounded.

As soon as the Confederates ceased firing we were ordered to march out of the stockade; but before starting a number of our men broke the stocks of their guns, and several of the other boys, with myself, threw ours into the inside ditch, which had six or eight inches of water in it, and jumped in on them and stamped them into the mud as deep as we could.

As we marched out of the stockade that evening in the darkness, between 8 and 9 o'clock, we found ourselves prisoners of war surrounded by a howling mob of Confederates, who unceremoniously relieved us of our watches, etc., and made all kinds of one-sided trades for our clothing, hats, caps, boots, and shoes, and would not allow us to return to our quarters for our knapsacks, haversacks, blankets, or other belongings.

As soon as we were out some Confederate general rode up and called for our commanding officer. When Captain Wiesner stepped out he severely criticised him for not surrendering before so many lives were lost. But the captain informed him he had simply obeyed his orders to hold the post as long as he could, and that with the commanding Confederate officer rested the responsibility of the loss of life.

At the time the Johnnies were robbing us of our effects they found me rather poorly clad, for I had not drawn any clothing since leaving Vicksburg, over six months before, and my pantaloons and blouse were quite threadbare, besides being considerably soiled. These they did not appear to want, but I had on a very good black felt army hat which seemed attractive to them, and I had not taken more than one step out of the opening leading from the stockade when a Johnnie about six feet tall, with long sandy hair, said: "Say, you young Yank, you have got a purty good hat," and with that jerked it from my head and handed me his old quilted cloth one instead.

I had no more than got this old quilted rag placed on my head when another Johnnie stepped up to me and said: " Yank, let's trade hats," and jerked mine off and handed me his old broken-billed gray cap; and before I had gone ten steps farther into the crowd another Johnnie said: " Yank, you have no business with a Confederate cap," and, snatching it off my head, handed me his hat, saying: " Hayre, take one of yere un culler."

When I examined the old black and blue limp thing he handed me I found the crown was a piece of an old blue army overcoat which he had " whanged " on with cotton cord, and the limp black rim was looped up to this on all sides with the same kind of cord to hold it from falling down over his face.

As no other Confederate seemed inclined to trade hats with me after this exchange, I concluded my youthful brow was now graced with the poorest makeshift of a hat Hood's army could produce. Yet while that was my candid opinion, and I felt insulted and highly indignant at every Johnnie who so unceremoniously jerked my succession of hats from my head, to-day I would give more for that old Confederate hat than I would for the best hat that can be produced in America; and I never think of this episode without a hearty laugh. Furthermore, as time obliterates the bitterness engendered by war, and the mollifying influences of a quarter of a century have subdued its heated passions and strife, we can throw the mantle of charity over many things which then seemed harsh and cruel.

As we were being relieved of our clothing and other possessions, ruthlessly, as we thought, many hot words were exchanged, and in some instances it seemed as if they would terminate in blows.

We had not been out of the stockade over five minutes when a long mysterious line of battle, like a phantom column, stretching to right and left as far as we could see, made its sudden appearance amid the evening's shadows, coming in on the double-quick. Their colors or uniforms I could not make out, but from the first glimpse I caught of the long line in the protecting gloom it seemed to me I could discern the Union blue. New and buoyant hopes at once sprang up within my breast, for all through that eventful afternoon and evening, not knowing of the orders the captain had received nor that Hood's whole army was in the valley between us and our main forces, I had momentarily expected the appearance of a relief column from Marietta. Was not this our line of boys in blue I saw swinging over the crest of the hill? and were they not coming in on a charge to relieve us? It seemed to me it must be so, for they were coming from the right direction, and my young heart fairly leaped within me at the thought; and my powder-stained finger tips pressed my brow beneath the old Confederate hat to assist my straining eyes in piercing the evening's gloom to discover, if possible, whether the advancing column was the blue or the gray.

As I thus stood, with trembling frame and heaving breast, what a Yankee shout of joy would have burst from my young throat had I caught a fair glimpse of the stars and stripes held aloft by a boy in blue. But in this cherished hope I met a bitter disappointment, for, alas! the colors were the stars and bars borne by a boy in gray.

At this bitter revelation a heart twinge nearly took my breath, for not until then did I fully realize the terrible weight of my situation. Having confidently and momentarily expected relief during all the afternoon and evening, it was not until this advancing column of gray drew their lines closer and tighter around us that I fully abandoned all hope and allowed myself to believe and admit that we were prisoners. When at last the sad, sad fact fully broke upon me my wrought-up nerves were completely unstrung, and thoughts of home and dear ones from whom I felt I was going, perhaps forever, came in rapid succession. I gave way to boyish grief, and a heavy gloom, deeper than that of the night, settled down upon me. I however gave way to this despair but for a moment when hope and determination came to my relief, and, brushing the streaming tears from my smoke-begrimed face, I firmly resolved to make the best of my sad situation and not again give way to emotions of despondency and grief.

CHAPTER XXI.

Marching to Prison.

A FEW moments after the new line of battle at the railroad below us had halted, the prisoners were ordered to fall in line, double file, and were surrounded by a cordon of gray-coated guards. Then this blue and gray procession at the order, "Forward! March!" crossed the railroad and headed for Big Shanty, and as in the gloom of the night we bade adieu to our dead and wounded comrades, some of them in a dying condition, I am sure I never saw a more sad and sullen set of blue and gray. I think, however, we respected each other's courage, and each had but one grim satisfaction—the Johnnies, that they had captured us and had possession of Moon Station, and we, that they had paid dear for their Yankee prey.

By this time we prisoners were dressed in all manner of old ragged Confederate coats, hats, and caps, and now, as we left our dead and wounded comrades, and were starting for prison, disarmed of our guns, having but three or four blankets all told, which happened to be carried into the stockade, compelled to leave behind all of our haversacks and knapsacks in which were kept our letters, pictures of friends, and little keepsakes from home, we marched out of Moon Station a saddened set of captives, with gloomy forebodings. Every man in our company had been killed or captured, excepting Uncle Billie Ward, an Irishman, who did not enter the stockade when our pickets were fired upon, and who made his way into our lines at Marietta. The poor colored men, Jack, Toney, Oliver, and one other cook, who were captured with the rest of us, the Johnnies nearly frightened to death, but otherwise did not injure.

As our road to Big Shanty lay through heavy timber and brush, and the night was dark, our guards, before starting, provided themselves with a number of pitch pine torches, with which to light the column on its way, and as a precaution against any of us making our escape. After these torches were lighted we were afforded a better view of our new uniforms, and a more comical, woe-begone looking set of Yankee soldiers, or queerer torchlight procession, I never saw or marched with. We could barely recognize each other ten steps apart, and when there was a recognition, notwithstanding our dismal plight, we could not suppress a laugh or a joke over each other's comical appearance.

We reached Big Shanty near midnight, where we found a number of dead and wounded comrades of Companies A and B in the depot, where we were held until morning. One of the living, an Irishman, whose name I have forgotten, who deserted from the Confederate army at Vicksburg, and who joined our regiment while there, during the morning's engagement had an arm broken. A short time after we arrived his old Confederate captain came in the depot, and, recognizing his former subordinate, had the poor fellow taken out and shot. Companies A and B were not all captured, a part of them under Captain Gillespie escaping to Marietta.

At daylight, along with our comrades of Companies A and B who were able to march, we were started southwest under a heavy guard. About 8 A. M. on this the 4th day of October we heard heavy musketry firing northeast of us, and were satisfied Ackworth was attacked, as was the case; and the three companies of our battalion stationed there held the post until 2 P. M., when, greatly outnumbered and overpowered, they were forced to surrender.

All during that day on our march we were passing Confederate troops, principally infantry and artillery, with long trains of ambulance and provision wagons of every conceivable shape, from light spring and old farm wagons to an occasional good United States army wagon which had been captured from some of our trains. The mules and horses were as poor and motley-looking as were the vehicles. The most of them had on chain harness, cotton cloth back-bands, and cornhusk collars. The troops were poorly clad in brown and gray cotton suits, and but for the flags they carried looked as if they might have been a section of the old Continental army.

Hood's troops seemed to be in good spirits, and as we passed regiment after regiment they would sing out, "Well, Yanks, old Sherman has got flanked this time;" and we would retort, "Yes, and you will catch it up at Altoona." But, notwithstanding their seeming good spirits, from their general appearance, as compared with the Union army, we took considerable comfort in believing the Confederacy was on its last pegs.

That evening just at sundown we went into camp in the vicinity of Lost Mountain, where we found a number of Confederates encamped in advance of us. As we passed these troops, camped along both sides of the road under the tall pines, we noticed long piles of corn dodgers ricked up on the wire grass ready to be issued to the troops. Dozens and dozens of Negroes were engaged in baking this bread in Dutch ovens. The dodgers were about the size of a brick, though a little different in shape, were nicely browned, and, being hot, gave out a savory flavor to a tired and hungry soldier boy. We were corraled in a cow pen that night on the same plantation where these Confederate troops were encamped. Just outside the bars stood an old empty white-topped wagon, the rear end gate of which was out—a Confederate portable secretary. On the floor of the bed, at the rear end, were pen and ink and a large blank book, one of old Jeff's autograph albums. In this book each Yankee prisoner was invited by a crusty Confederate sergeant to inscribe his name, company, and regiment, and, this done, he passed on into the pen, around which was stationed a strong guard. In recording his name in that book many a brave comrade signed his death-warrant.

Surrounded as we were by Confederates, General Hood at the time seated on his horse within a few feet of us, the Confederate stars and bars in sight, I could but contrast the scene and occasion with the one when, in the old church at home, surrounded by warm patriotic friends, I had gone forward with Hardin and other associates and signed the enlistment papers as they lay on the communion table o'erspread with the stars and stripes. There we were heartily cheered, and called brave boys; here we were called Yanks derisively, with qualifying adjectives that we considered quite inappropriate, and on we were hurried like cattle into the pen.

Once inside that high rail inclosure, we began to speculate as to what kind of rations they were going to give their new herd. As for myself, I had my mouth fixed for one of the toothsome corn dodgers. But none of them came, and in their stead Confederate hard-tack was issued to us, three pieces to each man, designed as a day's rations. These were unlike any Yankee hard-tack we had ever tackled. They were made out of ground rice and water without any shortening or salt. There were no molars in our squad of prisoners that could grind them, and the only way we could manage them was by pulverizing them between two stones, of which there were a good many in the pen. I ground mine in that way and ate but a part of them that night, putting what was left in my blouse pocket for the next day.

During the night one of our boys was awakened by a Johnnie taking his shoes from under his head. The alarm was at once given, and the entire squad, over one hundred in all, awoke. Then, although our feet needed the rest, we sat up on the ground where we had been lying with nothing under us but our shoes for pillows, and put them on, and tied them in hard knots, so that we lost no more that night.

Once awake I found it difficult to get to sleep again, and as I lay there in the old cow pen on my back, gazing at the stars through the tops of the gently swaying pines, I thought of many things. What would the dear ones at home think when they should hear that their only boy was a prisoner? How would father and mother take it? And my sisters—Nellie, May, and Georgia—then quite small, and all younger than myself? How I wished for their pictures, which I had received but a short time before my capture— a splendid photograph it was of the three in a smiling group. I wondered if some Johnnie would send it to his home as a memento of the fight. Then I tried to imagine what kind of a prison we were going to, supposing it would be some large building like a barrack, surrounded by a strong guard.

I finally dropped to sleep, however, thinking that for a boy only a little over sixteen years old I had made a record I need not be ashamed of, though I was a prisoner. I had been at my post of duty and filled my place ever since my enlistment, and, since signing the prison record the evening before, my name was inscribed in both Federal and Confederate war records, in the latter of which signatures, however, there was not much comfort.

The morning of the 5th dawned bright and clear. Some time during the night previous the other three companies of our battalion, which had been captured at Ackworth, joined us, Dr. Chaffee, our regimental surgeon, being with them. As surgeons were not held as prisoners of war he was released, but before leaving us he took a list of all our names, companies, and regiments for publication in the Northern papers for the information of our friends.

At an early hour the bars of the pen were let down, and we were turned out into the road and took up our line of march toward a point on the Chattahoochee River, to the southwest of Atlanta. As we started we passed a Confederate regiment that was just taking up its line of march in the opposite direction. In passing this gray column I noticed one of the men with a frolicsome pet that wore a uniform which was in pleasing harmony with that of its owner, and which, from its sprightly maneuvers as it skipped about from shoulder to shoulder along the whole line of the regiment, at last hiding itself snugly away in its owner's pocket, seemed imbued with the spirit of that most glorious October morning. This nimble little creature was a sprightly gray squirrel, and I venture to say, while he has not the national reputation of "Old Abe," the proud eagle of the Eighth Wisconsin Regiment, that he is by no means forgotten by this old Confederate regiment.

About 8 A. M. that 5th day of October, as we were swinging along at a good gait over a rolling country covered with stately pines whose lofty evergreen crowns were gently swaying in the clear morning air, our ears caught the faint reverberations of the booming of a cannon, undoubtedly the opening gun at Altoona Pass; then came another and another, and as the rumble of distant thunder is the presage of the coming storm, this, to our keen ears, was the premonition of the fearful tempest which was breaking upon Altoona Pass. We knew every inch of the ground there, rifle-pits, barricades, and redoubts, for we had helped make them. If prayer is the sincere, earnest desire of the heart, "uttered or unexpressed," everyone in our captured company must have prayed effectually for the success of our boys there that day as we were marching away to prison under the sound of those guns.

It will be remembered that on the 4th of October, the day previous, the stirring revival song, "Hold the fort!" had its birth, or rather the event which inspired it occurred. That was the day on which General Sherman signaled from Vining Station, below Marietta, to the top of Kennesaw Mountain, the message which was signaled from there to Altoona, that he was sending reinforcements to Altoona, and for them to hold the post without fail. At the very time this signal was given we were in the valley between the two mountains, and the message was sent over our heads and over Hood's army, although all unknown to them and us.

I desire here to record my belief, which I think no one who is informed about the matter will question, that Altoona Pass would not have been saved by the brave General Corse and his gallant men but for the desperate fighting of the Veteran Battalion of the Fourteenth and Fifteenth Illinois Infantry on the 3d and 4th of October in the valley below Altoona. By their stubborn resistance the Confederates were held in check at least thirty-five hours, and twenty hours of this time engaged them in actual fighting. This, with the time required in taking care of their dead and wounded, gave General Corse time to get down from Rome to Altoona with his forces, which he did just as the outposts at the latter place were being attacked by Hood's troops at 1 A. M. the morning of the 5th.

Hood attacked this place with three brigades, numbering between four and five thousand men. Altoona, previous to Corse's arrival, had but eight hundred and ninety men, under command of Colonel Tourtelotte, who could not have held the place eighteen hours without assistance. Hood sent but one division to strike and destroy the railroad in the valley where we were stationed, and bore off to the left or west with his main army. This division took our stations one at a time, commencing at Big Shanty between 9 and 10 A. M. the 3d of October, and striking us at Moon Station the same day at 2 P. M. We held our position until 9 P. M. Ackworth was attacked at 8 A. M. the morning of the 4th, and was held until 2 P. M. the same day, the troops at these three stations all being portions of our Veteran Battalion. After taking these points Hood's troops could not, and did not, reach Altoona until 1 A. M. the 5th of October, as previously stated, just as General Corse arrived with his troops from Rome. Thus, it will be seen, it took Hood's forces forty hours to make fifteen miles. Now, suppose our little battalion had surrendered post after post as we were attacked by that division of determined Confederates. Had such been the case it can be readily seen that Hood's forces could have reached and taken Altoona Pass, where Sherman's provisions for his march to the sea were stored, at least twenty-four hours before General Corse arrived there.

This being the fact, and no mention of the important work of our Veteran Battalion having been made in any war history, must be my only apology for making this record here. I feel that this much is justly due our brave boys who fought so stubbornly and held their posts so persistently against great odds in defense of this line of railroad leading to Sherman's base of supplies, and who indirectly saved Altoona Pass.

General Corse and his men were a band of brave and gallant heroes, and this statement is not intended to, nor can it, detract in the least from their glory. I dare say the general would readily grant all that is here claimed, and would accord due merit and praise to our brave battalion. It is not surprising that members of our battalion should have felt somewhat disappointed when General Sherman's *Memoirs* came out to find that no mention was made of our services. But we attributed this to his lack of information respecting the work done.

This record, therefore, of the gallant defense of important posts by our brave old Veteran Battalion is the first that has ever appeared, so far as the writer's knowledge extends.

CHAPTER XXII.

Arrival at Andersonville.

JUST as the sun was setting on the evening of the 5th of October, 1864, we went into camp for the night on the south bank of the Chattahoochee River, some twenty-five miles distant from the cow pen near Lost Mountain where we spent the previous night, and twenty odd miles southwest from Atlanta. Our camp was just a few yards to the right of the pontoon bridge on which we crossed.

As we were going into camp General Beauregard and staff crossed to the north bank of the river, and, when over, Hood's entire army, excepting our guards, was on the north side of the Chattahoochee. The bridge was then taken up. After being marched to our camp on the bank of the river a guard line was formed around us in the shape of a crescent with each horn touching the edge of the water. In our front in the river was quite a growth of buck brush extending about twenty yards out into the stream. The ground on which we were camped was open, sloping gently to the river's brink. After the turn of the night I was awakened and noticed a dozen or so objects, about six feet long and somewhat the shape and color of logs, quietly rolling down the slope over the sandy beach into the river and disappearing in the buck brush.

Across the river, on the opposite bank from where we were, Confederate forces were encamped, while just beyond the skirting of buck brush I could see guards as they were paddling up and down the stream with lighted torches as though afraid some of us might be somnambulists, and that walking in our sleep we might get drowned. But while the brush formed a pretty good hiding place, which some of our boys were disposed to avail themselves of in an attempt to escape, I concluded, when by the light of his torch I caught a glimpse of one of the Johnnies in a skiff with fixed bayonet, that I would prefer my chances on land.

In the evening when we went into camp we were carefully counted, and on the morning of the 6th as we started out the counting was repeated, which disclosed the fact that they were short some thirty odd prisoners. We were then halted and marched back into camp. The officers in charge questioned the guards as to whether they had seen any of the Yanks escape or not. Finding that none had been discovered the Confederate officer felt sure they were either in the ground or in the water, and instituted a careful search for Yankee graves. Being unable to resurrect any from the sandy beach, he stepped down to the river's edge and called aloud for them to come up out of the watery deep, but not a ripple or a sound came from the placid stream, and the waters of the beautiful Chattahoochee continued their onward flow all unmindful of the excited Confederates.

This unruffled serenity of the stream seemed very exasperating to the officer, who was now fairly frothing at the mouth, and indulging in the use of inelegant descriptive adjectives concerning us Yankees which we did not particularly enjoy. However, after he cooled down enough to use his brains with some degree of intelligence, he ordered some of his guards to get into the boats and institute a vigorous spearing campaign with bayonets in search of the missing prisoners. It was not long until they started their game, and as one after another came bounding to the shore from their hiding places, dripping from head to foot, they were greeted with hearty cheers and shouts as though they were proud conquerors instead of skulking prisoners. When the officer found his full complement of prisoners we took up our line of march again and started south at a lively gait in the direction of West Point. About noon we halted for dinner near a large log warehouse that stood alone in the pine woods, several miles from any other building, so far as we could see. One end of this building was stored to the depth of some three feet with bacon packed in charcoal. In the other end was a great quantity of meal in sacks. That noon we had issued to us about a pint of good meal to each man and a half pound of bacon. The bacon had but the slightest trace of salt, but was preserved by the charcoal, and tasted quite delicious when broiled. The meal we found somewhat difficult to manage. Some took theirs in hats, others, who were fortunate enough to have any left, took theirs in their handkerchiefs, and still others in their pockets or on pieces of bark. We used the meal by mixing it with water, and then put the saltless dough on pieces of bark or chips, which we propped up in front of the fire until baked.

About 4 P. M. that day we passed a fine-looking spring which was some twenty feet from the road. Being quite tired and thirsty, I asked one of the guards, a kind-looking old man, if he would not go with me to the spring and let me get a drink. This he consented to, and, dropping out of ranks, he told me to go on in advance of him. Reaching the spring, I satiated my thirst with its delicious cooling waters. On the opposite side of the road from the spring was a canefield, and while lying on the grass beneath the large bushy-topped chestnut tree which shaded the crystal fountain, I wondered if the clever old guard, who was standing a few feet back of me leaning on his rifle, would allow me to climb over the fence into the field and get us a stalk of sugar cane apiece. When we got back into the road alongside the field, without halting I glanced back over my shoulder, and said: "Guard, let's have some of that cane. If you will let me I will go over and get us each a good stalk."

All Southerners are fond of cane, and, being in an accommodating mood, the old gentleman consented to my proposition. Being unencumbered, I quickly bounded over into the field. The freedom thus given seemed to beget within me a keen desire for more, and as I stepped out into the canefield I determined, if possible, to have it. But I thought it would be best to work my way out several rows before undertaking it. With the view of throwing the old man off his guard, while I was going out I carefully examined the different hills as I passed them as if in search of the best. When I reached the fourth row, some twenty-five or thirty feet from the fence, I decided that that was the time for making the break for liberty. However, before doing so I concluded I had better cut a stalk of cane, and while doing so to look back and see what the old guard, whom I left standing in the middle of the road, was doing. I soon discovered that the accommodating old man had shifted position, and was then near the fence, and at that instant had his rifle run through the top crack of the fence, hammer cocked, with a carefully drawn bead on me, ready to fire at my first attempt to escape.

At this uninspiring sight the two nimble members which I had expected to carry me off so rapidly in my flight for freedom became so demoralized and untrustworthy that I abandoned the project, and at the same time it occurred to me that after all the cane near the fence might be the sweetest; so, leaving the stalk I had been hacking at with my dull knife as unconcerned as possible, I walked back to the outside row near where the guard was standing and cut off two good stalks. While doing this the guard let down the hammer of his gun, withdrew it from the fence, and quietly waited for me to return with the cane. Climbing the fence, I handed him the better stalk of the two, and then we hastened on to catch up with the prisoners and guards in advance. But neither of us made any mention of what we thought the other's intentions were when I was getting the cane. Had I succeeded in escaping from the guard I would have had a fair chance to reach our lines near Atlanta, for, as I have before mentioned, at that time all of Hood's forces were north of the Chattahoochee except our guards, a fact which the boys who tried to make their escape the night before well understood.

After a long, hard march we reached West Point the evening of the 6th, about sundown. Marching into town, we were halted on a street in front of the large brick courthouse. While halted here for a few moments until it should be determined what to do with us for the night several of the boys who had a little money secreted about their persons obtained permission, and, under guard, went to some of the stores and purchased some bread, crackers, and cheese.

These guards were old soldiers from Hood's army direct from the front, and I trust the reader of these lines will take special note of the fact that I do not enter one word of complaint against their treatment while we were guarded by them. Indeed, if the old guard had shot me had I attempted to escape he would have done his simple duty. I mention this here because this was our last day with these soldierly guards.

While in the street before the courthouse, the evening being a pleasant one, a large crowd of citizens, principally women and children, gathered on the sidewalks to see the live Yankee prisoners. From the comments of some of the ladies, both old and young, I am afraid the ragged and dirty appearance of our old battalion made an unfavorable impression upon their minds. Our woe-begone appearance seemed conclusive to their minds that the Union was about ready to collapse, and that "old Sherman" would soon be compelled to succumb. One elderly matron, pointing her finger toward us, as she was talking to another excited woman, said, "Nobody needn't tell me old Lincoln's soldiers are clothed and fed better than our brave boys are. I've seen thousands of our soldiers, and I have never seen as ragged and dirty a looking set as these Yankees are. You jist mark what I say, our boys will drive 'em out of Georgia yit."

We had been halted but about twenty-five minutes when we were marched into the courthouse and held in the large court room over night. On the morning of the 7th our guards were changed, some mounted Georgia militia relieving the old soldiers who had brought us to West Point. We very much regretted this change, for we soon discovered that the militia, composed of young upstarts who knew nothing of the hardships of military life, were going to give us trouble. The commander of the new guards kept his revolver in his hands continually, all the while threatening to shoot the first Yank that didn't hop when he spoke to him, or who would attempt to retort to his gruff commands; and he ordered all his subordinates to treat us in like manner.

It was just a little after sunrise when we started that clear morning for Columbus surrounded by those mounted boy militia. We had not proceeded very far when we learned from some of the guards that the captain, a young fellow about twenty-two or twenty three, had a sweetheart living near Columbus, and that he was going to drive us through to her father's plantation before camping for the night, which would require a twenty-eight or twenty-nine mile march under a hot sun over dusty roads for men already much fatigued from hard fighting, poor rations, and severe marches.

We were started off on a trot, an unnatural gait, which both worried us and stirred up the dust as our long swinging gait to which we were accustomed did not. By 10 A. M. the sun was beaming down upon us very hot and some of the older men began to fag. For their sakes the commander was courteously requested to slacken our gait by a sergeant of our company, but for this respectful and modest request he received a terrible cursing and came near being shot.

Several times during the day, when we were almost famishing and choking with the dust, we crossed streams, but this inhuman officer would not allow a halt so that we could get a drink, and galloped his horse around from one side of the column to another, urging his men to crowd us on, and all the while flourishing his revolver. This rush was continued from early morning until sundown, when we went into camp on some open ground belonging to the plantation referred to, and within a mile or so of Columbus. It was the most trying day's march I ever experienced while in an able-bodied condition. When we halted some of our men fell down from sheer exhaustion, apparently more dead than alive. In justice to some of the young men who helped to drive us that day I wish to say that I do not believe they were in sympathy with their inhuman officer, but were afraid to object lest they should bring upon themselves his cowardly malignity.

We broke camp the following morning and marched

into Columbus, entering the town about 9 o'clock, where we were the sensation of the day, and were viewed and interviewed by hundreds of citizens, who seemed, however, more respectful than those at West Point.

We were held in Columbus until about 5 A. M. the following day, October 9, when, under heavy infantry guard, we were placed on board a train of flat cars and at once started thumpety-bump over an old rotten railroad for Fort Valley, some ninety miles east, arriving there about 1 P. M. the same day. There we were at once transferred to a train of box cars on the Macon and Albany Railroad and headed south for Andersonville, distant about forty-five miles.

At Columbus there was put on the train with us one of the scrawniest, raggedest, and most filthy Union soldiers I had ever seen. We all tried to shun him for fear of becoming stocked with vermin and of catching some disease. On our way from Fort Valley to Andersonville, as we thumped along in the old box cars over the loose joints of another dilapidated road, this filthy skeleton of a fellow, listening to our erroneous surmisings about Andersonville, said, "Comrades, you will not believe my story, but I escaped from that place two weeks ago, and I tell you now you are all going to hell."

Then he proceeded to give us, as we afterward found to our great sorrow, a true picture of Andersonville Prison, with its unspeakable horrors; and his description was a better picture of this prison than any I have ever seen penned or penciled on paper. Although he was one of our comrades in blue, yet I think there was not a man in the car who believed his story. As for myself, I entirely discredited it, and thought he was either a great liar or a deranged person who had been wandering around among the swamps and pine forests until he had become nearly starved and naked. To fortify this thought his long matted hair and filthy look gave him a decidedly maniacal appearance, and made him repulsive to everyone.

About 4 o'clock that bright afternoon, October 9, 1864, a day on which the harmonies of nature would banish all thoughts of gloom and horror, our train stopped in an opening in the pine forest, where could be seen nine or ten log houses whose roof boards were held in place by long poles. To the east of the railroad track, about a quarter of a mile from this point, over some gently rolling clay hills which were partially cleared of timber, we could see a large log stockade. This station, in the heart of this great Southern forest, our emaciated companion informed us, was Andersonville, so named before the war, as I have since learned upon reliable authority, for our noble Major Anderson, of Fort Sumter fame, by a friend of his who surveyed the railroad.

To me, having listened to my grandmother's Indian stories, and read books on frontier life among the Indians, as I landed here, and listened to the distant baying of hounds in the forest, and saw the prison pen, the place appeared like a new settlement in the wilds of the Far West, with a stockade for the protection of settlers in case of an attack by the redskins.

When our train came to a stop we were ordered out

of the cars, and were at once turned over to the prison guards, who marched us a short distance east to an open space, where we were halted and, taken separately, were carefully searched by several Confederate sergeants. They took every valuable they could find from our mouths, buttons, shoes, and the various places where we had them secreted in the lining of our clothing.

While this search was in progress a small, wry-faced Confederate captain with a foreign countenance walked over to where we were from one of the log huts, over which a Confederate flag floated from the top of a pole planted in front of it. This individual, whose frame was somewhat stooped, hair shaggy, beard a grizzly gray, wearing a very common suit of Confederate gray and crowned with a small gray cap whose large, black bill was all out of proportion, his mouth filled with uncommonly long tobacco-stained snags of teeth, and with an enormous revolver in hand, was the old Swiss captain, Henry Wirz, of Andersonville notoriety—to my mind a very poor representative of the land of William Tell. When he came to where we were he said, "I vill shows you Yankees 'pout 'Uncle Sam.' You shust vait I keeps you six months, you no more fights for 'Uncle Sam.' —— —— 'Uncle Sam!'"

These words are in his exact language, except that he filled the blanks with curses, and they were burned into my young mind so deeply at the time that they seem to ring in my ears to this day.

This narrow-minded, shallow-souled, malicious man was commander of the interior of the prison, and

ARRIVAL AT ANDERSONVILLE.

directed our treatment and how we should be fed, watered, clothed, and sheltered. It is but fair to say that he was detested by some of his own guards as well as hated by all the prisoners. Neither the Confederate soldiers in the front nor the masses of the people of the South knew any more about what was done in Andersonville and other Southern prisons, and the inhuman treatment we were receiving, than we know of what is going on in the prisons of Russia, and were in no way responsible for such treatment, and such is the universal belief of those who were incarcerated in these prison dens. The record of the coming chapters will simply give some of the actual experiences and observations of a boy prisoner, as nearly as language can convey a correct idea of them.

CHAPTER XXIII.

Entering Andersonville Prison.

WHEN the search for valuables was over, inasmuch as commissioned officers were not confined in Andersonville, those belonging to our battalion were ordered out of the ranks to be sent to some prison kept especially for such officers. Our acting lieutenants, Kieffer and Bostwick, not having received their commissions at the time, had to enter the prison with the rest of us. Here we bade adieu to our gallant captain, Tom Wiesner, and other commissioned officers, and, although Captain Wiesner is still living, and now resides at Rock Bridge, Ill., I have never seen him since.

After the officers were separated from us our old battalion, three hundred strong, was taken east toward the stockade, surrounded by a strong guard of old men and boys belonging to a Georgia militia regiment.

At the time of our entrance the prison consisted of a strong stockade twenty feet in height, inclosing twenty-seven acres of ground. This stockade was formed of large pine logs firmly planted in the ground some five feet deep. The main stockade was surrounded by two other similar rows of pine logs, the middle stockade being sixteen feet high and the outer one twelve feet high. These were designed for both offensive and defensive operations. If the inner stockade should be forced by the prisoners the middle one would form another line of defense. In case of an attempt to deliver the prisoners by a force operating from the outside the outer stockade formed an excellent protection for Confederate troops, and a most formidable obstacle to the approach of Union cavalry or infantry. The four angles of the outer line were strengthened by earth forts on commanding eminences from which the cannon, in case of an uprising among the prisoners, might sweep the entire inclosure. The ground inclosed by the innermost stockade lay in the form of a parallelogram, extending lengthwise almost due north and south. This space included the northern and southern slopes of two hills, between which a stream of water five or six inches deep and six or seven feet wide ran from west to east. The surface soil of these two hills was composed chiefly of sand with varying admixtures of clay, which was sufficiently tenacious to give a good degree of consistency to the soil. On the west side of the stockade, the side next to the railroad, there were two entrances, one on each side of the small creek midway between it and the corners of the inclosure on the same side. These were known as the north and south gates, and were the only entrances into the prison. Around these two gates on the outside were small stockades with other sets of gates. Around the inner stockade and just outside of it at regular intervals were forty-four sentry posts, or little perches, which were reached by ladders and were covered with board roofs. On these the guards stood, the greater portions of their bodies rising above the stockade, which gave them a full view of the inside of the prison. Twenty feet inside the inner stockade, entirely around the inclosure, was the dead line, which consisted of a strip one inch thick by four inches wide nailed on the top of stakes driven into the ground, and which were about three and a half feet high. To attempt to pass or reach over or under this line was certain death.

A portion of this description of Andersonville Prison, which accords with my knowledge of the place, I have copied from a report of a Confederate surgeon given at the Wirz trial after the close of the war. The illustration on the opposite page is a fair representation of it, so far as it can be pictured.

On our way to this pen, a little to the right of the southwest corner of the stockade, we saw four ragged, skeleton-looking Union prisoners confined in stocks, with hands, feet, and neck securely fastened. As they lay there motionless, their blackened faces upturned toward the clear sky, they were in appearance much like the poor fellow we picked up at Columbus, and looked as if they might be dead.

As we went through the second or middle stockade a little to the right of the south gate we passed a brush shelter made with poles resting on stakes, which were covered with pine boughs, having open sides and no floor. Lying on the ground under this shade we counted over twenty emaciated, blackened human forms. The most of them were covered from head

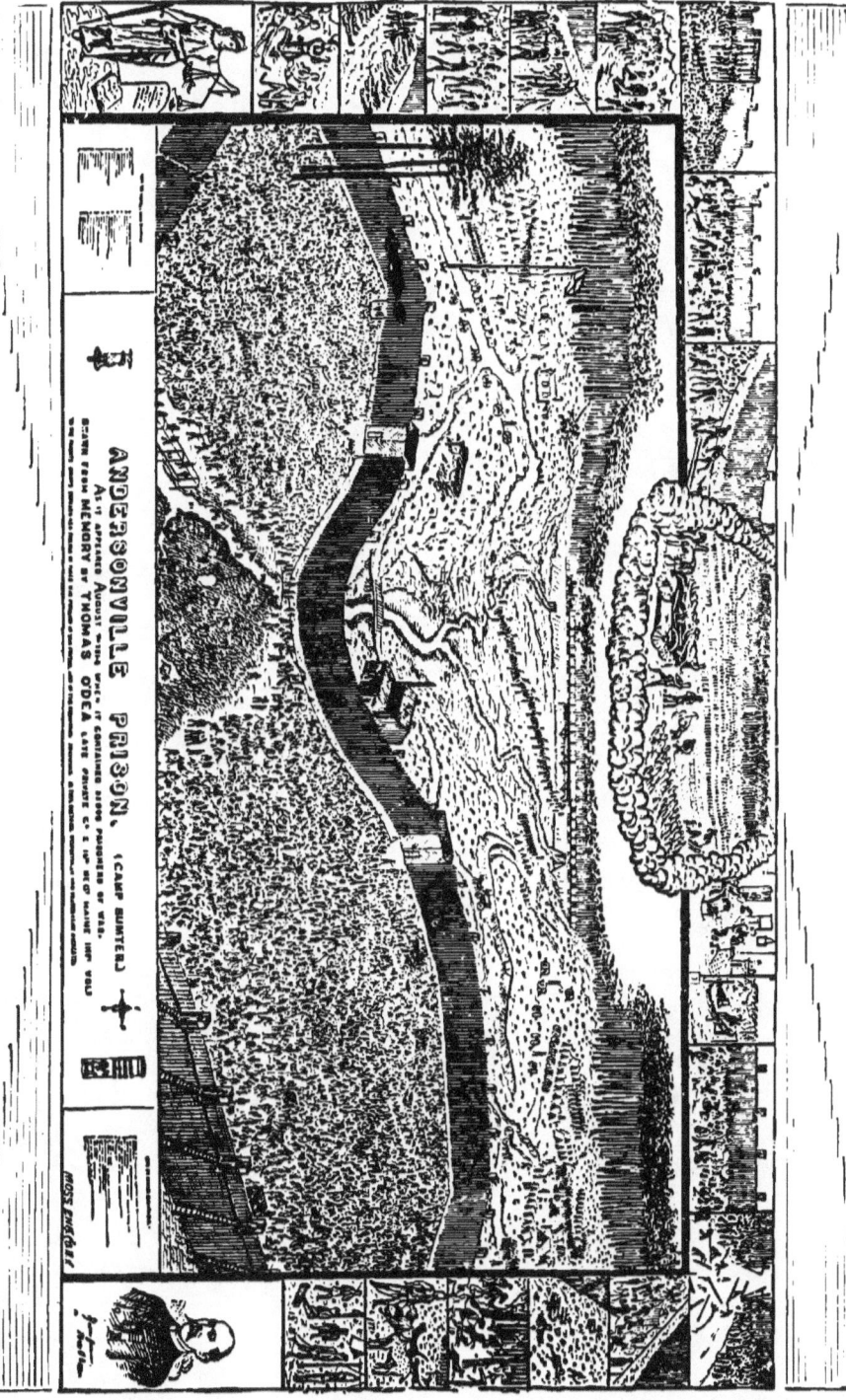

to foot with angry looking sores. They were lying side by side and were entirely destitute of clothing. This was the Andersonville dead-house, through which, during twelve months, between twelve and thirteen thousand Union soldiers were carried, whose graves in the national cemetery at that place are all marked by small white marble slabs, all provided and kept in order by the United States government. Many more who were confined in Andersonville, in attempting to escape, perished in the surrounding forests and swamps, and so were not buried in the cemetery, and a record of whose death was never made.

This shroudless squad of emaciated bodies was the last sight that met our wondering gaze before the heavy iron bolt was drawn and the massive wooden doors swung open to admit us into the small stockade by which the south gate was inclosed. When these were opened the head of our column, perhaps one half of it—the section in which I was marching—was taken inside this ante-chamber of the main stockade. It was about twenty-five feet square, inclosed by a wall of logs which were from a foot and a half to two feet in diameter, and about twenty feet high. These had been sawed on the sides which came together so that they fitted so closely that those within could not see out without placing their eyes close up to the small crack between them. The logs forming the main stockade were scored and fitted in like manner.

When the small pen was crowded as full as it could hold of prisoners a tall Confederate sergeant, by the name of Johnston, entered with us while the rest of the guards remained in heavy lines around the prisoners who were left outside. The gates were then closed and fastened securely behind us.

If a portion of a drove of cattle hemmed in on the scales, just before entering the slaughter pen, could think and feel as we do, I believe the emotions of the dumb brutes, ready to go to the shambles, would be akin to ours as we were crowded into that small pen, with the words of old Captain Wirz ringing in our ears, with added emphasis from the ghastly sights we had but a moment before witnessed.

At the time we could see nothing outside save the blue sky above us and the gray-coated sentinels on their perches, and as we looked into each other's blanched and troubled faces we felt indeed that we were in the very jaws of death and gates of hell with no one to deliver us.

When the gates behind us had been closed and made secure the Confederate sergeant who had entered with us unlocked the massive wooden gates of the inner stockade, threw back the heavy iron bar that secured them, and shoved the heavy doors inward on their creaking hinges, and we were marched in. As we entered through the open door Johnston ordered us to keep in line. To the left of the gate were to be seen twelve or fifteen more shroudless dead, covered with filth and vermin, lying in a row near and with their heads against the stockade.

Once inside, what an immense volume of suffering was opened before us! The horrible sights which met our view seemed to daze us completely, and men exclaimed: "Is this hell?" Verily, the great mass of gaunt, unnatural-looking beings, soot-begrimed, and clad in filthy tatters, that we saw stalking about inside this pen looked, indeed, as if they might belong to a world of lost spirits.

Our battalion was marched east from the gates on a street to a point near the center of the stockade, east and west, and there we were allotted a piece of ground adjoining and just to the south of the creek. As we marched to the center of this literal valley of destruction and halted we were engulfed in an ocean of black, grimy, emaciated beings, covered with sores, vermin, rags, and filth, who, with their smoke-blackened faces, matted hair, and weak, strange-sounding voices, crowded around us inquiring about Grant and Sherman, about news of exchange, and wanting to know if we had any hard-tack or coffee to trade for corn bread. Could it be possible, we thought, that these gaunt, filthy creatures, with half-naked, bony limbs, lusterless eyes, and feeble voices, some of them in their starving condition having lost their minds, were ever able-bodied Union soldiers? If so, alas! for our fate.

In this great throng I could see some who were hatless and naked, except for old ragged shirts, two with nothing on but an old tattered pair of drawers each. One man was with the whole top of his head raw, and in an unspeakably horrible condition. The man had no coat, was clad in filthy tatters, and, as I stood within four or five feet of him, the sight almost fastened me to the spot.

Dozens of men were there with their lower limbs burst open from dropsy, and others with their teeth and gums falling out from scurvy. In another crowd that evening I saw three men whose feet and hands were gangrened to such a degree that the bones and sinews were in full view, and the joints were separating. In any direction we might go south of the creek, where the most of the prisoners were congregated at the time we entered the prison, these poor creatures could be seen lying on the ground unable to get up.

The swamp near where we were camped, embracing two or three acres, was covered to the depth of several feet with filth in a fomenting condition, which prevented the growth of any vegetation in it, and was literally alive with millions of wriggling maggots. It emitted a sickening odor, and the old prisoners told us to keep away from it as far as possible for fear of gangrene.

This representation of Andersonville Prison is as we found it, and is in no way overdrawn. Indeed, it is a milder representation of it than any I have ever seen as written either by other Union men who were confined therein, or by Confederate surgeons who visited the place and in official reports gave descriptions of it and recommended changes for the improvement of the condition of the prisoners, which changes, however, were never made. Some of the commonest prison sights could not be described here.

Before we entered the prison we had been separated into companies of ninety each, according to one of the prison regulations, with one of our own sergeants placed over each squad, whose duty it was to draw rations for his company and account for his men. That evening was the last time our old Veteran Battalion ever stood together in ranks, and before we scattered, as we stood there beside the shallow creek, which was used for prison sinks, and into which the washings from the cook house and the Confederate camps above flowed, often covering it with a greasy slime, I believe that every man in the battalion felt as if we had entered the valley of despair, and were camped on the river of death.

As for myself, I never felt so utterly depressed, crushed, and God-forsaken in all my life before. All my former experiences in battles, on marches, and at my capture were not a drop in the bucket as compared with this. I was utterly appalled at the sight of the misery and death I saw on every hand, and the very logs of the stockade appeared as if ready to march in over the frail dead lines and crush us between their high walls. By this time we all felt that the skeleton-looking companion on the train had not pictured the horrors of the prison nearly so terribly as we found them, and that Wirz meant every word he uttered when he told us that if he kept us six months we would never fight for "Uncle Sam" again.

That evening I was sixteen years four months and five days old, and all that I had with which to meet the horrors of that prison and to battle against grim death, outside of my physical force and resolute will, was my old Confederate hat, my blue woolen blouse and pantaloons, my gray woolen shirt, one pair of cotton drawers, one pair of woolen socks, and one pair of army brogans; and every piece of this outfit was at least half worn. In my pockets I had an old jack-knife, a piece of coarse comb, and the silk handkerchief previously mentioned. The latter, from frequent washings, was almost colorless, and was rent in several places.

As soon as we broke ranks that evening we formed messes. My old mess, which was composed of Charles Paine and his cousin, Charles Harper, William and Peter Gross (brothers), Frank Durant, and myself, hung together. These messmates were all as destitute as myself, excepting Charles Paine, who at the time of our capture had his blanket with him in the stockade, and still retained it. Having but the one blanket among this mess of six, we persuaded Will Clark, who also had a blanket, to join our mess, which gave us two for the mess.

When we broke ranks that evening it was about half past four o'clock. Soon after this I heard some one over near the gate we had entered sing out, "Limber Jim at the gate!" This refrain was at once taken up by every old prisoner that could pipe above a whisper, and "Limber Jim at the gate! Limber Jim at the gate!" was heard all over the pen. Seeing a crowd start for the gate, and having nothing to look after, I started in the same direction to see what "Limber Jim at the gate" meant.

On my way up the street along which we were marched in I was passed by the cleanest and best looking old prisoner I had seen. Everybody seemed to be trying to get out of the way of this man, whose tall, lithe, sinewy form, as he strode by me, caused me to think he was the limberest old prisoner I had met, whether it was Jim or not. Arriving at the gate, I found that this man really was "Limber Jim," one of the old regulators, who at the time was chief of the prison police, and that he was wanted at the gate to clear the way for the ration wagon, which was standing just outside.

As soon as he had made an opening through the famine-pinched crowd the inner gates were thrown open, which revealed in the small stockade a mule team hitched to an old wagon, in which were some greasy looking barrels. This wagon was driven inside and started east on the street which led across the pen, and as it moved along it was followed by crowds of eager, hungry prisoners. At each narrow cross-street along the way it halted, and the sergeants in charge of the groups of nineties received the rations of corn bread and pea soup for their respective companies.

The bread was in cakes, or loaves, about two feet square and four inches thick. The soup was received in buckets which the prisoners had made out of wood, using strips of leather cut from their belts for hoops. Some carried their soup away in boots, others in bootleg buckets, others in drawer and pantaloon legs, made secure at the bottoms, and which had become so coated inside from the sediment adhering to them that they leaked but very little.

As each sergeant received the rations for his company he was followed off to his quarters by the men belonging thereto. There he divided the rations into four parts, and gave them to four other sergeants for distribution among as many different squads. These squad sergeants cut the corn bread up into as many pieces as they had men in their squads, and as the names or numbers of the men were called the final distribution was made. Meat, when we had any, was distributed in the same way. Beans and mush were divided in many different ways.

This ration wagon, Wirz's portable cupboard, was also Andersonville's hearse, used to haul the dead from the gates to the place of burial, as I was informed.

On evenings when we drew meat, which was generally poor boiled beef, about two or three ounces to each man, lively trading scenes would follow. Dozens of unsightly specimens of humanity in all manner of tattered garments could be seen, with the different kinds of rations they had drawn, making exchanges as best suited the traders. The men who had lost their teeth from scurvy wanted soup, mush, or meal in exchange for their hard corn bread. Those with dysentery wanted a soup bone or soup in place of their corn bread, and thus the trading was carried on until each man had done the best he could for himself.

When our mess of seven drew rations that evening, not having any vessel but a two-pound peach or oyster can bucket, we hardly knew how to manage. But Charlie Paine came to our rescue with a piece of old red and brown colored damask, about twenty inches square, which he had used as a handkerchief. This we soon converted into a soup tureen, in which we drew our cow-pea soup. It required four pairs of hands to hold up the corners and sides of this flexible tureen the first evening while we were getting our soup. After that we lapped the corners and secured them with wooden pins, and it was not long until our improvised dish could stand alone, and thus we used it all the time of our prison life for our soup and mush, and during all that time the only cleansing it received was an occasional scraping.

I was very hungry that evening, but from the amount of bugs in the soup, hundreds of which I saw while helping hold the tureen, my rather particular stomach became as much demoralized as had my lower limbs on a former occasion. So I decided I would not eat any pea soup while a boarder at the "Wirz Hotel." But that evening I fished the peas out of my soup, took them in my hands and my cornbread in my pockets, and went to the creek. There I washed my peas, losing a number of them in the process, and, when through, could hold all I had left in one hand. I then crushed every pea in a skirmish for bugs, in which I was quite successful, for every pea but a dozen or so was full of them. I ate the good ones, but threw the rest away, and as fast as I threw them away they were picked up and eaten by an old prisoner, who, I thought, must be crazy.

It takes some people quite a while to learn to eat oysters or some other articles of diet, but it only required about three days for us new prisoners to change our minds about eating pea soup, and our daily increasing appetites, made keen by short rations, soon prepared us for all we could get, with craving for more.

While at the creek that evening washing my peas, lying on the sand, I saw a prisoner dying just across the narrow stream from where I was. Near by him were two skeleton prisoners almost naked, who were quarreling about who should have the dying man's clothes, and, indeed, fought over it. Which of the two obtained the clothes I never knew, for when they came to blows it was more than I could endure, and I left. It was amid such scenes and horrible experiences that the curtains of our first night in Andersonville closed around us, but far deeper than the shades of the night was the gloom that settled down upon us.

CHAPTER XXIV.

Andersonville Experiences.

THE evening was warm and pleasant, and, as the stars came out one by one, all of us being weary, we lay down with the bare sand for our couch and our two blankets for a covering, a sad, hungry, and thirsty mess of boys. We had not yet learned of the wonderful Providence Spring, and, rather than drink the water from the filthy little creek, we had scooped out some shallow holes back from the stream a little ways and tried to drink the tepid, boggy-tasting water which oozed into them, but it gagged us quite as badly as the soup.

We had not been lying down long when, in addition to the wicked mosquitoes, which came in vast numbers from the adjoining swamps, we were attacked in force by the fleas and graybacks, which were in the sand by the millions—I mean by the millions! They seemed to relish the "fresh fish," as new prisoners were called, and, while they had pestered us greatly before retiring, now that we were down on a common level with them their crawling and gnawing nearly set us wild.

It now seemed to me that all of my five senses, sight, smell, taste, hearing, and touch, were so shocked and outraged that I could not possibly exist in that horrible place. Nor do I believe I could had not those senses in a great measure become blunted and so less susceptible to the many terribly obnoxious things that we came in contact with. Indeed, it was not long until we became so accustomed to our poor quality and scanty quantity of rations that our empty stomachs craved anything eatable; and so accustomed to scenes of suffering and death did we become that they made less impression upon us than does the suffering and death of dumb brutes now.

About eight o'clock, as we lay there on the sand deploring our condition and trying to beat off the fierce and persistent attacks of insects, our minds were diverted from the skirmish for a few moments by the announcement of the sentinels from their posts. First we heard: "Post numbah one, eight o'clock, and a-l-l-'s w-e-l-l!" A similar announcement was made from post number two, and so from all the others until the entire circle of forty-four had reported. This indicated to the officers in charge of the guards that none of them were asleep or neglecting their duty.

I shall never forget my feelings when I heard the voice of that first guard ringing out, "Post numbah one, eight o'clock, and a-l-l-'s w-e-l-l!" To me it seemed a hollow mockery, and that everything was all wrong instead of well; and so it ever seemed to me through all the months of my confinement there, which dragged so wearily by.

Occasionally this cry would be varied a little, and to me it was a great relief when a guard would cry out: "Post numbah foah, nine o'clock, and h-y-a-r-'s y-e-r m-u-l-e!" and the next one follow it up with, "Post numbah five, nine o'clock, and h-y-a-r-'s y-e-r r-i-d-a-h!

When that first call of the night had gone the rounds of the sentinels, and its sound had died away from the lips of the last guard, the most of the prisoners were lying down and the prison was comparatively quiet. Then as we lay and gazed up into the clear, starlit sky, away from the misery by which we were surrounded, and were comparatively free from the sights and sounds which had so horrified us by the light of day, our nerves began to reassert themselves, and we seven boys, none of us of age, began coolly and resolutely to look our situation in the face; and there on the sand we talked the matter all over. But one opinion seeming to prevail among us, namely, that no man could live to get out of that prison who should become broken spirited, abandon hope, or lose his grit, then and there I believe our nerves became as rigid as those of the most stolid Indian. Then we pledged to keep our persons as clean as possible, and to stand by each other in all that might befall us—a vow that was never broken.

The sun was shining brightly the following morning when we awoke from a night of restless dreamy slumbers. For boys unaccustomed to such sights it was well we had set our wills to firmly endure all while the shades of night curtained from our view the acres of misery by which we were surrounded. With no breakfast, the vermin constantly pestering us, and the sight of filthy, ragged prisoners, with old weatherbeaten boards about fourteen inches wide and eight feet long, going in all directions over the pen, picking up and carrying out the stripped and almost fleshless forms of those who had died during the night, required the strongest nerves. Not less than thirty-five bodies were thus carried to the gate that morning, and before night sixty stiffened forms had been placed there side by side on the sand. From there they were carried to the pinebough dead-house, previously mentioned. Then they were placed in a wagon and piled up as long as they would lay on, and hauled away to the trenches, about half a mile distant, and placed in their coffinless graves. This was a daily occurrence.

During that month of October, 1864, was recorded the heaviest death rate, in proportion to the numbers in confinement, of any month in the history of Andersonville. This was occasioned by the fact that, becoming alarmed lest Sherman should release the prisoners, the authorities removed the bulk of the inmates to other prisons, leaving the sick and more feeble ones at Andersonville. During the month there were 4,208 confined in the prison, and out of this number 1,595 perished, an average of 51 a day.

I have now given but a glimpse of the horrors which I witnessed during that month, and have only described a few cases that I saw the evening I entered the prison.

Having nothing to eat that first morning in Andersonville, and nothing to do but answer at roll call, fight insects, and take care of our small stock of possessions, our quart cup, soup dish, and two blankets, and having heard of the Providence Spring, we left one comrade to guard our position and possessions, while the rest of us made our way to where it was located, on the west side of the stockade, half way up the hill toward the north gate, between the dead line and the inner wall. The waters of this spring were conducted through a trough under the dead line into a larger trough but a few feet within the dead line.

When we reached the spring we found hundreds of the prisoners there, each very particular about drinking out of his own bucket, cup, cowhorn, boot, or bootleg, for fear of catching the scurvy, which was generally considered by the prisoners to be contagious.

In order to reach the spring from the south side of the creek we had to pick our way to the small log foot-bridge which spanned the stream near the dead line on the west side, passing through a wilderness of low mud huts and tattered tents. The huts were made out of clay balls, and the tents of old army blankets, fragments of old clothing, oilcloths, etc., and seemed to be arranged in no particular order. On the north side of the creek hundreds of these huts and tents were vacant, a few only being occupied.

There were no buildings of any kind within the entire inclosure excepting six long sheds with open ends and sides. These were located along the north end of the stockade within a few feet of the dead line, each having double rows of bunks. These were known as the hospital sheds. There were, however, but few of the sick in them, and this for several reasons; the bunks having no bedding, not even a straw, were harder than the sand; having no sides, and the roofs being high, the rains would drive through them; then they were too far from the water, and from where the rations were issued, and from roll call, which all were required to answer every morning.

The two great events of Andersonville's history—the appearance of Providence Spring and the hanging of the notorious six raiders—had occurred before our battalion entered.

If you will now refer to the plan of the prison you can readily locate the spring. The cook house, you will notice, stands just outside the stockade, on the north side of the creek, between the two gates. The spring was directly opposite the cook house, inside the pen, between the stockade and the dead line. At that time I was not a professed Christain, but, like thousands of the prisoners, I then believed, as I now believe, that Divine Providence placed that spring there in answer to prayer.

The reader can but faintly imagine the condition of things when, in the month of August, 1864, according to the report of a Confederate surgeon who was there and examined the prison, there were 32,899 prisoners confined on 1,176,120 square feet, a little less than six feet square to each. With the exception of a few wells which the prisoners had managed to dig with old cans, half canteens, etc., and which afforded but little water, and a very poor article at that, the creek was the only source of supply for water to drink. All over the grounds holes as deep as an arm's length had been dug and were used for sinks, as was the creek also. From these and the sewage from the cook house and the Confederate camps above the water in the creek could not be otherwise than foul and poisonous, and most terribly so after a big rain.

Is it any wonder that the prisoners, compelled to drink this filthy water during the hot summer months, were dying by the hundreds? or that they should pray for a supply of pure water? It was when the situation was at its worst, in that month of August, that this magnificent spring appeared and sent forth its flow of the pure, life-sustaining beverage, not in scanty measure, but most copiously, supplying the needs of the entire thirty-two thousand prisoners.

Its location was providential, being at a point where its waters could not become foul, where it was easy of access to all, where it occupied the least possible space of the limited grounds, and where it was near the only thoroughfare which led across the creek north and south. Had it appeared on the opposite or east side of the pen it would have been below the swamp, and hence where the impurities of the prison would have been carried toward it, and where it would have been most difficult of access. Every circumstance indicates it as sent of God as certainly as were the waters from the smitten rock in the wilderness to the famishing Israelites, and rightly has it been named "Providence Spring."

To us prisoners it was a great boon, and you can imagine how much we relished and enjoyed its pure waters that first morning in prison; and after fully satisfying our thirst we carried a bucketful to our sentinel comrade whom we left in charge of our meager possessions. Many hundreds of times did our little can-bucket do similar service while we were guests at the "Wirz Hotel."

That morning some of our mess got hold of three small tent stakes in some way, and four pegs for the corners. We then whittled out some little wooden pins, with which we pinned our two blankets together, and then set up our little tent, so that the lower edge of our blankets came within six or eight inches of the ground. Once up, we crawled under our shelter, and thus our blankets gave us protection from the hot sun during the day, while at night, still pinned together (it was the only way they could be made to cover all seven of us), they gave us protection from the damp dews and chilly air.

You can readily see that with seven of us under the two blankets it was necessary for us to lie on our sides spoon fashion, and that when one got tired and turned over all the rest would have to turn with him, and lying on the hard ground made this movement necessary about every half hour. This constant shifting process was by no means easy on our scanty garments, and every week brought them nearer to the point of becoming threadbare.

That first day I thought I would go to the creek and wash my shirt. Arriving, I found a number of old prisoners there indulging in the luxury of a bath, who advised me not to wash my shirt, for the reason that it would wear out fast enough without it. I accordingly took their advice, and did no laundrying all the time I was a prisoner.

The same morning, up on the street which led in from the south gate, I saw six old prisoners bucked and gagged, as a punishment by our prison police for violating the prison rules. It is a sad comment on humanity that even in this prison community of comrades in blue there were found raiders—prisoners who would steal from their unfortunate mates if they could. These men were some of these despicable raiders, and they were punished by having sticks tied in their mouths so they could not talk. Their wrists were tied together securely and slipped down over the front of their knees, and, being placed in a squatting condition side by side, a small pole was run through between their knees and elbows, and thus they were all strung out together. Such punishments, I am sorry to record, were not infrequently made necessary.

The first night of our prison life one of the raiders stole a pair of shoes from one of our battalion. When the alarm was given several men started after the fleeing thief, who, after crossing the creek to the north side, fell into one of the open wells there, which was about twenty feet deep. He was left there until the next afternoon, when he was taken out by means of a rope made of blankets tied together. He was not hurt much, and when taken out was given his turn on the pole, which had been worn smooth in such service.

The second day we were in the prison was sunshiny and hot, and dragged wearily away. During the day we made several trips to the spring, and, besides, quite thoroughly explored and inspected the pen. We could not see out of it except when standing on the upper hillsides at the north or south ends, and then only over the stockade at or near where the creek entered and left it. Over these places we could get a glimpse of the outside world to the extent, perhaps, of one hundred acres. And, O! how attractive it was to see the carpet of green grass, the tall pines, and men walking about in freedom! The very birds which winged their flight over the prison pen caused us almost to envy them of their freedom, and to wish for wings, that we, too, might soar away.

When rations came that evening we felt more interest in them than we had the evening before, and threw nothing away except the bugs, and we all kept back a little for breakfast. This, however, we ate during the night, and we were not long in finding out that our rations did us much more good when we ate them all for our evening meal, rather than try to make several meals out of what was not more than a third of one good one. Reserving any to eat the following day left our dissatisfied stomachs craving what was left, and these gnawings greatly interfered with our sleep and rest; whereas, with the cravings of our stomachs more nearly satisfied, we could sleep more soundly, and our rest, consequently, was much more beneficial, and we had need to conserve every particle of vital energy we had while besieged by disease and death. So our mess, as did the majority of the prisoners, ate our rations soon after drawing them, and during the rest of the time made out on water as best we could, tightening up our belts as we grew more and more gaunt. My belt, being the breast strap from my knapsack, which I happened to have on the day I was captured, is the only article I have left that I wore while in Andersonville.

After we had been in the prison a few days one of

our company, though not of our mess, was taken out to work in the cook house, and was placed on parole for that purpose. By this arrangement he went out of the pen each morning and came back at night, and when returning he would carry in pieces of wood, boards, etc. He gave me a piece of a board an inch thick and about six inches square, out of which, after several days' work, I succeeded in scooping a plate. I also made me a wooden spoon, and these, with my old jackknife, comprised my entire culinary outfit, which I zealously guarded all through my prison life.

We had been in confinement but a few days when we settled down into the common humdrum, everyday life of prisoners, which, in addition to drawing and eating our rations, consisted in many tramps to the spring each day and one lively skirmish in search of vermin, during which each garment was turned inside out, and every seam was carefully fingered over and every insect found exterminated. These occasions were sometimes playfully and quite appropriately called "knitting parties," and sometimes "skirmishing parties." The rest of the time, with nothing to read and nothing to do, we devoted to lounging and talking over and over our old stories of army experiences, until repetition wore them as threadbare as our clothing was worn by the sand on which we slept.

When talking over probabilities it was the prevailing opinion of our battalion that, on learning how we had fought to save his base of supplies, General Sherman would arrange some special exchange for us and we would soon be given our freedom. But, alas! "the wish was father to the thought."

CHAPTER XXV.

Removed to Millen Prison.

ON the evening of November 8 a Confederate sergeant came into the prison and announced the welcome news that we were to be exchanged, and that Union ships were at Savannah awaiting our arrival. On the announcement of this news I made a spectacle of myself and gave a shout that was enough to alarm a Comanche chief. Old prisoners with pain-racked bodies, some of whom had been scheming, hoping, and praying for this happy event in that and other prisons for over a year, were wild with excitement, and wept and shouted for joy.

Never before had I witnessed such a scene or passed through such an experience. Everybody seemed frantic over the joyous information. Men prayed, shouted, sang, wept, and hugged each other in their joyous frenzy. "Now for God's country," could be heard from many lips which had well-nigh become sealed in death. Indeed, the news seemed to electrify the whole prison, even those whose lives had almost ebbed away, and if you had seen some who were in the procession the following day as they made their way out of the pen to the railroad, hobbling along on their old tent stakes, and supported by their stronger comrades, you would have thought it was almost like raising the dead.

The 9th of November, about 11 A. M., when it came our division's time to march out, all our mess had to do, as we had not put up our tent that morning, was to unpin our blankets and roll them up and pick up our soup tureen, quart bucket, and wooden plates—a task only too simple for seven. As we marched out those old gates that morning we considered we were a lucky set of boys thus to get out of old Wirz's clutches so easy, for, although our month's confinement had very much reduced us in flesh, and we were considerably weakened as compared with what we were when we entered, yet none of us were down sick, like hundreds of others, too weak to walk to the train.

On our way from the prison to the railroad we passed a group of some seven or eight ladies, who treated us with respect and gave some of the worst cases a few little sugar cakes. But I and my mess were too hale and hearty looking prisoners to draw any of the cookies. When we arrived at the railroad we were at once taken into box cars which were in waiting for us, and soon we were off, headed toward Macon. We were packed into these cars as tightly as we could be jammed between each other's knees, and sat in rows across the cars, facing the door from each end. This was very uncomfortable and had a tendency to make hungry men cross, and some brutal fights were witnessed in our car that day.

We had not been running along over the rough road a great distance when some of the old prisoners in the car began to weaken in their faith about the exchange news. This was decidedly dampening to our hopes, for they said they had been told they were going to be exchanged when they were taken to Andersonville. We reached Macon that afternoon about five o'clock, where for some purpose unknown to us we were switched onto a side track. While there Tony and Oliver, two of our colored cooks, from whom we had gotten separated at Columbus, found us and gave their old mess something to eat. They told us they thought Jack had been sent back to his old master.

Just before the train pulled out that evening, a little after sundown, I was sitting near the car door by Henry Cowan, of Company A. He had on an old Confederate suit of gray, and, his faith in the exchange matter being on the wane, he very slyly dropped out of the car onto the ground among the guards, and I soon lost sight of him in the fading twilight. Twenty-five years afterward, in July, 1889, in Springfield, Ill., while returning with my family to our hotel from the State House, where we had visited Memorial Hall, we stepped into a drug store to refresh ourselves with soda water, the heat being oppressive. As I wheeled up to the counter in my chair and received my glass from the hands of the clerk, I thought I could detect something familiar in his countenance, and while I was drinking the soda water I located him. It was Henry Cowan, of whom I had heard nothing since the day he jumped out of the car at Macon, Ga. You can imagine our hearty greeting and hand-shaking on this revelation. He then informed me that he succeeded in eluding the guards at Macon, and made his way to our lines near Atlanta in safety.

But a few minutes after Cowan left us the whistle blew and our train headed eastward. I was awake nearly all night, getting only an occasional doze, and could see that we were running through a poor, sparsely settled pine region, and also that we were making very poor time.

Just as the sun was making his appearance above the eastern horizon our train came to a stop in the midst of an immense pinery, and where, I had not the remotest idea. Here we were ordered out of the cars. I hoped it was for the purpose of issuing to us some rations, and that we would have an opportunity to get a drink and stretch our cramped limbs, which we had had no opportunity of doing since we left Andersonville. When we did get out we found our lower limbs so stiff that we had great difficulty in getting them straightened out.

As soon as we were all out of the cars, except a few who had died *en route*, and others who were too feeble to alight, we were ordered to fall in line and were started into the woods. We had marched but a short distance, perhaps one hundred yards, when, to our dismay, right before us there loomed up another horrible stockade, which was known as Millen Prison. Just before entering this prison we noticed on the right side of the road near the gate three emaciated forms in the stocks. We passed within ten feet of them, and could see that they were fastened the same as those we had seen at Andersonville, neck, hands, and feet. They were all dead and were covered with a white frost. This sight as we were entering another miserable log pen called a prison.

coupled with our knowledge of Andersonville horrors, sent our declining spirits down to the lowest degree.

On entering the pen we found it very similar to the one we had just left, with the exception that it was comparatively new, and hence cleaner, and the creek which ran through it was several times as large as the one at Andersonville. Here we found some seven or eight thousand old prisoners who had previously been moved from Andersonville. Among them was John McElroy, afterward author of *Andersonville; or, A Story of Rebel Prisons*.

Our sufferings here were greater than they were in Andersonville, for now frosty weather and cold rains had set in, and, our flesh, blood, and clothing all being thinner, our two old blankets afforded us but little protection as we lay on the bare ground, much of the time soaked to the skin and having very little fuel for fires. The rations here were but very little better than those at Andersonville. I do not know what the death rate was here, but it was fearful among the old prisoners, who, by the hundreds, almost naked and with no protection, were compelled to lie on the ground in the November storms. I do not mean to say that none had protection, for some who entered the pen when it was new, when such things could be picked up inside, had little shanties made out of pine boughs and slabs. But when we entered there was not so much as a splinter to be had without stealing or buying it, so that we and hundreds of others had to lie on the bare ground as at Andersonville.

I was near the gate our first day there when rations, consisting of meal and fresh beef, were brought in.

Instead of driving around through the pen with them as they did at Andersonville, the meat was issued that day at the gate to division sergeants, who called for men to carry the meat to the different quarters. Being close to the wagon, I took a small hind quarter that would weigh, perhaps, seventy-five or eighty pounds to carry to our division. It was quite a distance to where we were located, and I hardly expected to carry the meat so far, but I thought that while it was in my possession I could secure a good chunk of tallow. Failing to get any while I had it on my shoulder, after I had gone a little distance I fell down, managing to fall with the meat under me; and, while struggling to get up with it, succeeded in pulling off a full half pound of tallow, which I stuck in between my blouse and shirt, having left the former open for that purpose before starting. After securing the tallow and making an unsuccessful attempt or two to get up with the meat, I finally got up without it, and told our division sergeant I was too weak to carry it. He let me off with a reprimand for attempting to carry the meat and dropping it in the dirt, which I thought a very reasonable price for a good half pound of tallow.

I did not say anything to my mess about my exploit until they were cooking their mush, which was done by each taking his turn cooking it in the quart bucket. As this was being done I gave each one a piece of tallow about the size of a quail egg, with which to season his mush. My mess lauded my achievement as much as if I had been some great general who had gained an important victory.

While we were in Millen Prison there was an exchange of the sick and disabled, and I suddenly became so lame it required two sticks for me to walk with, and I know I never tried so hard in all my life to appear sick. But my attempt failed, and I was ordered out of the ranks twice and told there was nothing the matter with me, which, in comparison with many others, was true.

On one of these exchange occasions I saw in the ranks a huge bony giant. I believe if he had been straightened up he would have stood at least six feet and four inches in his bare feet. He had no clothing on him but an old ragged pair of drawers, which reached but a little below his knees. Between two other large soldiers, with his arms around their necks, resting his weight on their shoulders, he was being slowly walked out to the gate. He was nothing but skin and bones. On his great bony hips a hat might have been hung, and I am sure I could have compassed his wasplike waist with my two hands. How the man, in his condition, could live in that place at all was a mystery to me.

One day while in Millen I was near the gate, just inside of which there were several guards watching a pile of meal bags. It was just a few days after Mr. Lincoln was elected to the presidency of the United States the second time—a fact which at that time we were not apprised of, though, I think, the Confederates were, and felt crusty over it. Politics had been running high among the prisoners, and elections held had given Mr. Lincoln large majorities. One guard, as if endeavoring to raise his drooping spirits, and dampen mine, as I thought, broke out on that occasion with this jingle:

> "Davis on a white horse,
> Lincoln on a mule;
> Davis is the President,
> And Lincoln is a fool."

Not knowing whether Lincoln had been reelected or not this sentimental poetry rather nonplused me for the instant, and the only retort I could make was that they would find out before a great while that Lincoln's mule could kick the hardest.

But this reply did not seem to be relished by my Confederate friend any more than I had relished his poetry, and I was summarily ordered to shut up. This I did, for we had orders not to talk to the guards, and to do so was dangerous. However, the way we two boys, Johnnie and Yank, eyed each other, like two sullen curs, gave evidence that we were willing to settle our part of the war right then and there.

One night, about the first of December, a signal gun was fired from the fort, and the guards were all gotten under arms. What it meant we did not know, but afterward learned it was because Kilpatrick's cavalry, which was with Sherman on his march to the sea, was heading for Millen, and was approaching a little nearer than seemed safe. So, as they had run us from Andersonville to prevent Sherman from releasing us there, they were now going to hurry us out of Millen for the same purpose.

CHAPTER XXVI.

Removal to Blackshear Prison.

THE night was cold and dreary, and the rain was coming down in torrents, when, about 4 A. M., a Confederate sergeant entered the pen and ordered us to get up and fall into line.

We were soaked to the skin, and our teeth were chattering when we got up in the dark and fumbled around on the wet ground in search of our few belongings. We then fell in line and were marched outside, where we were told there had been some misunderstanding before about our exchange, but that this time our vessels, without any mistake, were at Savannah awaiting us.

Though we were taken out so early it was fully noon before the division I was in was packed into cattle cars as tightly as we had been in coming from Andersonville. Then we started toward Savannah. It had rained during the entire morning while we were waiting, yet we had no shelter and no fire by which to dry or warm ourselves, and as the tall pine trees were madly lashing their branches in the wild November winds the big cold drops of water as they came down in perfect sheets upon us seemed as if they would drive entirely through us.

The guards had been quite careless with us that morning, and it did really look as if we were going to be exchanged. Near the railroad track there were several large sugar kettles set up in the woods uncovered. They would hold, perhaps, one hundred gallons each, and were, as we passed, about two thirds full of hot mush. As we were going by them I broke ranks, and, taking my wooden plate, scooped up about a pint of hot mush, and with it got a badly burned hand. Many others, also, helped themselves to the mush in the same way, and the guards made no attempt to check us.

After getting aboard the cars and thumping and pounding along over the rough railroad, if you could have caught a sight of us, soot-begrimed and huddled on the floor, as we ate our saltless mush and licked our burned and sticky hands, trying all the while to protect ourselves against the cold and pitiless rainstorm which was driving through the car, you might have taken us for a load of colored slaves just imported from the wilds of Africa and being conveyed to Southern plantations.

The road was rough, the train long, and the breath of the old rickety engine short, so we did not reach Savannah, some ninety miles south of Millen, until the next morning about sunrise, where we were ordered out of the cars and marched up into the city to a square, a number while on our way having perished on the trains, which were composed of flat, box, and cattle cars.

It was not raining when we arrived, but it was cloudy, and a northeast gale from the ocean was blowing, which, as we huddled around in groups with no fires, chilled us through and through. Here we received three crackers apiece—imitation of United States hard-tack, but not so large or good as "Uncle Sam's."

Dozens of generous, tender-hearted ladies, with baskets full of bread, sweet potatoes, and other provisions, visited us, but the heartless militia officer forbade their giving them to us. These ladies, however, told him they had husbands and sons at the front, and that they were better Confederates than he, and paid no attention to his orders, but threw the provisions over the guard line to us, so that we felt we would much rather be guarded by the husbands and sons of such women than by such a wretch as this merciless militia officer.

This act of kindness indicated that there were many within the bounds of the Confederacy who were considerate of others' good, and tender-hearted even toward their antagonists, and was a most timely benefaction to us, for we had just learned that no vessels were there to receive us, and, being deceived again about our exchange, our drooping spirits, now almost crushed, needed something to brace them up. To me it was the worst disappointment I experienced, in the matter of exchange, during all my imprisonment. The Confederates may have failed in their expectations about exchanges, but evidently with every removal they held out their promise, and thus deceived us in order to prevent any attempt on our part to escape and thus make it easier to guard us.

The afternoon of that day we were marched to the

Atlantic and Gulf Railroad in the city, and were taken aboard a train of old flat cars which experienced no little difficulty in getting under way, the old wheezy engine having more dry boxes and hungry Yanks than it was able to move readily or keep under way on this, the rottenest, most dilapidated road we had struck in the Confederacy.

This road, which seemed to be abandoned, or used but little, ran in a southwesterly direction almost parallel with the Atlantic coast, through a flat, poor, sandy pine region, covered with swamps, and almost destitute of either vegetation or live stock. All we saw of the latter along these two streaks of rusty track were turtles, snakes, and alligators, such as could easily slide out into the adjoining swamps when their lazy lollings were disturbed; excepting a few very small bony cattle, which looked about as poor as the small bunches of hard, dead, wiregrass at which they were nibbling, and a few pioneer razorback hogs, which looked as if they might be outlaws that had been run out of upper Georgia, where I had seen some very good swine, by their more respectable neighbors.

These razorbacks were of variegated colors, ranging from a dull red to black. They were sharp featured and of compressed frame, and nearly all that I saw appeared as if standing on their heads with a pile of sand around them, which they seemed to bore out with a peculiar motion they had while lacerating the ground for something I never could see them get. The general impression that one would form from this animal's build is that he has been designed by nature to loosen hard soil and slide through narrow crevices. From his motion and the way he shoveled out the sand, he looked a good deal as if he might be a self-acting post auger and spade combined, and, if he had a pair of handles attached, that he would make an excellent self-propelling garden plow.

On this rickety, wabbly railroad no provisions seemed to be made for feeding or watering the "iron horse." When he became thirsty he was halted near some stream or pool of water, and then the colored hostlers would climb down with buckets and supply him with water. When he became hungry he was reined up near some adjacent field, from which arm-loads of dry rails, or dry logs chopped and split up, were obtained and carried aboard for him to devour.

On coming to the foot of a small grade he would seem utterly exhausted and unable to proceed, and to aid him we prisoners would have to climb down from the old flats and foot it to the top of the grade.

These little foot excursions, however, afforded us an opportunity for getting hold of something green, which we seized with great avidity. Scrub palmetto roots were pulled up for buds, from the lower end of which about a bite of a white tender substance could be obtained, with about as much flavor and strength as a piece of raw turnip contains after lying in the water over night.

Thus we traveled by day and night for forty-eight hours to compass eighty-five or ninety miles. Finally the train came to a stop in what seemed the very heart of the pine forest, at a point called Blackshear.

Why we should stop there I was at a loss to understand, unless it was from sheer exhaustion. No buildings were to be seen, and, apparently, no provison had been made for our reception. We were marched out into the pine woods again as at Millen, and I kept looking for another duplicate of Andersonville, but none appeared.

When we were brought to a halt, about half a mile from the railroad track, it was on the bank of a good-sized stream in a body of tall, open pine timber. Here the guards and some artillery were placed around us. Stakes were driven down around the square we were occupying to mark the dead line.

Our grounds did not extend to the borders of the creek, but from the nearest point of the square to it, which was about twenty yards, a lane about twenty feet wide was staked off down to the stream, which was well guarded on both sides. This allowed us free access to the water.

At Savannah we had eaten up our three small crackers and such provisions as the generous ladies had brought us, and we had not drawn an ounce of anything since we left there, forty-eight hours before. All I had eaten since leaving Savannah was the three or four palmetto buds secured along the way, and a turnip top which a guard had thrown away; and when we arrived at Blackshear I was almost exhausted from hunger and cold, and was but barely able to march out to camp; and there we were kept twenty-four hours longer without a morsel to eat. In the endeavor to appease our hunger we split up pieces of fat pine wood into splinters, boiled these in our buckets and cups, and skimmed off the resin which raised to the top, and chewed it for gum. This was evidently an injury to us, and in many instances was followed by severe pain.

During the second afternoon there, which was the third day since we left Savannah, or seventy-two hours since I had eaten any rations, after drinking my fill of creek water, being very weak and faint, I lay down, passed off into a stupor, and became unconscious. In this condition I certainly would have perished but for the fact that in an hour or so after I became unconscious beef rations were issued, from which my comrades made some hot broth and poured down my throat with wooden spoons, I being entirely unconscious at the time.

On that occasion I passed through all the pangs of starvation to the limits of consciousness as certainly as did any of my comrades in Andersonville or elsewhere, and I am confident that but for the timely ministrations of my faithful comrades referred to, and the tender watchful care "of Him whose eye never slumbers or sleeps," and without whose notice not even a sparrow falls, I never should have revived. By these, and these alone, my life has been spared, and I live to make this grateful record.

At Blackshear we had plenty of fuel, the timber protected us from the winds, and as there was no rain while we were in camp there it was decidely the best place we had found in our prison quarters. After my starving experience I had the good fortune to trade my old silk handkerchief for five or six good-sized sweet potatoes, which, added to my meager rations, in connection with our favorable situation, improved my physical condition quite rapidly.

While here I witnessed, for the first and only time, the killing of a prisoner by a guard. This prisoner was a Pennsylvanian. He had been to the creek for water, and was returning up the guarded lane, and when he came to the mouth of the lane opening into the square he turned a little too short to the left and stepped just outside the corner stake, which was about a foot high. The guard, a heartless young militiaman, was standing about ten feet away, and so that the prisoner came between him and the corner stake. When the unsuspecting Pennsylvanian, recovering from his mistake, had gotten two or three steps inside of our camp lines the guard threw his gun to his shoulder and shot the poor fellow in the back just below the ribs, the ball tearing an ugly hole entirely through his body.

I was on my way to the creek at the time and was within twenty-five or thirty feet of the man when he was shot. I saw it all, and it made my very blood run cold. He was not killed instantly, and was picked up by his comrades and carried to their quarters, where he suffered for an hour or two in terrible agony, and then died. Let me say here that I do not believe that such horrible deeds as this would have been committed by soldiers at the front on either side. None but heartless cowards, who were never found in the bloody contests at the front, ever perpetrated such cruelties on defenseless prisoners.

We had been at Blackshear but about a week when news came that we were going to be sent back to Savannah for exchange, and eight or ten hundred left us at that time for that point, much elated at being the first to leave and start for "God's country," as they termed it. Those of us left behind expected we should follow as soon as the trains could make the trip to Savannah and return for us. In this, however, we were disappointed, and afterward learned that the first train load had been taken right through Savannah on their way to Florence Prison in South Carolina, to which place they had, no doubt, intended to take us also, in order to keep us out of Sherman's way, when "Uncle Billy" and his boys interfered by entering Savannah.

About this time General Sherman's movements had these prison authorities completely outwitted, and they were evidently puzzled to know what to do with those of us who were still at Blackshear. The Union forces having occupied Savannah, their principal base of supplies, it became a serious question as to where they should get provisions to feed themselves and prisoners. Furthermore, when Savannah fell it cut off their only route for getting us up into Carolina; therefore, the only two things that seemed to remain for them to do were to hold us at Blackshear, and all starve together, or push farther to the southwest with us. They decided to do the latter.

CHAPTER XXVII.

Flying from Sherman.

HAVING determined to move us in a southerly direction, they took us over the same road on which we had entered Blackshear to Thomasville, which is situated in the southwestern part of Georgia, reaching there the early part of December, 1864.

Here they had made some preparation for us outside the town limits by digging a deep, wide ditch around a square inclosure of four or five acres, covered with heavy pine timber. The ditch was five or six feet deep and too wide for us to jump across, the dirt from it being thrown up on the opposite side from our camping ground. Along this embankment guards were posted. At one place on the side next to the town a space wide enough for the ration wagon to drive over was not ditched. This was securely guarded by cannon.

Thomasville was not a large town, but was quite a good looking one for southern Georgia. While on the streets of this place, before we were taken to our camp, I saw a man purchase a small raw-boned bay pony, paying for him twelve hundred dollars in Confederate currency. I saw the money counted, the bills being mostly in denominations of two, five, and ten dollars. It was a large bundle of bills, and if they had been hay or fodder they would have made the little scrub pony a pretty good supper, which he looked as if he needed.

The Confederacy at that time seemed to have more money, such as it was, than anything else. It was then estimated as worth about five cents on the dollar. It was made on such poor thin paper, with such a sickly, ashen color, that it looked to me as if it might be in the last stages of consumption, and not worth anything as compared with our government greenbacks, which, with their rich green and red tints, looked as if they were backed by the whole vegetable and animal kingdoms.

It was about noon on a raw, cloudy day when we arrived at Thomasville. On our way out to camp we passed a wagon containing crackers, which was backed up to the road, and as we passed by each man was handed three crackers, the same kind we drew at Savannah. When I drew mine I put them in my blouse pocket. Then I broke ranks, managed to elude the guards, made my way back past the wagon, dropped into the lines again, and as I marched by the wagon again I received three more crackers. This I did twice while the column was passing, and thus obtained nine crackers in all. This was the only successful flanking I ever did while I was a prisoner, and I tried it many times.

We reached our ditch inclosure soon after noon, and marched inside. We had not been there more than an hour when a cold rain and sleet set in. The guards threw over a lot of axes into the inclosure, so that we could chop down the trees for shelter and fuel. I picked up one of these axes, but a big fellow jerked it out of my hands. Then the next best thing I could do was to watch the trees as they fell and run in and pick up limbs which broke off, and drag them to where one of our mess was in charge of our camp outfit, and of the brush and limbs as they were brought in. The other boys of our mess were collecting material for shelter and fuel in the same manner.

While this work was going on, the prisoners being quite thick in the inclosure, several were killed, and others were wounded by the falling trees. I was among the latter. The end of a large limb, which had been broken from a pine tree about forty feet from the ground by a tall tree falling against it, struck my right side and broke three of my ribs, the ends of which, driven inward, punctured my right lung. This knocked me insensible, and my comrades picked me up and carried me to our quarters, where Sergeant Will Close, one of my best friends, who had belonged to my former mess, took off the only pair of drawers he had, made a bandage six or seven inches wide out of them, and bandaged me up as tightly as he could, with the assistance of my messmates. This bandage was fastened together with wooden pins, and was held in place by strips running over my shoulders, attached to it with the same kind of pins. In this condition I lay on some pine boughs, in the rain and sleet, for two days before I returned to consciousness, my only protection during this time being such as my messmates could make out of the brush and our two old blankets. This, however, did not keep us dry, for a part of the time there was a driving rain and sleet storm; but having plenty of fire, when the storm was not too severe, helped us out some. During the time I was insensible my messmates kindly drew and took care of my rations for me.

It was about a week before I was able to be up at all, and then I would not have been had not a Confederate officer informed us that they were going to march us across the country sixty miles to Albany. He wanted no prisoners to start who were not able to endure the march, for there would be no wagons along, and the route lay through an unsettled pine forest most of the way, hence there would be no means of caring for any who might give out along the road. This placed me in a very critical situation, and my mess held a council over my case. It was certain they would all have to go. For me to stay behind with none of them to look after me would be certain death, the Confederates offering no assistance. Accordingly, it was decided that I had but one chance for life, and that was to stick with my mess and try to make the trip with their assistance.

It was an icy morning toward the latter part of December when we broke camp and started on that long march. I was still so weak that I had to be supported the greater part of the time between two of my comrades, and my side and punctured lung were so inflamed that every step I took I suffered as severely as if a knife had been thrust into them.

The second day on this trip, about 10 A. M., we

came to a creek, the water in which was about waist deep, and was covered with ice at least a half inch thick. The creek was not very wide, and across it two large trees were felled for the guards to walk over on, the prisoners being required to ford the stream. As I approached the stream and saw my comrades passing through the icy water, from the way my side and lung were paining me it seemed to me that if I should go in I should perish. I then foolishly broke ranks without asking permission of the guards and stepped upon the log between two of them as they were crossing over. It was with great difficulty that I balanced myself at all on the log, and could not walk fast enough to keep out of the way of the guard behind me. I had not taken more than four or five steps over the creek when the one immediately behind me, who was carrying his gun at a right shoulder shift, gave me a push with the butt of it in my back, and knocked me headlong into the water. The blow with which I was struck took the breath out of me, and, although I was a good swimmer, I went entirely under the water and nearly strangled before my comrades could get me out.

The weather was freezing cold at this time, and my clothing soon froze on me, as did that of all who got wet. I was now so nearly exhausted and so racked with pain from my wounded side that my comrades were required to almost carry me the remainder of the day, which they kindly did.

The moon was casting her first faint, silvery beams through the Southern forest, and the tall pines, fantastically festooned with long gray moss, were gently nodding and moaning above us with ghostly sounds, when we went into camp for the night, and all the prisoners were so completely worn out that it seemed as if we could not have gone a step farther.

Our camp was bountifully supplied with fallen pine, and we soon had rousing fires against logs fed with rich pine knots, the warmth of which soon thawed us out and dried us off.

That evening some of the cattle which had been brought along for the purpose were butchered, and when the beef was issued to us we made some saltless soup, which, together with our friendly fires, very much revived us.

At these camps we were always counted as we went in and as we came out. At this one, the situation appearing favorable, some of the boys dug holes, got into them, and were covered over with brush and dirt during the night by some of their comrades. The next morning when we were counted out of camp five or six of the prisoners were missing.

The officer, not wishing to detain the entire command (the dodge being one to which he had become accustomed), secreted a few guards around the deserted camp to await developments, while we pressed on. As these secreted Yanks, when they thought all were at a safe distance, resurrected themselves one by one, these guards arrested them until they had all the missing prisoners. Then, taking our trail through the woods with their Yankee prey, they overtook us about noon, and, although we were all suffering more or less, and felt sorry for the boys, we could but laugh at their failure and woe-begone appearance.

During the morning of the day before we reached Albany we passed by the only plantation of any consequence we saw anywhere along our trip. There a lady, one of God's own jewels, who had in some way learned that we were going to pass by her place, came out to the road at her front gate as we passed, having with her three tidily-dressed slave women, and all four of them were loaded down with baskets and large pans full of boiled sweet potatoes, which she wanted to give to us. This the Confederate major who was in command, whose name I well remember, but withhold, refused to allow her to do, and when she insisted on carrying out her wishes this rude and heartless officer cursed her, and told her she was not loyal to the South, ordering her back into the house, and the guards to take the sweet potatoes, which they did, and not one of them did we get. However, when she got inside of her gate she gave this cowardly, inhuman wretch a scoring which was far more cutting than was his profanity.

She did not hesitate to tell him that he was a coward, or he would not be where he was; that her husband and son were in the army, and if she had any more sons they would be there too. To us starving prisoners she said she had a son who was a prisoner at Camp Duncan, Ill., and if any of our mothers should see him in our condition she hoped God would put it into their hearts to give him something to eat, as he had moved her to give to us. Had it been in our power we would gladly have placed that precious boy in his mother's loving arms.

Reaching Albany the next day about 9 A. M. we were

halted for a short time just outside the town beside a stream of water which flowed from a spring some twenty-five or thirty feet across, and which looked as if it might be forty or fifty feet deep. Within the open space where we were halted there was a feed lot, containing a little over an acre, in which corn-fed cattle had been kept. We had no sooner halted than our company of starving prisoners, ready to devour anything eatable, climbed over the fence into this lot to obtain the corn which had dropped over the ground from the cattle. Considerable quantities were thus secured, some getting as much as a half pint or more. Before eating this, however, it was taken to the creek and washed, and when thus cleansed it tasted much like unhulled hominy about half boiled. This strange repast was scarcely finished when we were ordered into line, and were then marched to the Macon and Albany Railroad, taken aboard a train of box cars, and headed toward Andersonville, some sixty miles north, where we arrived the afternoon of the same day.

We had now been out of this dreadful prison just a month and a half, and, in the meantime, had swung around a circle of five hundred miles to prevent Sherman's forces from releasing us, and during that time there was not a place where we camped but was strewn with the bodies of our comrades who had died. During our sixty miles' march from Thomasville to Albany many perished on the way, and I am of the firm belief that the sufferings on that long march, during those bleak December days, through those forests and swamps, taking the half naked and starving condition of our men into account, are unequaled in the annals of our country. Considering my weakened condition and my severe wound, how I ever endured the trip is a mystery that eternity only can unfold.

CHAPTER XXVIII.

AGAIN IN ANDERSONVILLE.

ENTERING the Wirz Hotel the second time on Christmas Eve, December, 24, 1864, we found the same old landlord there to receive us. But we had been buffeted around so much by him and others we had become somewhat calloused, so that his bluster and profanity now did not seem to affect or alarm us as it had done before. Even going through the great gates into the pen, from which it now looked as if I had less prospect of getting out alive than I had before, did not seem to horrify me as the same thing did on my first entrance.

Arriving inside of our old quarters, we found that the landlord had just cleaned house. All our old tent stakes, pegs, etc., had been picked up and thrown over between the dead line and the inner stockade, all the mud huts torn down, spooning holes filled up, and the twenty-five acre floor freshly plowed, but not swept nor even harrowed down.

We had not been inside fifteen minutes when a prisoner, reaching under the dead line, near the creek, for some tent stakes, was killed by one of the guards. I did not witness this, but heard the report of the gun, and some of my mess saw the man after he was shot. An ounce ball and three buckshot had torn a hole through the upper part of his body and killed him instantly.

While we had been out of this prison on our tour two sheds, each about thirty feet wide and one hundred and fifty long, had been built inside the prison on the south side of the creek. These, unlike the ones on the north side, stood lengthwise north and south. They had no bunks, the ends and sides were open, and about all the protection they afforded was from the sun and from a straight downpour of rain.

It appeared that Wirz, in putting up buildings for his guests, could never get it into his head that we needed more than a roof or a wall. If he put up a wall he left off the roof, and if he put up a roof he left off the wall. His style of architecture, however, had this redeeming feature, namely, it afforded us a bountiful supply of fresh air, the only life-giving and life-preserving element he allowed us to have in unstinted measure while we boarded with him.

We had been in the pen but a short time that Christmas Eve when the wagon drove in with rations. We each drew a half pint of cold mush and two or three tablespoonfuls of some kind of concoction called vinegar, which was made out of sorghum molasses, and was intended as an antidote for scurvy. A few times while there we drew about the same quantity of sour water which came off of fermented meal, and was designed for the same purpose.

That night my mess was placed in with the Tenth Division, which was not fortunate enough to get under the sheds. These new sheds stood in the southwest corner of the stockade lengthwise with the slope Our mess had quarters near these and within five or six feet of the dead line.

The evening we entered the second time was cloudy, raw, and blustery. At Albany, knowing that we were returning to Andersonville, and that we should need them, while on our way to the railroad we picked up chips, sticks, and pine knots, and carried as many into the cars with us as the guards would permit. As night came on a cold rain set in, which soon turned to sleet. Our chips, sticks, and pine knots came into good play, and, splitting them up into little splinters about the size of ordinary leadpencils, we built us small individual fires which we crouched over and protected as best we could with our bodies. In order to save fuel we fed our fires just enough to keep up a little blaze, over which we held our aching hands, which, together with all exposed parts of our bodies, were smarting, for the sleet was almost like hail and was driving against us with stinging force.

The suffering and agony of that Christmas Eve in that prison pen can never be told. The cold mush that we drew and ate in the evening seemed as nothing in our gnawing stomachs, and the vinegar seemed as if it had turned to aquafortis and was consuming our very vitals. We were so benumbed from the cold and pelted with the driving sleet it appeared as if we should freeze and that the flesh would be cut from our bones before the dawning of the coming Christmas morning. Men moaned and groaned and shrieked all over the south side of the pen where we were congregated, as if in wild accord with the cold, fierce, dark night and with the warring elements.

About 11 P. M. we became so exhausted that we could sit up no longer, and we were forced to lie down on the newly plowed ground now thoroughly soaked with water and turned into a mixture of clay and sand-mud and covered with sleet, which, as it melted from the heat of our bodies—having nothing under us—stuck to our clothing on all sides, for we were compelled to turn frequently from side to side during those awful hours.

My recollections of that terrible night while lying in that mud and sleet, with no protection but our two old blankets, are vivid, and I recall it as the most horrible experience in all my prison life. We lay spooning as closely as if glued together with the mud in order to keep warm. I doubt if we lay in one position to exceed fifteen minutes any time during the night, when some one of the seven, being full of pain, would have to change position, and that would necessitate a change for all. Every time we spooned to right or left, and especially when my wounded side was down, it seemed as if it would take my life, and I believe that but for a quart of blackberry bush and corn soup that I made and ate at Albany the previous morning—all I had to eat the entire day except the mush and vinegar mentioned—and the fact that the boys kindly let me sleep near the middle of our group, I should have perished, as indeed many did.

During this awful night of woe death reaped a rich harvest, and Christmas morning, which should have been the brightest and happiest of all the year, revealed the stiffened forms of those who perished during the night in greater numbers than I noticed at any time afterward, and the monarch there seemed to be the king of terrors rather than the Prince of Life.

Toward morning the weather turned colder, the rain and sleet ceased, and it froze to some extent, but by 10 A. M. the sun appeared and thawed everything out, and from its warming rays and the heat of our little fires we got pretty well dried out by night, and the mud scraped off.

That Christmas Day, 1864, with empty, craving stomachs, while we thought and talked of the dear ones at home, filled stockings, rich presents, roasted turkeys, mince pies, and fruit-cakes, we were at work—thousands of us in the south side of the stockade, busy as beavers in the mud—constructing mud huts out of clay balls and digging out "spooning holes," as they were called, with our hands, half canteens, old cups, and pans.

The rain had only wet the ground as deep as it was plowed, and by night our mess had completed an excavation two feet deep, five feet wide, and eight feet long. With the dirt which we took out of this excavation we made an embankment all around it on the outside, which made it about three and a half feet deep and gave us a good protection from the cold winds. After a time we obtained tent stakes, and then we could cover our mud hut over with our blankets, which would turn off most of an ordinary rain. The blankets we kept up during the daytime only, excepting when it rained, taking them down, when dry, at night for a covering while asleep.

Scores of mornings they were covered with frost. Indeed, a number of times during that winter while we were at Andersonville the little creek running through the prison was frozen over so that it would bear a man.

When our Christmas dinner was brought in that afternoon we all quit work for a short time. That day each prisoner received three or four ounces of cold boiled beef and a chunk of coarse unsalted corn bread about two inches thick and some four inches square.

The sun, at that time one of our warmest friends, the coming of whose bright beams cheered us in the morning, and the departing of whose rays depressed us in the evening, was rapidly sinking in the west. The December air becoming quite chilly, we all needed something with which to warm us up, so in the absence of any warm rations to eat or drink we improved our Christmas repast somewhat by removing the thick upper and lower crusts from our corn bread, which we toasted brown by our little fires, broke up into small bits, and in our can bucket each made for himself a quart of smoking hot Andersonville coffee. This we drank and ate, grounds and all, and I venture that no tea, or chocolate, or coffee drank in any Northern home that Christmas evening was relished as we shivering prisoners, huddled around our little fires sipping our warm beverage out of our black buckets, cups, wooden plates, or cow horns, did our improvised Andersonville coffee, all the while slowly nibbling our cold beef and corn bread so as to make them last as long as possible, and the meanwhile talking over the probable features of Christmas dinners at our homes and wondering if we should ever live to join the dear ones again on these festive occasions.

At that period of the war neither the Federal nor Confederate authorities were willing to exchange prisoners on the terms the others offered, and it seemed to us that in the midst of this bitter contest the die of death was cast against us by both friend and foe. But we well understood the desperate situation, and that either many precious lives must be sacrificed or that of the nation. Hundreds and thousands of as brave men as ever trod the earth were incarcerated in Andersonville and other prisons, and literally starved and rotted to death that our benign government, the grandest and best of the ages, founded by Washington and his noble band of compatriots in precious blood, might not perish from the face of the earth, but be perpetuated as they left it, a strong, united country, a refuge for the oppressed and a terror to oppressors.

Desperate bravery in the midst of the carnage of the battlefield is a great quality in a soldier, but the quality of patient endurance under privation and suffering, without the inspiration of battle, is a still higher virtue. Add to this the will and nerve to yield up young, hopeful life in loving devotion to country by a tedious, torturing death—a death often lingering through months of captivity, months when the brave prisoners slept on the bare cold ground and saw their hands and feet becoming unjointed and rotting off, when, too, by taking the non-combatant's oath they might obtain liberty and life, but deliberately and resolutely deciding to endure all in true loyalty to their government—this, I say, constitutes an exhibition of determined bravery and self-sacrificing patriotism that never has been and never can be excelled.

The Confederates offered us three ways by which we might be released from confinement in Andersonville. The first was by parole to work outside in the prison hospital or cookhouse and in burying our dead. Comparatively few, however, were required for these purposes, and those accepting this parole were not considered traitorous in so doing, but were respected by their comrades. The second was by taking the oath of allegiance to the Confederate government, which involved taking up arms against our government. I remember but three or four whom I saw go out for this purpose, and they were under guard, or I believe they would have been lynched by their comrades. As it was they were jeered and called "galvanized Yanks." No doubt some who took this oath did so with the view of making their escape to our lines after reaching the front. But such "galvanized Yanks" had little prospect of escaping in this way, for they were scattered about in the Confederate army where they could be well watched. The third method was by taking the noncombatant's oath. This required neutrality—that is, the individual taking this oath thereby agreed that he would not enter either army, but was bound himself to make no attempt to escape and to work for the Confederate government in some capacity.

The Confederates were quite eager for our men to

take this oath, particularly artisans such as blacksmiths, wagonmakers, tailors, shoemakers, etc. These would have been valuable acquisitions to the Confederacy, and in many instances would have taken the place of Southern men, who would have been armed and sent to the front—men who would have made better soldiers than the "galvanized Yanks."

As this oath offered liberty and life to the prisoner, with exemption from risk of battle, the young reader will understand that the refusal to take it involved a rejection of its proffered liberty and life on the one hand, and, on the other, acceptance of starvation, suffering, and not improbable death.

During the time I was a prisoner I saw hundreds and thousands reject that oath and thus accept the inevitable and yield to severest sufferings and a most dreadful death, actuated by the most exalted patriotism and most unswerving devotion to the nation.

CHAPTER XXIX.

Diversions of Prison Life.

AFTER making the most of our Christmas rations we resumed our work on our "spooning hole" with renewed energy, and we finished it by starlight about 8 o'clock in the evening.

After a trip to the spring—for it was always customary to fill up on water before retiring for the night—we all lay down in the bottom of our newly prepared quarters, spooned together as closely as possible, covered with our old blankets, and found ourselves much more comfortable than we were the night previous, when lying in the mud and sleet with no protection from the cold wind. This hole in the ground was our home as long as we stayed at Andersonville.

If old Wirz had come around about that time with a spade when we seven boys were lying so snugly in the bottom of our excavation, with the dirt banked up around so conveniently, I am afraid he would have been strongly tempted to entomb us and thereby deplete the number of his free boarders.

Not oftener than every twenty or twenty-five days during that winter each prisoner was permitted to go out, under guard, to carry in wood, going about a quarter of a mile for it. It was astonishing to see the great logs brought in by some of the boys who looked as if they could scarcely stand on their feet.

When any of our mess went out for wood he would fill up his pockets, and between his blouse and shirt, with pine needles, until we obtained of them a covering about a half an inch thick for the bottom or floor of our spooning hole. This made a decided improvement over the bare ground for a couch on which to rest.

Several times during the winter we were driven out of our spooning hole by heavy rains filling it with water. At such time many of the mud huts caved in on their occupants, often completely entombing and smothering them. One morning, after a terrible night of rain, I saw one which had stood near our quarters in such a collapsed condition, with three pairs of feet sticking out of the mud and water from the front end. These men had scooped out a hole and set up a small ridge-pole with other poles leaning against it. These they had thinly thatched with pine boughs covered with clay about six inches thick. As this roof became saturated with water it was heavier than the little ridge-pole could bear, and, sleeping with their heads at the rear end, when it fell in on them they were entombed and smothered to death.

Now that winter had set in we were rid of two pests, namely, flies and mosquitoes, and had the advantage, to a certain extent, of two others, the fleas and graybacks, which the cool weather made more sluggish and hence much more easily captured.

In order to protect our pine-needle bedding each

morning it was carefully gathered up and placed in one corner of our den, where it remained until bedtime, when it was very carefully and evenly spread out again. While gathering up our bedding we carefully examined every square inch of ground on the bottom of our spooning hole in our search for vermin, and we never failed in finding and killing hundreds.

Prize fights, which occurred quite frequently down on the flat near the creek, were quite a source of amusement for the prisoners during that winter. The stakes were usually a few chews of tobacco, and why men would pound each other up for such insignificant and worthless things was a puzzle to me. The principals and seconds in these encounters were always too particular and deliberate to suit me. The contestants were usually city toughs who seemed to be posted on the rules of the prize ring, and often they would consume an hour in doing the work I had seen accomplished in a rough and tumble fight up in Illinois in five minutes' time.

Occupying a part of one of the long sheds near us was a squad of twelve or fifteen Wisconsin Indians, who always seemed interested in these prize fights, but never more than two of them attended them at a time, and as soon as the contest was ended the two would return to the shed and repeat it for the amusement of their comrades. I always followed them at such times, and considered their performances the best part of the show, for their gesticulations and the grimaces of their comrades were always very comical, especially their big grunts after a good play by one of the contestants.

Singing and speech-making was another of our pastimes. These were frequently led by a short, heavy-set old man, who went by the name of "Baldy." This sobriquet was given him on account of his bald head. But if that smooth pate, fringed with a circle of gray hair, possessing piercing black eyes, and which sat on his shoulders like a bald eagle on a mountain crag, was bald on top it was not by any means a blank within, as his singing and patriotic speeches evinced. At such times he never failed to collect about him large crowds or to keep them awake. I remember one afternoon in particular, when old "Baldy" seemed to get unusually warmed up, while he had several thousand of us ragged, emaciated prisoners around him nearly splitting our throats singing "Rally round the flag," that the guards on the south side of the stockade seemed to become exasperated at this patriotic demonstration in a Confederate prison and ordered us to desist and disperse, threatening to fire into our assembly in case we did not. Who this old man was I never knew, but he was an Illinois soldier, for I met him in July, 1865, at Springfield, Ill., whither we had gone to be discharged.

Another prison diversion was that of making crazy-patchwork, and it would not be surprising if some one of the inmates of Andersonville should turn out to be the inventor of the kind so much in vogue in these days, for the stitches, material, and shape of prison patches were all on the crazy order. An outfit for the work was a bone needle, hand made, thread raveled from a piece of a meal bag foraged from a ration wagon, or otherwise obtained, and old rags for crazy patches taken from the bodies of dead comrades.

I remember one fellow who stole two meal sacks, out of which he made him a pair of trousers, the seat of which he decorated with a piece of old wool carpet eight or nine inches square, and which had a large red rose in the center. Where he ever gathered that wool bouquet I never knew, but he always said that he was no common boarder, but one of the gentlemen who occupied the parlor bed room at the Wirz Hotel.

After we had been back in Andersonville the second time about two months the scurvy attacked me, and oftentimes from that on until our release this terrible disease and my severe wound would get the advantage of me. Indeed, I was frequently so helpless that my mess would have to draw and prepare my rations for me and protect me from the ravenous insects. I was the youngest by several years of my mess, and they all treated me with the same tender care and gave me the same kindly attentions they would have extended toward a younger brother.

Sometime in January, the sleeves of my blouse being completely worn out, in some way my messmates obtained the red and green linsey lining out of an old blue overcoat and made me a new pair of sleeves out and out.

One sunshiny day in January Will Gross, one of my messmates, being very hungry, decided, since it looked as if spring was opening, that his system needed something within more than protection from without, and, having the best coat of our mess, he concluded he would try to trade it to one of the guards for some meal. Accordingly he started out and soon found one who said he would give him a haversack full of meal for the coat, which Will had pulled off and was displaying by holding it up as near the dead line as it was safe to approach. When the bargain was concluded the guard told Will to toss the coat over to him, and he would throw the haversack and meal over into the stockade to Will. So, rolling his coat up and tying it in as small a compass as possible with the sleeves, Will tossed it over to him. After the guard went down and picked it up from where it landed he kept Will in suspense for several minutes, then, returning to his sentinel stand with the haversack, he pitched it to Will, who, on picking it up, found it to be full of sand.

Seeing he had been deceived and robbed of his coat, he plead with the guard to take his haversack back and return the coat, but this the guard refused to do and ordered him to leave if he didn't want to get into more serious trouble. Will looked quite dejected when he returned to us without his coat, carrying in its stead the old limp haversack minus the meal.

One afternoon near that time, becoming almost frantic for some salt with which to season my mush, for we were not drawing a particle nor did our little ration of boiled beef contain any, I cut the three brass buttons off of my blouse, which at that time were considered worth five cents, and traded them to a guard for a teaspoonful of coarse salt, which was also valued at the same price. The exchange was effected on this wise: I tied the buttons together with a raveling and tossed them up to the guard in his perch, and he tossed the salt down to me tied up in a small rag.

Toward the latter part of January I met with a fine opportunity to supplement my scanty rations for a few days. It was at a time when several hundred new prisoners came in, who had been captured at Franklin, Tenn. While *en route* to Andersonville they had been held a few weeks at Meridian, Miss., and while there had been pretty well fed, receiving among their rations meat from the offals from a slaughter house. The first evening they drew rations at Andersonville among them was some boiled beef, the bones of which they threw away. Seeing this I was not slow in improving this unusual opportunity. Indeed, without waiting for them to throw the bones away, I engaged four or five good soup bones from the men as they drew them, which they turned over to me as soon as they had eaten the meat from them. Some of these bones were richer than, and worth double, the meat which was issued with them, and afforded us richer dumpling soup for a few days than I ever ate before or afterward at Andersonville.

The dumplings I made out of my meal ration by working it into a stiff dough and rolling it out into little balls about the size of quail eggs. These little meal marbles, cooked with the broken up soup bones, and without any salt, tasted so very *very* delicious that I was never more positive of anything in my life than that, if I should live to get home, I would have my mother cook some for me. Indeed, I thought they were far superior to any flour dumplings cooked in chicken soup that I had ever tasted, and that it must have been an oversight in my mother that she had never tried them. But, surprising as it may seem, when I got home where there were mills full of meal, I never had my mother try her skill on Andersonville dumplings.

The new prisoners referred to gave us our first news of the result of the Altoona and Franklin battles, which we received with lusty cheers. But, as these prisoners had been captured the 30th of November, two weeks before Sherman started from Atlanta on his march to the sea, we were still in doubt as to his whereabouts, for the Confederates had not informed us of the fall of Savannah.

Among the new prisoners who came in at this time was an acquaintance of mine from Naples, Ill., by the name of Hiram Rader, who belonged to Company B, Twenty-seventh Illinois Infantry. The first night he was in the pen near midnight a raider stole something from some one near the gate. He was detected just as he was starting off with his booty, and immediately the alarm was given : " Raider at the gate !" " Hi," as he was called for short, happened to be awake at the time, and, hearing so many calling his name, supposed he was wanted at the gate to be exchanged or to receive some important news. He hurriedly bounced up and started in that direction as rapidly as his long legs could carry him. But he had not proceeded very far on his starlit journey among the old prisoners, who were always on the alert for running raiders, especially at night, until he found himself sprawling on the ground with several piles of old bones on top of him, holding him down and calling at the top of their voices for the police. He had a difficult time explaining to these detectives how he could be a Rader in Andersonville and not be a thief, and ever after, while a guest at the Wirz Hotel, he was very cautious about answering to his surname, and especially at night.

19

CHAPTER XXX.

The Fate of a Beefhead at Andersonville, as Witnessed by a Boy Prisoner.

DURING this, to me, never to be forgotten winter of 1864–65, several regiments of Confederates on their way to the front were camped for several days at Andersonville, and during this time had fresh beef issued to them, the heads and offals of which were issued to the prisoners inside the stockade.

During this stay of these Confederate regiments the company of ninety to which I belonged two days in succession drew one beefhead minus the tongue for its meat ration. Each head was taken charge of by the sergeant who had command of our company and divided into ninety equal parts, or as nearly so as it was possible for human ingenuity to get at it without the aid of a food chart, giving the relative value of brains, eyes, bones, horns, and hide, as compared with beef flesh.

The sergeant had a board which he kept on which to divide our rations, and I shall never forget watching him as he dissected these heads on that board. He had a puzzled look, as with an old case knife he taxed his ingenuity in skinning and dividing the heads into ninety different parts so as to be fair for all. To add to his perplexity, we ninety starving, emaciated prisoners in our wretchedness encircled him, keenly scrutinizing the operation and intensely impatient at his slowness.

The skin once off, an old ax was borrowed and the horns were knocked off. Then the eyes were dug out, with from a half inch to an inch of the eyebrow attached to each, and, after all the meat was taken off that possibly could be, the head was broken up and the brains taken out. The manual part of the task, which had proved to be no easy one, was now about over, but the difficult part of all, the scientific division of it, yet remained. To determine for ninety starving comrades the relative nutritive value of bones, brains, eyes, horns, meat, and hide was, I surmise, one of the knottiest problems our sergeant ever tried to solve. The meat and the brains he eyed with an intelligent and confident expression, and seemed to say to himself: "I know what meat is, and have heard that brains are very rich, worth, ounce for ounce, about as much as the marrow in bones; these the boys can cook with a spoonful of meal in their blickers and have quite a relishable, nutritive dish." But when he picked up a bone, eye, or horn, and looked at it or turned the hairy, bloody hide over and examined it, the intelligent and confident look deserted him, and one of perplexity mingled with uncertainty spread over his smoke-begrimed face; and, shaking his puzzled, shaggy pate in a vain endeavor to arouse some dormant idea to his aid, you could read on his countenance: "Comrades, I want to do the square thing by every man, but I never dealt out such rations before, and I am at a loss to know the relative nutritive value of these different parts, and if I did know it how can you cook these horns and large pieces of jawbone which you cannot get into your quart cups?"

However, he finally got a starting point by laying the horns and eyes on one end of the board, calling each one a ration. The brains were then placed alongside of these in little piles containing one and a half or two ounces each; next came small piles of meat containing an ounce or two each with bones, the larger the bone the less the meat; next were several large pieces of jawbones with the teeth in them, and with scarcely a trace of meat on them; finally the hairy and bloody hide, including the ears, all pretty well sanded, was then spread, mapped out with his knife several times, and then cut up into two-inch square pieces. Now, the head, which was not a large one, for cattle are small in that country, was divided into ninety rations as nearly equal as the sergeant could get them.

This miniature meat market, with its meager furnishings and impoverished customers, was an odd-looking affair. There was the old weather-beaten board counter, about six or seven feet long and ten or twelve inches wide, lying flat on the sand with the divided rations dotted over it, but destitute of either scales or cash drawer, the grim prison-pinched butcher squatting beside his counter with case knife in hand, inspecting his precious stock, taking away a little here and adding a little there, then recounting to make sure there were the ninety rations; and, lastly, we ninety penniless, starving, and half naked customers, with faces and all exposed parts of our shriveled forms so heavily veiled with thick, black, sticky pine soot that, had our mothers stood beside us looking for the boys they sent to the war, their keen vision could not have detected our identity, all eager for the market to open, but having no choice or preference of the divided stock when it was, made a grotesque prison picture I would to-day like to possess as a war relic.

After the sergeant succeeded in dividing the beef-head into ninety rations they were then rearranged on the board in four divisions, two portions containing twenty-three each and two twenty-two each, the only way the awkward arrangement of companies into nineties could well be suited, the rations still being separate, and each of the four divisions containing its proper proportion of the different kinds. The eyes and horns, which gave the sergeant the most trouble, were managed by balancing an eye against a horn, so that the portion receiving a hooker was minus an optic, and *vice versa*. The tedious hair-splitting division now over, except for the extra ration in the two groups of twenty-three each, our most critical prison judge would be slow to make a choice.

The company sergeant now being ready for the four squad sergeants to cast lots for their several portions, we all gave back a little so as to enlarge the circle. The four squad sergeants stepped forward with smaller boards in hand and stood waiting to receive their portions. Squads one and two had twenty-two members each, squads three and four had twenty-three each. That there might be no possible unfairness, a comrade was chosen who turned his back toward the company sergeant and the rations. To this one who was willing to turn his hollow eyes away from the board for a brief time, the sergeant said: "We will decide one and two first." Then resting the point of the faithful old case-knife on one of the boards containing twenty-two rations, he inquired: "Which shall this be?" to which the chosen comrade responded: "Number two." The other board containing twenty-two rations went to number one. The remaining two were disposed of in like manner to squads number three and number four.

The trusted and patient company sergeant now rose slowly to his feet, his cramped, benumbed and scurvied limbs almost refusing to act. But he got up from his difficult task with the satisfaction of believing he had performed his duty faithfully and had fairly earned the extra ration which he received for the labor of drawing and issuing rations for the company.

The squad sergeants now stooped down and placed their boards alongside the larger one, and the four sets of rations were transferred from the latter to the former. The large board was handed up to its owner, and as our squad sergeants rose with their four wooden trays the weary, eager, anxious throng of depleted Yankees began to disperse, each group, like a pack of hungry wolves, following closely on the heels of the sergeant having their rations. Arriving in front of our dens and spooning holes, we halted and formed a smaller circle around him. His board was now again deposited

on the sand, revealing to some of the weaker ones
who could not get near the larger board, and who just
brought up the rear, that our squad had received in
our portion a horn instead of an eye. Now another
comrade was chosen to call off our numbers, and turned
his back. The distribution was now getting nearer
home to us. Were we eager before? Our eagerness
was now intensified tenfold.

The boys and girls who read these lines may, if
they wish, make a guess, as I did at that time, as to
which was the best ration on the board, and which
one they would have chosen had they been there. I
picked out a little pile near the center of the board
which looked as if it had more clear meat in it than
any other. This I did not get, however, and if I
had I should have been badly deceived, for there was
one ration there, if no more, that was far superior to it.

Each evening the beefheads were distributed when
my number, fifteen, was called the sergeant's finger
was resting on one of the two-inch square pieces of
the hide, which was, perhaps, the poorest ration in
the lot. The first ration of this kind I drew I hardly
knew how to manage, but seeing an older comrade
with a similar one squat down by a little fire and
hold his ration over it until the hair was all singed off,
and then keep on scorching it until he got it so he
could bite it off a little at a time, I did the same.
But, during the barbecue I felt indignant at the
friendly fire for shrinking up my ration and lapping
up the precious juice, which I was unable to save.

When my ration was done my part of the beef-
head, as the result of the numerous divisions and of

the contractions made by the fire, was shrunken and rolled up to about the size and shape of a cigar stump. It made just three small bites and was tough, but I have never tasted a sweeter morsel before nor since, and I chewed it at least an hour before I gave up to let the last of it slide into my pinched and collapsed stomach; and, alas! when it was gone and it was too late to remedy it, I ran across a more ingenious comrade than the one I had patterned after, who had a ration precisely like mine, but had an improved method of cooking it. After singeing the hair off of his piece of hide, he then scorched it but about half as much as I had mine, then he put it into a quart cup and boiled it with a little meal. He was just taking it out when I saw it, and I discovered he had actually gotten a little meat seasoning into his meal gruel for I could see little particles of grease floating around on top of it, and his piece of hide had swollen up until it was at least four times as large as mine, and it looked as if it might taste much better. You will not wonder then when I tell you that my stomach is at war with my brains yet for the inconsiderate method of cooking my beefhide ration that day.

The next day, when I drew my small square of beefhide, I profited by the experience and observation of the day previous and followed the method of cook number two in preparing my meager meal, which I found a decided improvement on that of number one, and resulted in a little wholesome fullness under my belt which I did not experience the day before.

My comrades who drew the large pieces of jawbone had a difficult contract on hand to make them eatable, but they did, and consumed every particle of them. There was, however, but little marrow in them, and if there had been more they were so large they would not go into their quart blickers so as to get the benefit of it, and these were the largest cooking vessels they had. The best they could do, therefore, was to sit around the small fires and charr the edge of the bones and gnaw the charred portions off, which they did until the bones were entirely eaten up.

And now, boys and girls, have you made your choice of rations yet? And are you sure you have the best? Here it comes, a genuine prize package, in the shape of a horn, and worth any four or five other rations on the board. No one knew its value until one of my messmates, Charles Harper, who drew a horn, let the secret slip out by boiling the horn in our blicker, one end at a time, until the inside, by a little jarring, slipped out, and was a genuine prize almost the full size of the horn, and nearly all marrow. Such portion of it as was not marrow was so soft, that, after being boiled, it could be readily eaten. The horn contained a quantity of rich, gluey substance, which was scraped out and eaten, and the horn itself was left to charr and be eaten as the jawbones were, or to be made up into spoons or combs. This rich horn was by far the most valuable ration secured by any of my mess during the seven months we were guests at the Wirz Hotel, and excepting several blank days, the small square piece of hide was the poorest.

CHAPTER XXXI.

Last Days in Prison.

THE very last prisoners who ever entered Andersonville were three handsome looking sailors, who came in the latter part of February, 1865. These "Jack tars" were dressed in new suits of sailor blue, and wore pretty dark-blue Tam O'Shanter caps with black ribbon streamers reaching to their shoulders. The youngest one of them, a finely formed young fellow about twenty years of age, with a sweet, noble countenance, whose clear eyes were as deep blue as the sky, and whose wavy auburn hair crowned a shapely head, was one of the handsomest young men I ever saw. His complexion was as clear and fine as that of the fairest maiden, and his jaunty garb set it off to the best possible advantage. The few weeks before he and his suit became soiled and faded he was the admired of all and the prince of the pen. He looked about as much out of place in that filthy den, among us ragged, dirty, prisoners, as a fair Easter lily would in a frog pond, among tadpoles. Nor did it require a much longer time for him to wilt and fade than it would the fair lily, if plucked and thrown out on the muddy bank in the scorching sun.

These sailors belonged to a man-of-war which was anchored off the coast at Brunswick, Ga. The town at that time was deserted, but some Confederate militia were secreted along the shore, two or three of whom left their guns with their comrades, went down to the beach, and waved a signal of distress to the ship's crew. The captain observing this signal desired to rescue them if in need, but knowing there was danger attached to the undertaking he called for volunteers to make the attempt. In response to this call these three noble hearted fellows, ready to make sacrifice for any in distress, volunteered. On reaching the beach, however, where the men with their signal of distress were standing, the other Confederates rushed from their ambush and took these sailors captive, and thus they were ruthlessly snatched from their proud ship and genial comrades and carried away to one of the deadliest of prison pens.

These sailors brought us the news of the fall of Savannah and that General Sherman had started up into South Carolina. This we were glad to hear, but, learning that Atlanta was evacuated, we felt that we were a long way from our friends, with no possible hope of release, and as they brought no news of exchange, the future looked dark and gloomy, indeed, to us.

The severe winter and exposures were telling on the old battalion with fearful effect. Hardly a day passed but we would see some of our comrades on the dead pile, while others were becoming demented from their sufferings. To add to my troubles, by the middle of March the scurvy had broken out so badly all over me that neither my shirt nor bandage could be removed, nor did I have either of them off from that time until after I was released.

About the 1st of April, 1865, the Confederates began sending prisoners from Andersonville to Vicksburg. Some of our battalion got out at that time and were on the ill-fated steamer *Sultana*, which blew up on the Mississippi River soon after. The division to which I belonged at one time early in April received marching orders and went over to the railroad to board a train of cars which was in waiting to carry us to Vicksburg. On reaching the railroad, however, just as we were about to board the cars, a dispatch was received, stating that the Union cavalry under General Wilson had made a bad cut in the railroad near Selma, Ala., and that, consequently, we could not be gotten through that way. So we were marched back into the horrible old pen again.

But while we were out we were halted by a cornpen made out of pine poles, in which were eight or ten bushels of nubbin corn, and, while Wirz was foaming around and the guards were excited over the news, we improved our opportunity by raking out every nubbin; and when I marched back into the stockade seven or eight of them were stowed away between my blouse and the shirt, raking and scraping my angry scurvy sores. Wirz, for a wonder, was not wound up on the striking side that day, else, when he missed the corn, he would have cut off our rations for a day or two to pay for it.

General Lee surrendered on April 9. The war was then practically over, but we knew nothing of the event. President Lincoln was assassinated April 14, of which the guards, on the 16th or 17th, told us, but they gave us no information whatever about Lee's surrender. They had deceived us so often, however, that we gave no credit to the statement that Lincoln was murdered.

The news of the collapse of the Confederacy they withheld from us, I think, to keep us from clamoring to be released. They evidently did not want to turn us loose on the country, and desired to keep us quiet until they could devise some way of getting us to our lines.

Before President Lincoln was assassinated he had ordered a celebration at Fort Sumter to take place on the 14th day of April, 1865, just four years to a day from the time the fort was surrendered to the Confederate forces. The celebration, consisting of an oration by Rev. Henry Ward Beecher, the raising by Brevet Major General Anderson of the same United States flag which he had so gallantly defended, and its salutes from Fort Sumter and from every fort and battery which had fired upon it in 1861, actually occurred on the day of Mr. Lincoln's assassination.

But while this great national demonstration was going on we were still lying in Andersonville, entirely ignorant of the glorious victories our armies had achieved. It was April 18th or 19th, I think, when the Confederates told us to be ready the following morning to start for our lines. We hardly knew whether to believe them or not, but old Wirz being so easy about the loss of his corn, and the actions of the guards, made it appear to us that something unusual had occurred. Still we did not allow ourselves to get very much excited, as we were afraid it would turn out to be another hoax.

The following morning all who were able to hobble marched over to the railroad, and these were physically the dregs of Andersonville, excepting the very lowest sediment of prisoners who were unable to be moved and were left lying on the ground in the pen or in the hospital. Several of our old battalion were included in this number, among them old Uncle Jimmie Vevers, whom I never expected to meet again, but who was found by our cavalry a day or two later, and who finally reached Illinois five or six months afterward.

We had now been in Andersonville the second time from December 24, 1864, until April 19 or 20, 1865, or nearly four months. During this time we had a great deal of rain and sleet and freezing weather, and none of the time did we have one tenth enough fuel for cooking and warming purposes. Our rations all this time were very meager, also, barely sufficient to keep us alive.

Our mess during all these lingering months of suffering occupied our spooning hole in the ground which we dug on Christmas day. Lying on the sand so constantly had by this time worn our clothes into shreds, and we were reduced to skin and bones. The most of us were covered with scurvy sores and with the sticky pine soot until we were black as Negroes, for we had not drawn an ounce of soap nor had our clothes been washed since our capture, for the reason previously mentioned, to prevent wearing them out thereby.

At that time, in addition to my shirt and bandage being stuck to my back and chest with scurvy sores so that they could not be removed, the scurvy was also in my mouth and all over my limbs, particularly my lower limbs and feet. My left foot, which was the worst, was eaten to the bone. Had I not continually forced myself to walk a little every day when at all able, and when not able stretched my limbs and worked my joints, in two or three days' time they would have become so stiff I could not have moved. This stretching exercise was so painful it seemed as if it would almost take my life, and it required my utmost resolution to do it. This, however, was necessary or I must give up walking, and to do that I felt meant certain death, for I had known ever since the first of April that the railroads were cut all around Andersonville, and that to get away from there at all would require a march through miles of swamps and forests in order to reach our lines in any direction.

The weather now was fine, and my wounded lung and side, while yet very sore, had improved considerably since the mild weather of April had set in.

The day we received word we were going out, expecting we would have some marching to do, those who had shoes cobbled them up the best they could, while others made bandages for their feet out of old rags. At that time my shoes were worn and cut all to pieces, though some of the soles were left, for the last month of my confinement I did not walk much. The entire feet of my socks were gone, but the boys took the legs and made coverings for my feet out of them, and I made bandages for them and my ankles out of the lower part of my drawers' legs. Now, if you can imagine the condition of my old, limp rimmed Confederate hat, my ragged trousers, and my blouse, with its red and green linsey sleeves now full of holes, my smoke-begrimed face and hands, pinched frame, and matted hair, which had not been cut for over eight months, and consider my age, as I marched along with a stick for a cane in one hand and my square wooden plate in the other, in company with the other prisoners, all surrounded by gray-coated militia guards, you will have a true picture of the author of these lines as he appeared on that April day as we marched out of prison—a picture which is not overdrawn in any particular.

As we passed through those old prison gates I believe we emerged from one of the most horrible, ghastly places the world has ever known, and in comparison with which the old Spanish Inquisition would pale into insignificance.

When Kemler was executed by electricity in the State of New York one of the chief newspapers of Florida published a list of thirty different modes of execution which have been in vogue in as many different countries. After carefully examining the article several times I could find no method of execution presented therein the cruelty of which was anything like the torturing deaths that Wirz, in his barbarous treatment, produced in Andersonville; no method but I would greatly prefer to some deaths which I saw there.

Now, having reached the time of my departure from Andersonville, not expecting to have any occasion to refer to it again, I wish to repeat with emphasis that we prisoners—we who endured the tortures of this horrible prison—do not hold the Confederate soldiers or the great mass of Southern people in any way responsible for the barbarities perpetrated on us by Wirz. This inhuman prison-keeper always entered the pen astride of an old sway-back gray mare, invariably carrying his revolver full of lead in his hand, and was always surrounded by an armed bodyguard on foot which, as he was seated on his horse, made him all the more conspicuous. The prisoners called him "death on a white horse."

But before taking leave of this anti-fat sanitarium I must say a word in favor of its notorious proprietor. He never ran a bar in connection with his hotel, nor did I ever see a drunken boarder or a drop of intoxicating liquor on the premises while I was his guest. Still, I could not recommend his bill of fare or lodging, and, besides, he had a most unsatisfactory way of claiming all the baggage of his boarders.

Farewell, Captain Wirz! Farewell, Andersonville!

CHAPTER XXXII.

Released from Prison.

THE glad day of our release from Andersonville's horrors had come. While we were on our way to the railroad that morning I had an opportunity to talk a little with an old guard. He was one who, on our march across the country from Thomasville to Albany, noticing that I was a mere boy and was severely wounded, seemed to sympathize with me, and advised me to take some kind of an oath and not reenter Andersonville prison, in case they should return with us to that place—advice against which my mind was steeled. But the old man gave it in a way which indicated that he had some feeling for me and really wanted to save my life. He knew I was so enfeebled physically that I could be of no benefit to the Confederacy even if I should take an oath and be released, and I have ever appreciated his sympathy.

On this, our last trip over to the railroad, he told me Lee had surrendered, and that the war was virtually ended, and that he believed we were going to our lines. This gave me renewed hope and made the walking much easier, but still there was a lingering doubt, for General Johnston had not been heard from, and, in fact, his final surrender did not occur until five or six days later, on April 26, 1865.

When we reached the railroad we found several trains of box cars in waiting for us, with their engines headed south, and we at once boarded them and started toward Albany. As we steamed away from this place of misery and death in the pine forest, and the stockade, the bloodhounds, and the brutal Wirz were lost to view, I never expected to look upon their hideous forms again. If we should, indeed, reach our lines I was sure I would not, and I knew I could not endure much more with the heavy odds against me, for, notwithstanding my hopeful nature and firm determination not to yield to the attacks of the enemy which was now fiercely preying upon me—the scurvy —yet I could plainly see that it was literally eating me up. As we bade adieu to Andersonville that day I was sure that, even if we did not go to our lines, I should never live through another prison experience anywhere else to be returned to Andersonville, so I was satisfied this was a final adieu.

If, however, it should prove true that we were going to our lines I was determined I would summon my courage anew and all my remnant of failing strength in order to reach them, even though I should have to crawl, for I regarded this as my last chance for life and freedom, and was resolved that no bodily pain should defraud me out of the precious prize; and God only knows what I suffered on that journey.

Arriving at Albany the evening of that day, we marched out of town and camped near the large spring beside which we were halted when we were there the previous December. This time, however, we were fed much better than usual, especially on corn meal. The next morning we received more rations, and, after an early breakfast of mush, we started into the forest on our former trail south, toward Thomasville, reaching that place one evening four or five days from the time we started, and there we tarried over night.

Up to this time the weather had been warm and fair, but that evening the angry clouds gathered, and I never saw a heavier rainfall than came down that night from 8 P. M. until about six the next morning. We were exposed to it all, and were soaked through and through, but it was a warm rain and so did not hurt us much. The greatest trouble we experienced from it was in being broken of our rest, occasioned by our camp ground becoming flooded with water.

The morning after this rain we received better rations of crackers than we had ever drawn from the Confederacy; and, breakfast over, we were immediately started into the forest again in a direction south from Thomasville, and, after wading through many flooded swamps and swollen streams, we came out the next forenoon at a point on a railroad running from Tallahassee to Jacksonville, Fla. Here we were soon placed aboard trains and started eastward.

This road was in bad condition, which necessitated a slow speed, and lying by over night, so that we did not arrive at Baldwin, situated about twenty miles west of Jacksonville, until the following day about 9 A. M. From this point to Jacksonville the railroad track had been torn up and the rails carried away by the Confederates, when they evacuated the latter named place.

Baldwin was a small station fortified by slight earthworks, and was as near to our lines at Jacksonville as any of the Confederate forces were stationed. As soon as we arrived there we were taken from the trains, formed into line on the railroad bed east of the station, and there informed by the Confederate officer in charge of us that he was going to remove the guards and leave us to march into our lines at Jacksonville. Those were the sweetest words I ever heard fall from a Confederate's lips, and the man actually looked better to me than any Confederate I had ever seen.

This welcome intelligence sent a thrill through my weak and emaciated body, now racked with severe pains from the hard struggle I had experienced in getting that far, which seemed to put new life, strength, and elasticity in every fiber, but the four or five minutes he was talking to us made it seem almost like an age before the guards were removed.

Before this was done, however, he turned the command of some three thousand prisoners over to one of our sergeants, with the instructions about marching us to Jacksonville, informing him that all he had to do was to follow the railroad track, and that we would be sure to find our friends when we reached there.

The guards were then removed, and before our sergeant had time to give the order, "Forward! March!" we all started off as rapidly as we could hobble or run. He tried to control us, but he had no more power to check us released prisoners and keep us in ranks, now that we were heading for life and freedom, than a child would have in controlling a herd of cattle, and this was because we had been deceived so often.

One moment we would think the Confederate officer was honest in what he said, and the next we would have our doubts and be fearful that he was going to deceive us again; and so when the guards were removed we determined to get as far away from him as we could, and that if he should attempt to throw the guards around us again we would try to make our escape by taking to the swamps on either side of the railroad.

While the officer was talking I stood, nervously and tremblingly, ready to start, like a boy with his toe to the mark at a foot race ready for the signal, only with an intensified eagerness on my part, as it was to be an effort for life and freedom.

For the first half mile as I hobbled along as rapidly as I could go with the aid of my stick, I nearly twisted my neck off looking back to see if any of the guards were following. The first half of this distance I could see there were none, but after that I could not tell but what there were some mingled with the prisoners behind me. Then my fears would cause me to press on until compelled to drop and rest for a few minutes.

There were quantities of ripe blackberries growing along the sides of the railroad embankment, and when I would become exhausted I would manage to drop down by a bush, or a pool of water found in the excavations from which the earth had been taken to form the railroad bed; but, at such times, I would remain for a moment or two only, just long enough to catch my breath, eat a few berries, or take a sip of the boggy water from these standing pools, which, at that time, abounded with snakes and alligators, then the thought of gaining the prize I had for so many weary months longed and prayed for, together with the fear that some of those I saw far back in the rear might be the guards coming, would incite me on, and sometimes I would barely get settled for a little rest when I would struggle up again and push forward as rapidly as I possibly could. What my gait lacked in style was made up in variety.

During this whole terrible trip from Andersonville, while marching through dense forests and wading deep swamps, my tortured body had been goaded on with mingled hopes, doubts, and fears, but now, as I neared the priceless goal, every milepost I put behind me seemed as a vanquished doubt or fear, and each one that I wearily approached seemed to beckon me on to liberty and begat within me a new and buoyant hope.

About half an hour before sundown, that 28th of April, 1865, when the company of stragglers with which I was marching had approached to within about a mile and a half of Jacksonville, we saw a man on a horse ride out of the timber and stop on the roadbed about a quarter of a mile in advance of us. When he came to a halt he looked in our direction, and seemed to be shading his eyes or looking through field glasses.

He remained on the track but a moment or two and then rode off into the pine forest to the right or south of the railroad. This greatly excited us, and put my heart all in a flutter. We could not discover whether he wore blue or gray, and did not know whether to be sad or glad, whether to proceed farther or take to the woods. As for myself, my oppressive doubts and fears began to troop back into my mind more rapidly than the successive mile posts had driven them away. I rather believed that man was clad in gray and began to doubt that our troops occupied Jacksonville, and thought that possibly, after all, the Confederates were in possession of the city.

While we were halted for a few moments, discussing the probabilities, I explored the interior of my cranium as carefully as its exterior needed going over, in an endeavor to rake up some idea about the location of Jacksonville and the probabilities of its being a favorable place for our troops to be stationed, but with my most careful search I could not remember the names and locations of any towns in Florida but the capital, Tallahassee, St. Augustine, Key West, and Pensacola. Jacksonville, so far as my memory served me, was a blank, as also it was with our entire squad.

We were then in great trouble and hardly knew what to do. To take to the woods offered us some possibilities of escape, to proceed and run into a line of Confederates our doom was sealed. However, as the majority of our squad of thirty or forty felt tolerably sure the man we saw was dressed in darker garb than the Confederate gray, and as some prisoners who preceded us had passed the point where we saw him cross the track without any commotion, so far as we could see, we decided we would proceed cautiously a little farther, and if we should then discover that our comrades in advance of us, were in any trouble, we would break for the timber.

I think my mind and nerves were never so wrought up as when we ventured to advance. Was it possible I should be cruelly robbed of life and freedom that I now felt was so nearly within my grasp, after all I had endured? I hardly knew what to do. Hope seemed to impel me forward, while doubt and fear seemed as strong cables drawing me into the sheltering woods.

When we had traveled along in this tortured state of mind for a short time, we came to the point where we had seen the unknown rider; then, glancing to our right, we saw that same man not more than a hundred yards distant, ride out toward us from under some large live oak trees, which were heavily and beautifully festooned with long Spanish moss.

Pen cannot describe our sudden transition of emotions as we passed from a state of killing suspense to one of supreme delight. The color of the rider's uniform settled the great problem of life or death for us; and, O glorious revelation, it is blue! He is a Union picket officer! See! he puts spur to his noble steed and is dashing forward to meet and greet us. Ah! never before did horse and rider look so grand to us prisoners as did this handsome young officer in Union blue, as he came dashing up to us on his noble bay steed, with outstretched hand, to welcome us back to a nation's protection and grateful benefactions. Never before had I seen a uniform that appeared so beautiful or the countenance of man that seemed more noble and true.

As he approached I raised my old Confederate hat to salute him and then made an attempt to speak, but now that the strain of months of anxious solicitude was over my voice failed me and I gave way to sobs, the first I had yielded to for months.

The voice of the noble young officer, also, was husky, and his eyes were dimmed with tears at the sight of our ragged and emaciated condition. In answer to our questions he informed us that the war was really over and the Union saved, and, notwithstanding our feebleness, we gave him a cheer. Then, with hearts lighter than air, we pressed on until we reached the city of Jacksonville, and for the first time during that awful trip did we seem to appreciate the beauty and fragrance of the blooming magnolia and the sweet, soft notes of the silver-tongued mockers as they warbled forth their evening lay.

But hark! what familiar strains are those which come floating to our ears on the soft evening air? Ah! they are the sweet strains of the inspiring "Star-spangled Banner," which we had not heard played by a band for months, and the soul-stirring notes almost set us wild. To add to the thrill of the moment, just then we caught our first glimpse of the dear old "Stars and Stripes" proudly floating at the masthead of a vessel lying in the harbor; and, as the glorious vision burst upon our view, the old tune and flag seem to lift us to the very skies. The fruition of fond hopes realized burst asunder the tomb of foreboding doubts and fears, and new joy came to life at a bound. Off came our hats, and we shouted, sang, and wept until we were hoarse and so exhausted we could scarcely stand on our feet. My throat did not seem large enough nor my lungs strong enough to greet that old tune and flag in an appropriate manner. Indeed, I do not believe that any Americans were ever in a position to appreciate more fully the patriotic sentiment of that glorious national air and the ample protection guaranteed by that beautiful Union flag than were we released prisoners.

To reach our lines after all the horrors of Andersonville Prison, to see these glorious visions and to hear cheering strains, these were as the effulgent brightness of a noon-day sun bursting with all its splendor upon our midnight of deep sorrow and almost utter hopelessness; and we were at once lifted from the valley of gloom and sadness to the highest mountain peak of joy and gladness.

May the boys and girls of this fair land, by the aid of Him who presides over the destinies of all nations, ever keep that grand old flag, the red, white, and blue, floating to the breeze, a perpetual pledge of freedom, so long as the beautiful, many-tinted bow of promise spans the fierce storm-cloud, the Father's pledge of unending care and protection.

CHAPTER XXXIII.

The Bliss of Freedom.

JACKSONVILLE, at the time of our entrance, was garrisoned with three regiments of United States colored troops officered by white men. None of the garrison were apprised of our approach until we began arriving at the picket lines.

When the one hundred or so of prisoners who had preceded us reached town the colored troops were about as much excited as were we. Their bands were brought out and they gave us a royal reception.

As we entered the city we met a colored sergeant with an armload of fresh baker's bread, not less than two dozen loaves in all, which he intended to issue to his mess; but when he saw our condition and how wistfully we looked at the bread, passing scarcely a word, he began pulling off the loaves and handing them out to us, and continued until he gave us all he had, and the generous fellow seemed sorry that he did not have enough to give to all the prisoners.

I received one of the soft, flaky loaves, which was the first wheat bread we had seen in seven months, except some rusty, Confederate hard-tack. When I received the loaf it looked as white as snow in my black hands, and, O! how good it smelled. And when I began breaking it off and put it in my mouth it felt as soft as velvet to my sore and tender gums, and to my taste it was as delicious and refreshing as must have been the manna to the hungry Israelites in the wilderness.

After receiving my loaf, in company with Theodore Maniley, another boy from Naples, Ill., who has since died from the effects of his prison treatment, I left the squad of comrades we were with, and together we went to where we saw two old colored women near a little shanty. They were washing clothes and just beginning to prepare their evening meal. When we approached they hardly knew what to make of us and could scarcely tell whether we were white or black. But after we explained who we were they kindly invited us to sit down on a log near by, and told us they would make us some coffee. We thought we would keep some of our bread to go with it, but when the coffee came the bread was all gone. We drank a quart apiece of the refreshing beverage, which gave our stomachs a satisfaction they had not known for months, the invigorating effects of which seemed to extend even to the entire surface of our bodies.

While we sat on the old pine log and chatted with these two kind-hearted old "aunties," they seemed about as much distressed over our terrible condition as did our mothers when we reached home. I shall never forget the deep pathetic feeling they manifested when addressing us as "po'r chillun," and saying, "Youse bof look like youse wuz dun beat out in dat ar' old prisun."

After drinking our coffee we bade adieu to the old

colored women and made our way on, into and through the town, to the St. John's River, where we had seen the vessel with the flag floating from its masthead. There on the bank the officers had corralled several hundred of the prisoners, and soon a wagon with soap arrived and was backed up with its rear end to the street we were on, which led down to the river. As soon as it came we were marched by the wagon toward the river, and as we passed it each man was handed a large cake of soap. We needed no further hint, and at once proceeded on down the sandy bank to the river, and there washed off so much prison dirt that it would not be surprising if it had something to do with the formation of the obstructing sandbar at the mouth of the St. John's River.

As I could not get my shirt off I did not go into the river as hundreds of others did, but confined my first scouring to my face and arms and tried to loosen up my matted hair, though the latter was not much of a success. It was a great luxury, indeed, to wash with this, the first soap we had seen in seven months, and with an unstinted quantity of water; and after we were through for that evening it had wrought such a change in our appearance we could scarcely recognize each other.

Some had better success than others in this cleansing process, and while we were all of one color before the bath, afterward, as we marched up the banks, we were of variegated hues, ranging from that of light quadroons to that of the darker coffee-colored Africans. The comical part of it was that nearly all were streaked with the dirty water dripping out of their long, sooty hair, for we had not the sign of a wiping towel.

After this introduction to the St. John's we were marched out to the east of the town, on the river bank, and there corralled, to prevent stocking the place with vermin, I presume; and as we marched out to camp each one of us held on to his chunk of soap as if it were a nugget of gold.

It was dusk when we reached camp. In a short time the colored soldiers began bringing us coffee and cooked provisions, and I ate and drank until I could not take another mouthful. Then, completely worn out and exhausted from the fatigue and the excitement of the day, I lay down on the sand to enjoy my first night of freedom.

The sun of a golden morning had been displaying his resplendent glory for at least two hours before I awoke the following day. When I opened my eyes I found I was within a new, clean, white tent, the opening of which was gently swaying to and fro in the morning breeze. Lying with me in the same tent were several men whom I did not know; and as I lay there on my back, gazing up at the snow-white canvas now flooded with mellow sunlight—the first time in nearly seven months I had awakened with anything obstructing my view of the sky—for several minutes I was completely dazed and lost. I seemed as if in a dream, and could not think who or where I was. I was still more mystified when I noticed my clothing, for in some unknown way to me mine had been changed during the night.

I think I lay there fully ten minutes before my

puzzled brain unraveled the mysterious problem. When the delightful revelation was unfolded to my mind that the awful struggle was over, and that I was actually safe within the Union lines and now in a government tent with clean clothes on and under the protecting folds of the Stars and Stripes, where I should starve no more, and would, no doubt, soon be home with loved ones, my cup of bliss was full to overflowing.

Then I lay quietly for a few moments looking at the pure white canvas above me, made brighter by the soft golden sunlight, which to me made it look heavenly. While I thus lay enjoying the bliss of my first morning of freedom, in peaceful reverie, I drank long and deep at the fountain of liberty. To me it was as the panting hart that had found the quiet water brook where there was no enemy to disturb, or as the tired infant peacefully resting in its mother's bosom; and, except later in life when my troubled sin-tossed soul first cast anchor in a more delightful, the spiritual, haven of rest, these were the softest, sweetest moments of my existence.

During the night tents had been hauled out to our camp and put up by the colored troops, and we had been picked up promiscuously and carried into them.

Many of the released prisoners became unconscious, some from sheer exhaustion, others from liquor which the surgeons brought out and ordered them to drink as a necessary stimulant in their enfeebled condition, and with which they had gorged themselves, some of them until they were in great misery.

The surgeons and a large force of colored troops

worked hard all night with the worst cases, and then dozens of them died before morning. Among the latter was my true friend and former messmate, Sergeant Will Close, who robbed himself of his only pair of drawers in the dead of winter to make a bandage for me when I was wounded at Thomasville. It was sad, very, very sad, to think that these poor prisoners, after all they had sacrificed and suffered, and were now at last landed within our lines, could not live to get home and enjoy the fruits of their sufferings.

It was fully a week or ten days before some of our comrades who had started with us from Andersonville ceased coming into Jacksonville. After leaving Albany, Ga., on that trip, we marched over one hundred painful miles, an experience that I doubt if any other body of prisoners were called to endure. There was scarcely a mile of the entire march but men fell out by the wayside. Many of these perished; others followed our trail and finally reached the railroad and were forwarded to Baldwin, and from there made their way into Jacksonville on foot or were picked up by ambulances, which were kept busy this week or ten days carrying out provisions and bringing back loads of straggling prisoners whom they found strung out all along the twenty miles of road between Baldwin and Jacksonville.

I think that that night, when the surgeons found me and discovered my condition, that before carrying me into the tent they must have administered to me some kind of opiate, and while I was under its influence had my wounds and sores dressed and clean clothes put on me. I knew the colored man who did the work and provided the clothes to put on me, for the next morning he brought me more clothes and bandages, an old pair of shoes and stockings, moss for a bed, and something to eat.

When I awoke that first morning in the tent I was not able to get up, and for a week I was confined to the tent, during which time this good Samaritan took the tenderest care of me.

The first morning, after a breakfast of fresh fried mullet, good coffee and bread, with an orange for dessert, he relieved me of my matted locks, and after he gave my head a good scouring and combing it felt most delightfully clean and cool.

That day a large number of kettles were brought out to camp, and those who did not burn their clothes gave them a good boiling. Those who had received changes from the colored soldiers—the only way we had of getting them—burned their old ones. By this process we soon got rid of the pestiferous vermin.

I was there a week before I was able to write a letter to the dear ones at home, whom I so longed to see. Then I got a teamster to let me ride with him down into Jacksonville and back, for I was not able to walk that distance. While the teamster was loading his wagon up with provisions, I entered the Commissary Department and begged a sheet of paper, an envelope, and a postage stamp, and wrote a letter home. This missive, which simply bore the information that I had reached our lines and expected to reach home in a month or six weeks, was the first I had written since my capture; and, on reaching home,

I learned that my parents had received that message as one from the dead, for they had heard of the horrors of Andersonville, and I, being so young, they did not think I could endure them.

We remained at Jacksonville between three and four weeks, recruiting until we should be strong enough to be sent home. During this time the colored troops, both officers and men, did everything in their power to alleviate our sufferings. They gave us money, clothing, and fruits without stint, and while there, in addition to other rations, there were issued to us fish, vegetables, and oranges. The latter were especially beneficial for our scurvy, and what delicious medicine they were to take!

After once reaching Jacksonville, it was very apparent we could not have been sent to a better place to recruit. The genial climate, abundant sunshine, balmy sea breezes, vegetables and fruits in abundance, were just what we needed, and enjoying them, together with the faithful care we received at the hands of the kind-hearted surgeons and colored men, we did recruit rapidly, considering our starved and diseased condition.

When the time arrived for our departure home, we were told that there was a large vessel lying at anchor out in the ocean at the mouth of the river, watered and provisioned, ready to take us to Annapolis, Md. This good news we received without question, and we gave a shout of gladness, for we were now eager to be off for home.

When all was in readiness we were taken on board steam lighters and carried down the broad, deep, beautiful St. John's River to its mouth, twenty miles distant. There catching my first view of the mighty ocean it looked to me as if it might be as vast and boundless as eternity.

Passing an earth fort, we proceeded out to sea a short distance to where the large black hulk, with its tall masts and reefed sails, lay rocking at anchor ready to receive us. As we neared the great monster our baby craft slowed up and approached it with care, for there was quite a high sea running, and there was some danger of the two crafts pounding. We were soon made fast to the *Cassandra*, the name of the large steam and sail freight vessel which was to carry us to Annapolis. The sailors on her stanch deck dropped rope ladders down to us, and we clambered up over her sides and were soon assigned quarters on her upper and lower decks, and were in readiness for our long-desired homeward trip.

CHAPTER XXXIV.

Homeward Bound.

AS soon as all were safely on board the great vessel the fastenings of the last steam lighter were cast loose, we waved them an adieu, orders were given, and the heavy anchors of our vessel were weighed, her bells rang and jingled, sharp whistles screeched and screamed, clouds of black coal smoke rolled out of the huge smokestack, and we steamed out to sea.

As we started the snow-white sails on the three tall masts were given to the breeze, and quickly filling with the stiff southwester, we were soon under full sail and head of steam on our way to our loved ones who were anxiously awaiting our coming with open arms to receive us.

The *Cassandra* was painted black as the night, the sails on her swaying masts were new and white as the driven snow, and as her shapely prow gracefully parted and plowed a deep foam furrow through the white-capped, tumbling waves she looked a thing of life like some mighty black sea fowl with enormous snow-white wings sporting on the mighty deep.

It was a lovely afternoon, the 20th of May, that we set sail northward, and as the low sandy shore of fair Florida faded from view behind us they appeared in danger of becoming a prey to the restless sea.

My mess, after getting on board, had the good fortune to have space or quarters assigned us on the upper deck.

We had not been long under way before hundreds were suffering from the deathly sea-sickness. One of my mess, Charlie Paine, took the cramp colic, and his agony was so intense it seemed as if he would certainly die; and I believe if it had not been for the prompt and vigorous efforts of the captain's wife he could not have survived. This noble lady of unselfish benevolence, had accompanied her husband on this voyage for the purpose of caring for the sick, and, being the first Northern lady we had seen since coming into our lines, it was indeed delightful to watch her as she cheerfully went about over the ship administering to their wants.

I had not been on the vessel a great while until I felt a serious disturbance in my stomach, but after a few hours this seemed to wear away, and I thought I had such a grip on my dinner that the old ocean could not break it loose.

On our way we touched at Hilton Head, S. C., and at Wilmington, N. C., at the latter place taking on fresh water. While lying there I saw a large blockading squadron which was one of the grandest sights I ever beheld.

We were favored with fair weather, and the trip was most delightful, until we neared Cape Hatteras. That morning black, portentous clouds began to gather in the west, soon the wind stiffened and great raindrops began to fall. At the time I was seated close up in the bow of the vessel, looking down into the sea at a school of large black porpoises which were sporting around the vessel's bow, and it was astonishing, at the rate of speed our vessel was going, how they could glide backward and forward and across the bow to within six inches of it apparently, and never seem to get a rub. These fish looked to be as large through the body as an ordinary horse. We threw meat and bread to them, to which they paid no attention, and seemed as if rollicking with some monster of the deep. The same fish would follow the vessel for miles and miles and never appear to tire of their play.

When the rain began to fall there was a bright flash of lightning which, to me, made the sea look more green than blue, and was followed by a terrific clap of thunder. I was so far forward at the time, and the winds were making such confusion, I could not hear the orders of the officers, but I discovered that some of the sailors were reefing the sails while others were lashing down the great water casks and everything that was loose on the deck; and the returning soldiers all appeared to be going below deck.

By this time the rain was coming down in torrents, and the storm increased with such sudden violence that before I hardly had time to take in the gravity of the situation, our vessel was rocking and plunging so furiously I could not stand on my feet and could only manage to reach the first hatchway where sailors stood and kneeled ready to batten the hatch down. By clinging to the outside railing until I reached a point nearly opposite them, then waiting for a favorable lurch of the vessel I slid the rest of the way.

The black, angry storm clouds now hung low, and it had suddenly become quite dark. The electric storm, while grand, was terrific. The forked lightnings shot and darted into the sea and about the black vessel until she seemed as if ablaze from stem to stern, and the rapid crashes of pealing thunder were more terrible than the hurried cross fire of artillery; and as the great *Cassandra* tossed in and out of the trough of the sea like a mere toy, nothing could be heard above the awful roar of the tempest. The waves were lashed into foam and were piling mountain high, and as the huge billows struck the ship they burst and engulfed the deck with spray.

Before I left the bow sometimes it seemed as if I was going to be lifted to the very skies, and the next instant as if I should be plunged to the very bottom of the deep. I had often thought I should like to witness a storm at sea, but since my experience on that occasion I have had no desire to behold the sublime and awful grandeur of another such scene. It seemed as if the black, angry heavens and the mighty turbulent ocean were in deadly combat, and as these warring elements roared and displayed, the one its fiery power and the other its maddened frenzy, our ship, with closely reefed sails, appeared but as a tossing straw to be ground to atoms between the enraged elements.

I was among the very last to go below, and, as I started down the ladder, I detected a variety of odors rising from the hold, where lay some two thousand seasick comrades. But among the various odors I failed to detect attar of roses, new-mown hay, or orange blossoms.

As I encountered the nauseous fumes which came up in the hot stifling air it was more than the strongest stomach could endure. I had not more than reached the lower deck among my heaving companions until I was compelled to make an unconditional surrender of the good things I had been recently storing away for purposes of nutrition.

All in the dimly lighted hold, probably about twenty-five hundred men, were sick, the hatches were all battened down tightly, and the air was stifling. It was certainly the most wretched place, for the time, I was ever in, Andersonville not excepted; and as the vessel tossed and rolled in the sea the most of us were so helpless that we tumbled and slid around on the floor almost like so many bags of boneless meat.

In this condition we were in the hold for some four or five hours without any fresh air before the storm had sufficiently abated so as to admit of the hatches being raised. I think I was there about twelve hours before I had strength to crawl up the ladder to the upper deck, and when I reached it, between 9 and 10 P. M., the stars were shining brightly and the vessel was plowing ahead as if nothing had happened, its only loss, apparently, being the large water casks which had been torn loose and swept into the sea. The captain said the gale was one of the heaviest he had encountered for a number of years, and that at several times during its progress the vessel was in great danger of foundering.

We were blown considerably out of our course by the storm, and did not enter Chesapeake Bay until about 10 P. M. the following day. There we found a perfect calm, which was a great relief after our experience at Hatteras; but, our vessel being large, and now having to depend entirely on her steam screw, she made poor time, so that we did not reach Annapolis until the following afternoon. We felt so safe and secure, however, in the great bay, that it was a luxury to lounge around on the deck and watch the fishing smacks and passing vessels on our way up to Annapolis.

When we arrived and steamed alongside the dock, looking over the railing or guard, our eyes were met by a sea of upturned faces of men, women, and children who were apprised of the coming of the vessel and had come to Annapolis to meet it and see if any of their friends or loved ones were on board.

Many were the happy meetings and cordial greetings we witnessed, and many, too, were the bitter disappointments; but it mattered not whether fond wives, mothers, and sisters, fathers and brothers were controlled by emotions of joy or sorrow, their lips were quivering and their eyes were bedewed with tears.

We were the last shipload of prisoners to come in, and those who were disappointed had but little to hope for, as there were none to follow us but a few sick, who were unable to travel when we left Jacksonville.

Descending the rope ladders to the dock, which was a scene of smiles and tears, we took our leave of the *Cassandra* and her crew and slowly made our way through the dense throngs of joyful and sorrowing ones, and marched up into the city a few blocks to some first-class barracks. From the effects of the roll of the sea, on our way up to the barracks we all seemed to have an inclination to step as high as a blind horse just after picking himself up out of a ditch. Indeed, it was several days before we entirely overcame this peculiar gait.

At Annapolis we drew ration money for all the time we were prisoners, at the rate of twenty-five cents a day. This gave me something over forty dollars—the hardest earned money I ever put into my pocket. Think of it! Only forty dollars for being incarcerated in open pens for seven months, exposed to storms and chilling frosts, and all the while on starvation rations, attacked by severe diseases and buffeted and most cruelly treated by guards and prison keepers. Though this was the first money we had drawn since our enlistment, yet there had been but the slightest complaint among the prisoners.

We sometimes hear of people who rob their stomachs to robe their backs. Well, you can make out a clear case of that kind of robbery against me, for I invested thirty-five dollars of that ration money for a new suit of nice blue clothes, including jacket, vest, trousers, and a soft black hat with cord and tassels. I did this because the suit the old colored soldier gave me at Jacksonville was badly patched and would not be as presentable as I desired on reaching home, and I did not wish to draw any more government clothing. I bought no shoes, because I could not wear anything in the shoe line having much more than soles.

At the barracks we found chairs on which to sit, the first thing of any kind we had to sit on for over seven months, save the ground. You may be assured that when I had taken a bath and had donned my new suit and sat down on one of the barrack chairs, crossed my legs, and hung my new hat, with its fine cord and tassels, on my knee where I could turn it around and observe it in all its beauty, I felt greatly elated. That easy camp chair was almost like a kingly throne in comparison with the dirt and sand I had been accustomed to sit on; and that jaunty black hat, with its gilt cord and tassels, resting on my new light-blue pantaloons, looked like a gorgeous crown in comparison with the old Confederate hat which was burned at Jacksonville.

At this time the government was feeding us well, and I had a few dollars in my pocket for luxuries. What more of earthly treasure could a boy desire?

CHAPTER XXXV.

Home at Last.

WE remained at Annapolis but four or five days before being sent out in all directions to our homes. The Western men, among whom I was placed, formed a train load, and started for the West over the Baltimore and Ohio Railroad; many of them left our train at Columbus, O., and Indianapolis, Ind. At Harper's Ferry, Wheeling, W. Va., and, indeed, all other points along the line where our train stopped, we were met by hundreds of citizens with baskets of provisions and bushels of the choicest flowers. At one place where we halted there were several large factories near the track which, on the arrival of our train at the station, quit running, and hundreds of young women and girls flocked around the train and almost deluged us with smiles and roses.

The journey home from Annapolis from beginning to end was a perfect ovation. Almost every place through which we passed had some one on the train who belonged there, and had written or telegraphed when we would pass; and their friends, and, apparently, all creation besides, within reach, would be at these stations with good things to eat and the choicest products of their flower gardens to meet and greet us.

Of course there were some great disappointments, and consequently some very sad scenes to witness, but taking it altogether I never expect to be on another tour attended with such greetings and welcomings and such joy and gladness as was this one.

At Indianapolis, Ind., we were held over Sunday, and were entertained at the Soldiers' Home. Thence we were taken to St. Louis, Mo., where we were quartered for a few days at Schofield barracks. While there the relatives or friends of many of the boys came to see us, and among them my father made me a visit. At the time I was unable to walk without great pain. The day my father came, and shortly before his arrival, I had been at the hospital and had the surgeon burn the proud flesh out of the sores on my feet and ankles, and when he entered I was lying in my bunk with my head to the door. You will remember that my father was a cripple, hence it was necessary for him to use a crutch in walking. Several times during that morning the boys had deceived me by telling me father was coming, when, on looking around, I discovered it was only crippled soldiers who came thumping along on the hard barracks floor with their crutches. So this time when they told me father was coming, I determined I would not look around, and did not until he had passed the head of my bunk and stopped in front of it.

I cannot describe our meeting, but when we clasped hands and kissed, as we always do after a long separation, it was several moments before either of us could speak. Then, with quivering lips and tremulous voice, father said: "My poor, poor boy; I should never have known you!"

Father and other friends remained with us until evening, and then returned home on the same boat on which they came down from Naples. We remained at Schofield barracks but two or three days and were then taken to Camp Butler near Springfield, Ill., where we were at once furloughed and permitted to go home, with instructions to return to Camp Butler or Springfield and report as soon as the government should notify us we were wanted there to be formally discharged.

Since we boys had responded to our country's call, bade adieu to our friends, and marched away with our rifles in the winter's snow and icy blasts in December, 1863, mother earth had twice changed her robe of white for one of green, and now with the olive branch of peace we returned amid the summer showers and fragrant blossoms of June, 1865.

How pleasing the contrast between winter and summer, war and peace, rifle and olive branch, sorrow at parting, and joy on returning; but no contrast was so pleasing to me as on arriving at home, instead of the troubled, anxious look my mother wore when she bade me adieu as I was leaving for the war, I beheld her smiles of joy beneath her tears as she clasped me in her loving arms.

I was accorded a hearty welcome back to our dear old home by father, mother, sisters, and friends, and received almost as one from the dead; and was in demand for dinners and suppers until I had gone the whole round of relatives and friends, and had attended a number of public receptions given for us returning prisoners and other soldiers, on which occasions we were required to relate over and over again our experiences in camp, on the march, in skirmish and battle, and while prisoners.

On the 12th of July I received notice from government officers to appear at Springfield the following day for the purpose of being formally discharged. Accordingly, I went, and on receiving my discharge papers I found that while they were signed July 13, 1865, they were dated May 30, 1865. I was born June 4, 1848, hence I had been to the war, through Confederate prisons, returned home, and discharged before I was seventeen years of age; and, during my absence had traveled over five thousand miles by land and water, and been through or on the borders of every slave State except Texas.

Up to the time of my capture I had never missed a march, skirmish, or battle in which my regiment was engaged. In fact I had never been absent from my regiment a single day or missed a single duty; and it is probable that few boys even in the army were called to pass through, or if so, lived to endure, the same amount of suffering from prison exposures and treatment from wounds and severe painful disease, as that which I was called to endure, and which in the Providence of God I have survived.

When I reached home my nervous system was so shattered and my general health so undermined, I could never resume my school studies. I tried various occupations at Naples, Perry, Sharpe's Landing, and Roseville, Ill., and had to abandon them all on account of my health. Finally in 1878, when living on a stock farm near Lathrop, Mo., which I owned, my old wound in my right lung reopened, a portion of the upper lobe of which I lost at that time. At the same time my spine was so seriously affected that I lost the use of my lower limbs for a short while.

Not regaining my strength so that I could even oversee my farming interests, I traded my farm for an interest in a family grocery business in Astoria, Ill., and removed there with my family in 1879, where I had been but a few months when I again lost the use of my lower limbs from disease of the spine, and my back became so weak I could not sit up in a chair without wearing a corsage, and being supported by straps around my shoulders hung over the top of my chair back, as can be seen in the frontispiece.

In that condition I have been ever since, and a number of times have been confined to my bed for months not able to sit up even with these supports. In addition to this trouble, while living in Illinois I had pneumonia and asthma at different times; and, finding I had a perpetual struggle for existence in that climate, remembering the sunny days, soft, balmy air, golden fruits, and fragrant flowers, which I so much enjoyed when released in Florida, my mind naturally turned in that direction; and, in October, 1881, with my family I removed to Lawtey, Bradford County, Fla., where I have since resided in peace and plenty, with the new lease of life Florida's genial, invigorating climate has given me, and where I number among my friends many old Confederates as well as Northern people and Union soldiers.

It seems a strange coincidence, indeed, that I should find myself located on the line of the Florida Central and Peninsular Railroad, but eighteen miles south of Baldwin, where I was released in 1865; and a kind Providence that has directed me thither where I am permitted to enjoy the benefits of one of the best climates in the world, without which I undoubtedly should have been in my grave years ago.

Up to the time of becoming totally disabled while living at Astoria, Ill., I had not made application for a pension, although I knew I had been entitled to one ever since I had been discharged. But when I lost the use of my lower limbs, being disqualified thereby for business, and, consequently, needing financial aid, I then made application for a pension. Friends wrote to Governor Cullom of Illinois—now United States Senator from that State—and stated my case in full to him. He in turn wrote to the United States Pension Department, and through his influence my claim was taken out of its regular order and received immediate action. The department generously allowed me a pension from the time I was discharged in 1865, amounting in all to $2,750, which was indeed a great blessing to myself and family, a wife and three small children.

When I was first enrolled as a pensioner I was placed on the list at twenty-four dollars per month. Within a year my pension was increased to fifty dollars per month; and in January, 1885, it was increased by special act of Congress to seventy-two dollars per month, of which special act the following is a verbatim copy:

48th Congress, } SENATE. { Report
2d Session. } { No. 953.

IN THE SENATE OF THE UNITED STATES.

January 6, 1885.—Ordered to be printed.

Mr. Cullom, from the Committee on Pensions, submitted the following

REPORT:

[To accompany bill H. R. 5004.]

The Committee on Pensions, to whom was referred the bill (H. R. 5004) for the relief of William B. Smith, have considered the same, and respectfully report as follows:

This bill proposes to increase the pension of William B. Smith from $50 to $72 per month, the rate which he would be allowed by the Pension Office under the act of June 16, 1880, if at the date of its approval he had been on the rolls at $50 per month. The writer of this report has seen Mr. Smith, and can certify from personal knowledge that the statement of the case made in the report of the House Committee is correct, as follows:

The papers in this case show that the petitioner's condition is most helpless and pitiable. It is impossible to conceive a case in which the full amount of $72 could be more worthily bestowed. We recommend the passage of the bill. The applicant, as is amply proved, is, and since October, 1881, has been, in a helpless condition, "requiring the constant assistance of another person to move, eat, undress, go to bed, get up, in fact, cannot help himself, and cannot sit up in his armchair without being strapped in to keep him from falling over." His present condition is but the aggravation of the disease for which he was originally pensioned.

We therefore recommend the passage of the bill.

In accordance with the provisions of this special act my rating has been and still continues as therein stated and thereby increased.

The very first money I used out of this generous aid by the government I sent to the New Haven Chair Company, of New Haven, Conn., for a reclining wheel chair, which I had noticed was highly recommended by the Hon. Alexander H. Stephens. When this chair arrived I found it a great luxury for an invalid, enabling me to get out into the open air and sunshine which I so much needed, and to be propelled from place to place, as I otherwise could not be.

And now, dear reader, having given you a plain, truthful account of some of the army and prison experiences and observations of a young boy soldier in the great American Civil War, I trust you have found it of some interest and profit, and that it clearly indicates why I am " On Wheels: and How I Came There."

www.ingramcontent.com/pod-product-compliance
Lightning Source LLC
Chambersburg PA
CBHW030003240426
43672CB00007B/806